WORDSWORTH CLASSICS
OF WORLD LITERATURE

General Editor: Tom Griffith MA, MPhil

MEDITATIONS

Marcus Aurelius

Meditations

Translation by Robin Hard
Introduction and Notes by Christopher Gill

WORDSWORTH CLASSICS
OF WORLD LITERATURE

The paper in this book is produced from pure wood
pulp, without the use of chlorine or any other substance
harmful to the environment. The energy used in its
production consists almost entirely of hydroelectricity
and heat generated from waste material, thereby
conserving fossil fuels and contributing little
to the greenhouse effect.

This edition published 1997 by Wordsworth Editions Limited
Cumberland House, Crib Street, Ware, Hertfordshire SG12 9ET

ISBN 1 85326 486 5

Typeset in Great Britain by Antony Gray
Printed and bound in Denmark by Nørhaven

CONTENTS

INTRODUCTION[*]

1. The *Meditations* of Marcus Aurelius is a work without parallel among writings surviving from Classical antiquity. It is the philosophical diary of a Roman emperor, probably written while he was campaigning in Germany near the end of his life. It gives us an unrivalled insight into the ideas on which such a person could draw to confront the challenges of being an emperor and the hard realities that every human being must face: loss of those loved, personal and social difficulties, making sense of the world, confronting old age and death.

Marcus Aurelius

2. Marcus (AD 121–180) was born in Rome as Marcus Annius Verus into a family of Spanish origin which had already achieved political distinction. His father died during Marcus' early childhood, and he was brought up by his grandfather, a relative of the emperor Hadrian. Hadrian admired the young Marcus, calling him *Verissimus* ('most truthful'). When Hadrian chose Antoninus Pius as his heir and successor, he made Antoninus adopt as his sons Marcus and another young man, Lucius Verus. Marcus was educated by a number of famous teachers, including the orator Fronto (much of whose correspondence with Marcus survives). From the age of twelve he showed a strong interest in philosophy; after an early introduction to Stoicism, Junius Rusticus guided him to Epictetus' *Discourses*, a key influence on the *Meditations*. In

* This introduction is divided into numbered paragraphs, which are used elsewhere in the book for cross-reference (e.g. 'see Introd. 5').

Book 1 of the *Meditations*, Marcus reviews the ethical and intellectual influence of his family, teachers and friends, giving special prominence to that of his adoptive father and predecessor as emperor, Antoninus Pius.

3. Antoninus' reign (138–61) was marked by good relations between emperor and senate and between the Roman Empire and other countries. Marcus held several of the major political posts (including consul) in preparation for his eventual status as emperor. He married Antoninus' daughter Faustina and seems to have had a largely happy marriage, with several children. After Antoninus' death, Marcus and Verus became co-emperors (with Marcus the more senior) and remained so until Verus' death on campaign in 169. Much of Marcus' reign was dominated by disturbance and warfare on the northern and eastern frontiers of the Roman empire. There was a serious invasion by German tribes in 170, and Marcus was on campaign in northern Italy and Germany for much of 168–80. In 175 Avidius Cassius, governor of Egypt and Syria, revolted unsuccessfully against Marcus; he was rumoured to have had an affair with Faustina and to have her support (though there is no mention of this in the *Meditations*). Another disaster of the reign was a plague at Rome in 166–7. Despite all these problems, the administration of the empire seems to have been handled well in this period, though it is difficult to make out significant long-term policies. In retrospect, Marcus' reign was regarded as a good one, especially by contrast with his son and successor, Commodus (emperor 180–92) who reigned badly and was finally assassinated as a tyrant.[1]

Meditations: Form and Purpose

4. The title *Meditations* (*Med.*) is modern; the manuscript used as the basis for the first printed edition (in the sixteenth century) has the title *To Himself*, which may not go back to the original.

---

1 The main sources for Marcus' life and reign, apart from the *Meditations* themselves, are Cassius Dio, *Roman History* 71–3 (in shortened form), written *c.*197–*c.*225, the biography of Marcus in the *Historia Augusta* (late fourth century and unreliable), and the letters between Marcus and Cornelius Fronto.

Probably the work had no title and was not intended for publication but served as a purely private notebook for Marcus' reflections. Apart from the first book (which records Marcus' ethical debts to those who have influenced him), the work consists of about five hundred short comments, with no clear principle of organisation. The division into twelve 'books' and of each book into numbered 'chapters' (the conventional way of subdividing ancient texts) was probably not made by Marcus himself. What seems most likely is that Marcus simply entered one or more comments at moments of leisure (for instance, at the end of the day), and that the resulting work is the sum of these comments. It is written in Greek, the main language of ancient philosophy, in which Marcus would have been fluent; the style is non-technical, though it alludes to many key ideas in Greek philosophy, especially in Stoicism. There are some indications that the work was written in the later years of Marcus' life; two books (2 and 3) have headings which refer to Marcus' German campaigns. Frequent, and increasing, references to his age, dissatisfaction with associates, and approaching death may suggest that the order of the books corresponds with the order in which they were written.[2]

5. Marcus' book largely takes the form of examining and advising himself. It is clear, especially from Seneca (c.4 BC–AD 65) and Epictetus (c.AD 55–c.135), as well as from Marcus' *Meditations*, that self-scrutiny was a well-marked feature of philosophical practice in this period, especially among Stoics. Recent scholars, including Michel Foucault, have sometimes seen this feature as anticipating Christian forms of meditation and self-examination as well as the modern practice of psychoanalysis. Some have also seen this feature as expressing a greater inwardness and a heightened concern with 'the self' in this period.[3] However, it is important to locate this type of ancient self-scrutiny in an appropriate intellectual and cultural context. It is probably best understood as the application to oneself of the types of practical ethics that play a

2 On the dating of *Med.*, see Brunt (1974), 18–19; Rutherford (1989), 45–7. For full details of all books referred to by author and date in these notes, see Bibliography below.
3 See Foucault (1988), esp. 46–7, 50–1; also Long (1996), ch. 12; Hadot (1995).

prominent role in philosophy in this period, especially in Stoicism. Key forms of practical ethics include protreptic (encouragement to engage in philosophy), therapy (typically understood as the removal, or 'cure', of false ethical beliefs), and advice (based on the principles of the relevant philosophical system). It was considered a mark of philosophical development if someone had learnt how to apply these techniques to himself, in internalised discourse; and Marcus' *Meditations* present a clear example of this type of self-advice and self-therapy.[4]

Stoic Ethics

6. Marcus does not claim to be a Stoic; and the *Meditations* are often thought to show the influence of other ancient thinkers, especially Heraclitus, Socrates, Plato, and the Cynics. However, those other philosophies had also helped to shape the development of Stoic thought; and Marcus' approach seems best understood as that of a (perhaps not wholly orthodox) Stoic, rather than an independent or eclectic thinker.[5] The key idea of Stoic ethics is that virtue is the only good; what are conventionally seen as the 'goods' of human life (health, wealth, social status) are 'matters of indifference' in comparison to virtue. While it is appropriate to treat health, etc. as 'preferable' to their alternatives, they should not be pursued as ends in themselves. An associated idea is that humans are naturally adapted to develop from an instinctive attraction to 'preferable indifferents', such as health and social status, towards the recognition that virtue is the only good. Stoics also believed that humans are naturally adapted to develop from an instinctive desire to benefit their own children, relatives and friends towards the desire to benefit other humans as such. Both these forms of development are conceived as ways of fulfilling the rationality which is fundamental to human nature (and which is also fundamental to the nature of the universe).

4 On practical ethics, see Long and Sedley (1987), section 66; on philosophical therapy, see Newman (1989), Nussbaum (1994); also (on Marcus) Rutherford (1989), 13–21.
5 See further Rist (1982); Asmis (1989); some of Marcus' apparent divergences from Stoicism may be a function of his style of expression, on which see para. 14 below.

'Wisdom' (which is the supreme virtue), in the fullest sense, includes understanding the rationality that is fundamental to the universe and to human nature and expressing it in one's life and character.[6]

Epictetus and Practical Ethics

7. To see the relevance of Stoic ethics to the *Meditations*, it is helpful to refer to the three-stage programme of practical ethics in Epictetus' *Discourses*, a work which strongly influenced Marcus. For Epictetus, the first stage is recognising that desire should be directed only at virtue (which is wholly 'up to us' or 'within our power') and not at the other so-called 'goods', such as health, wealth, and continued life (which are not 'up to us'). This move is crucial for avoiding the 'passions' (emotions, in ordinary terms) which, for Stoics, are the product of over-valuing these other things, and of failing to realise that, by comparison with virtue, they are merely 'matters of indifference' or 'externals'. The second stage is that of ensuring that our social relationships are conducted in a way that is socially appropriate and that also expresses our growing understanding that virtue is the only good. For Epictetus, the third stage is that of examining the logical relationship between the beliefs acquired in the first two stages, so as to move closer to the consistency and ethical understanding of the ideal 'wise' person or 'sage'.[7]

Meditations: Recurrent Themes

8. Recurrent features of Marcus' *Meditations* can be linked with this type of programme; these features show Marcus trying to carry forward his own ethical development by self-directed therapy and advice. One feature is the presentation of material

6 On Stoic ethics, see the useful summary in Sharples (1996), 100–13; also Long and Sedley (1987), sections 57–61; Inwood (1985), ch. 6; Annas (1993).

7 See Epictetus, *Discourses* 3.2.1–5; also 2.17.14–18, 3.12.8–15; on virtue as what is 'up to us', see e.g. 1.1, 1.4.1–4, *Handbook* 1. For translation and introduction see Gill and Hard (1995). On passions and freedom from passion (*apatheia*), see Long and Sedley (1987), section 65; Inwood (1985), ch. 5; Annas (1993), 61–6; Nussbaum (1994), ch. 10; Braund and Gill (1997).

wealth and social status as relatively worthless (not really 'good') and of illness and death as natural facts to be accepted (not really 'bad'). Another is the insistence that social relationships should be conducted appropriately and also in a way that recognises the low value of conventional 'goods' such as wealth and status. Epictetus' third stage has no precise equivalent in Marcus, in whom we do not find the orthodox Stoic stress on the idea that logic, ethics and 'physics' (study of nature) are interdependent areas of study. But the equivalent of Epictetus' third stage is the aspiration towards the 'cosmic' perspective in which one sees oneself as part of a providentially ordered universe, a perspective which is character-istic of the Stoic sage. In the *Meditations*, this aspiration to the cosmic perspective pervades the whole work; it also underlies the way in which Marcus presents the themes that correspond to the first two stages of Epictetus' programme in practical ethics.[8]

Meditations: Reason versus Indifferents

9. Unlike Epictetus, who professes to be a Stoic teacher, Marcus develops these ideas (for himself) in an unsystematic manner and in a style that sometimes assimilates Stoic ideas to those of other schools. This comes out, for instance, in the way Marcus develops the theme of Epictetus' first stage, that desire should only be directed towards virtue, that is, towards what is wholly 'up to us'. This theme is expressed in the idea that the mind or 'governing faculty', the seat of rationality and moral agency, is a *daimôn* ('guardian spirit') within you and that you should take care to preserve its rule. This is combined with a quasi-Platonic detachment from other physical objects. Marcus urges himself to be equally unconcerned with physical pleasure and wealth (conventionally seen as 'good things') and with physical pain and bodily decay (conventionally seen as 'bad things'). These attitudes are sometimes stated with an offensive bluntness that recalls ancient Cynicism – for instance, in his characterisation of luxurious food as 'the corpse of a fish' and of sexual love as 'the friction of a piece of gut, the expulsion of some mucus' (6.13). However, the essential point being made in this way (the contrast

8 On Epictetus and Marcus (also stressing the relevance of Epictetus' three-stage programme), see Gill (forthcoming); also Rutherford (1989), ch. 6.

in value between rationality and virtue, the only real 'goods', and the 'indifferents' normally valued as goods) is an essentially Stoic one and one that corresponds to the first stage of Epictetus' programme of practical ethics.[9]

Meditations: Social Relations

10. Marcus is more straightforwardly Stoic in discussing the virtuous conduct of social relations, the second topic in Epictetus' three-stage programme. Marcus often reminds himself to act in a way that is appropriate to the best standards of his social role: that is, acting 'as suits a Roman and a man' (2.5), and as 'a statesman, a Roman, and a ruler' (3.5). He reminds himself not to become 'turned into a Caesar' or 'stained with the purple' (6.30). He includes in Book 1 a long tribute to his adoptive father, Antoninus Pius, for showing him how to act in a way that is both virtuous and appropriate to an emperor (1.16, also 6.30). Also, perhaps more surprisingly, he includes a tribute to Roman politicians who had made a principled stand against imperial rule, and who pursued the idea of 'a government founded on equity and freedom of speech, and of a monarchy which values above all things the freedom of the subject' (1.14). However, he also refers frequently to certain universal ideals, such as being a 'citizen of the universe' (*kosmopolitês*), following 'natural law', and maintaining 'the brotherhood of humankind' (e.g. 3.11, 4.3-4, 4.29). The idea that we should live *both* by the best standards of our community *and* by objective, universal norms is one we find elsewhere in Stoicism, sometimes expressed as 'dual citizenship', belonging both to a local and a universal city. As Marcus puts it: 'As Antoninus, my city and fatherland is Rome; as a human being, it is the universe' (6.44).

11. This combination of ideas makes sense in the context of Stoic thinking about ethical development (outlined in para. 6 above). Human beings are naturally adapted to develop virtuous motives

9 For such Cynic realism, see also *Med.* 2.2, 8.24, 37, 9.36. On Marcus' use of the terms 'mind', 'soul', and 'body', see notes to 2.2, 3.6 below. See also Sandbach (1975), 173-4; Rist (1982), 31-2; Asmis (1989), 2238-44; Rutherford (1989), 143-7. On Cynicism, see Dudley (1937); Moles (forthcoming); on Cynicism and Stoicism, see Rist (1969), ch. 4.

by acting in line wth the best principles of their community, and so recognising that virtue is the only good. But human beings are also naturally adapted to extend the boundaries of their concern, and to see other human beings as fellow-citizens or 'brothers' in the cosmic city. Sometimes Stoic thinkers stress that the latter type of development can lead you to act virtuously outside the boundaries of your own community. At other times, they stress that playing your role virtuously within your community can itself be understood as a way of acting as a citizen of the universe; and this is the version of Stoic thinking that Marcus emphasises. Acting in this way is sometimes presented as a way of fulfilling our fundamental rationality ('the guardian spirit within us'): 'let the guardian spirit within you be the overseer of one who is manly and mature, a statesman, a Roman, and a ruler' (3.5). Marcus also stresses that adopting this attitude can help to free us from passions, such as anger, which arise in social relations from the failure to recognise that virtue and rationality are the only real 'goods'.[10]

Marcus: Theory and Practice

12. This way of understanding Marcus' thinking about his social role may help us to respond properly to an issue raised already in ancient times, whether Marcus' practice as emperor matched his philosophical ideas. Modern scholars have sometimes approached this question by asking whether Marcus' legislation reflected ethically advanced thinking about the status of women, children or slaves. This approach is based on the fact that Stoic thinkers sometimes questioned conventional ancient class divisions (such as between slave and free, men and women), and emphasised that all people are part of the brotherhood of humankind.[11] However, as

10 See e.g. 2.1, 3.4–6, 4.3, 11.1, 12.26. On reason as our inner guardian spirit, see para. 9 above. On Marcus' (typically Stoic) interest in anger, see Brunt (1974), 19–20. On Marcus' political thinking, see Gill (forthcoming); and on Stoic political theory generally, Long and Sedley (1987), section 67; Schofield (1991); Annas (1993), 302–12.

11 See the contrasting views of Noyen (1955) and Stanton (1969). Stanton sees Marcus' choice of his son Commodus as his successor as reflecting typical Roman attitudes, rather than Stoic ethics.

just noted, Stoic thinkers, including Marcus, also stress the idea that you can promote the brotherhood of humankind by acting virtuously *within* your conventional role. The *Meditations* suggest that Marcus regarded his objective as performing his role as emperor in a virtuous way and in line with the best Roman practice, and that he saw this as being a proper way of expressing human rationality and cosmic citizenship. So far as we can tell from the evidence of his civil and military practice during his rather difficult period of imperial rule, this (rather than social reform) is the objective he set himself, and one he largely fulfilled.[12]

Meditations: the Cosmic Perspective

13. In orthodox Stoic ethics, a further goal of human development is that of combining practical ethical understanding with an understanding of nature as a whole through the study of 'physics' or natural science. In this way, you could both live a 'natural' (rational) life and understand how rationality was fundamental to human life and to the cosmos. This could, in turn, help you to accept (what are normally seen as) disasters such as old age, illness and death, by understanding them as part of a larger providential pattern of which you are a part. The 'cosmic' perspective is very prominent in the *Meditations*, expressed in the ideas that we are 'only a part' of the cosmos and that we should aim for 'the view above' our normal standpoint.[13] As in Epictetus, we sometimes find in Marcus the idea that achieving the cosmic perspective depends partly on expressing in virtuous action and character the rationality we recognise in the cosmos, and in this way helping ourselves to see disasters as merely 'externals' or 'matters of indifference'.[14]

12 See para. 3 above; also Brunt (1975), 22–3; Birley (1987), chs. 5–9.

13 See further Rutherford (1989), 155–67; Annas (1993), 175–6; on the relationship between ethics and the study of nature in Greek philosophy, see Gill (1995), ch. 5.

14 See *Med.* refs in n. 10 above; also Rutherford (1989), 169–72; Epictetus *Discourses* 1.1.21–7, 1.17.21–8, 2.6.9–10.

14. Some of Marcus' ways of pursuing this idea seem less consistent with orthodox Stoicism. For instance, he sometimes seems to suggest that we can achieve inner peace of mind regardless of whether we see the universe as providentially ordered (as Stoics believed) or as a fortuitous combination of atoms (as the Epicureans believed).[15] He also seems to adopt the Heraclitean view that the universe consists of a perpetual flux rather than an ordered structure (though Heraclitus also believed that this flux contained its own underlying order).[16] And we find a quasi-Cynic stress on the ideas that nothing resists the passage of time and that life is an ever-changing pageant.[17] Marcus, as noted earlier, is not a Stoic teacher, and may have advised himself in a way that is not wholly consistent with orthodox Stoicism. However, the *Meditations* have a distinctive, lapidary (even oracular) style, combined with a fiercely determined, and often mordant, tone. It is not always easy to decide whether Marcus is presenting Stoic ideas in a personal way or offering a synthesis of Stoic and non-Stoic ideas. However, even allowing for some variations from orthodox Stoicism, the *Meditations* still reflect a predominantly Stoic pattern of thinking. They offer a powerful demonstration of how a Roman emperor, under extreme and continuing pressure, could find in Stoic philosophy a framework by which to live, and by which to achieve some degree of peace of mind despite recognising fully the inherent hardships of human life.

Meditations: Survival and Influence

15. The *Meditations* survived, we suppose, because the original notebook was preserved by Marcus' family or secretary. It is

15 See e.g. *Med*. 4.3, 6.10, 7.32, 8.17, 9.28, 9.39, 10.6, 11.18, 12.24; however, Marcus sometimes explicitly supports the Stoic (providential) alternative, e.g. in 4.3, 10.6, 11.18, the truth of which he generally presupposes in *Med*., see e.g. 2.3, 9.1. See Rist (1982), 29–30; Asmis (1989), 2250–1.

16 See e.g. *Med*. 4.43, 46, 6.42, 9.28, 10.18. See Long (1982), 999, who suggests Marcus' style is based on Heraclitus' aphoristic style; also Asmis (1989), 2246–9; Long (1996), ch. 2.

17 See *Med*. 4.32, 7.3, 9.29, 10.27, 12.36; also Rist (1982), 37–8; Rutherford (1989), 161–7. On Cynicism, see also n. 9 above.

virtually unknown in later antiquity; there is one apparent
reference to the work (as 'the *Instructions* of Marcus') in the fourth
century AD. However, scholars in the Byzantine era seem to have
had access to copies of the manuscript; the lexicon known as the
Suda (*c*. AD 950) refers to it as a twelve-book work and quotes
extracts from it. Several collections of extracts survive from the
Renaissance; the first printed edition (with Latin translation) was
published in 1559 (by Xylander), and modern editions are based
on this edition and on one other surviving manuscript from the
fourteenth or fifteenth century. The work was translated into
many European languages from the seventeenth century onwards;
important English translations include those of Casaubon (1634,
reprinted by Everyman in 1906) and Farquharson (1944, reprinted
as one of the O.U.P. World's Classics in 1989). The main English
commentaries are those of Gataker (1652) and Farquharson
(1944). Marcus' *Meditations* have influenced many modern
thinkers and writers, including Alexander Pope, Goethe and
Matthew Arnold. Frederick the Great of Prussia and U.S.
President Bill Clinton are politicians for whom the Roman
emperor's inner reflections have been a source of inspiration. A
preoccupation in earlier centuries was the relationship between
the ethical and spiritual thought-world of Stoicism and that of
Christianity. More recently, Marcus' work, along with other later
Greek and Roman philosophical works, has aroused interest
among scholars and intellectuals, as an example of ancient self-
scrutiny and of the practical application of ethics.[18]

CHRISTOPHER GILL
University of Exeter

---

18 See further Farquharson (1944), Introduction; on modern interest in self-
scrutiny and practical ethics, see para. 5 above, including refs to Foucault.

FURTHER READING

A. Birley, *Marcus Aurelius: A Biography*, London 1966, 2nd edn 1987

A. S. L. Farquharson, translation of *The Meditations of Marcus Aurelius*, with introduction and notes by R. B. Rutherford, Oxford 1989

A. A. Long, *Hellenistic Philosophy*, London 1974, 2nd edn 1986

R. B. Rutherford, *The Meditations of Marcus Aurelius: A Study*, Oxford 1989

R. W. Sharples, *Stoics, Epicureans and Sceptics: An Introduction to Hellenistic Philosophy*, London 1996

NOTE ON THE TRANSLATION

The *Meditations* are written not in Latin, Marcus' native language, but in Greek, the language of philosophy, so it is not altogether surprising that the author's style is often harsh and inelegant, and sometimes obscure; and he resorts all too frequently to the unappealing jargon of the Stoic school. To be sure, the defects of Marcus' style should not be exaggerated. He can write clearly and simply, and many of the more rhetorical passages are more effective and memorable, to the modern reader at least, than entire speeches by the rhetoricians of the period. At a time when such authors were concentrating their efforts on saying nothing very much in exquisite Greek, Marcus was at least trying to use the language to express thoughts which he considered to be of vital significance to the conduct of his own life. But the fact remains that he was not entirely the master of his instrument, and in many passages his Greek can be justly described as harsh, crabbed, odd or awkward (to select just a few of the epithets which have been applied to it by translators in the past).

It is this element in Marcus' style which presents the greatest problem to a translator. How far should it be reflected in an English version? Matthew Arnold was surely wrong to say that Marcus' style lacks a 'distinctive physiognomy', and to suggest that a good translator could, in effect, express Marcus' meaning better than the author himself; for the work owes much of its appeal to the distinctive sensibility of its author, and a translation is unlikely to convey this if it shows little or no respect for his mode of expression. On the other hand, a very literal translation, in which even the infelicities of Marcus' prose are fully reflected, will not only be hard to read but is unlikely to convey the vitality of the original. It seems to me that the classic Victorian translation by George Long, and that of C. R. Haines in the Loeb series, despite their value as cribs, can be criticised on both grounds.

The present translation steers a middle course. I have tried to provide a close translation in the sense that the sequence of thought and the phraseology of the original are respected as far as possible, and Marcus' thoughts have not been exclusively recast, let alone paraphrased, as in some of the more literary translations in the past. On the other hand, I have made no attempt to reproduce some of the less pleasing idiosyncrasies of Marcus' style, and its asperities and occasional obscurities, but have tried to present his thought in English which is (I hope) lucid and attractive throughout, and largely free of philosophical jargon, in such a way that it will be immediately intelligible to a reader with no special knowledge of Greek philosophy or culture.

The present translation owes a considerable debt to A. S. L. Farquharson's edition of the *Meditations* (Oxford, 1944, 2 vols), which contains the best English translation and invaluable notes on the Greek text. For the text, which is notoriously corrupt, I have generally followed Farquharson, although I have sometimes chosen other readings in uncertain passages.

ROBIN HARD

BIBLIOGRAPHY

Editions of the Meditations in Greek

J. Dalfen (ed.), *M. Aurelii Antonini ad se ipsum libri xii*, Teubner, Leipzig 1979, 2nd edn 1987

A. S. L. Farquharson (ed.) with translation and commentary, *The Meditations of Marcus Aurelius Antoninus*, 2 vols, Oxford 1944

C. R. Haines (ed. with translation), Loeb Classical Library, *The Communings with Himself of M. Aurelius Antoninus*, Cambridge, Mass. 1916

W. Theiler (ed. with translation into German), *Kaiser Marc Aurel, Wege zu sich selbst*, Zurich 1951

English Translations of the Meditations

M. Casaubon, London 1634, repr. Everyman, London 1906

A. S. L. Farquharson, Oxford 1944, repr. with introduction and notes by R. B. Rutherford, World's Classics, Oxford 1989 (the most useful previous translation)

C. R. Haines, Loeb Classical Library, Cambridge, Mass. 1916

J. Jackson, Oxford 1906

G. Long, London 1862; often reprinted

M. Staniforth, Penguin Classics, Harmondsworth 1964

Marcus Aurelius: Historical and Cultural Context

A. Birley, *Marcus Aurelius: A Biography*, London 1966, 2nd edn 1987

P. Brown, *The World of Late Antiquity*, London 1971

P. A. Brunt, 'Stoicism and the Principate', *Proceedings of the British School at Rome* 43 (1975), 7–39

P. A. Brunt, 'Marcus Aurelius and the Christians', in C. Deroux (ed.), *Studies in Latin Literature and Roman History 1*, Brussels 1979, 483–520

E. Champlin, *Fronto and Antonine Rome*, Cambridge, Mass. 1980

E. R. Dodds, *Pagan and Christian in an Age of Anxiety*, Cambridge 1965

M. Foucault, *The Care of the Self: The History of Sexuality vol. 3*, tr. R. Hurley, London 1988

M. T. Griffin, *Seneca: A Philosopher in Politics*, Oxford 1976, 2nd edn 1992

R. Lane Fox, *Pagans and Christians*, Harmondsworth 1986

P. Noyen, 'Marcus Aurelius, the Greatest Practician of Stoicism',
L' Antiquité classique 24 (1955), 372–83

J. H. Oliver, *Marcus Aurelius: Aspects of Civic and Cultural Policy*,
Hesperia Supplement 13, Princeton 1970

G. R. Stanton, 'Marcus Aurelius, Emperor and Philosopher',
Historia 18 (1969), 570–87

Philosophical Context

J. Annas, *The Morality of Happiness*, Oxford 1993

S. M. Braund and C. Gill (eds), *The Passions in Roman Thought
and Literature*, Cambridge 1997

D. R. Dudley, *A History of Cynicism*, London 1937

C. Gill, *Greek Thought*, Oxford 1995

C. Gill, with introduction and notes, *Epictetus: The Discourses,
Handbook, Fragments*, translated by R. Hard, Everyman,
London 1995

P. Hadot, *Philosophy as a Way of Life. Spiritual Exercises from
Socrates to Foucault*, ed. A. Davidson, trans. M. Chase, Oxford
1995

B. Inwood, *Ethics and Human Action in Early Stoicism*, Oxford
1985

A. A. Long, *Hellenistic Philosophy*, London 1974, 2nd edn 1986

A. A. Long, *Stoic Studies*, Cambridge 1996

A. A. Long and D. N. Sedley, *The Hellenistic Philosophers*, 2 vols,
Translations and Commentary, vol. 1, *Texts and Bibliography*,
vol. 2, Cambridge 1987 (standard abbreviation LS; the key
modern reference work for Hellenistic philosophy)

J. L. Moles, 'Cynicism', in C. J. Rowe and M. Schofield (eds),
Cambridge History of Greek and Roman Political Philosophy,
Cambridge, forthcoming

R. J. Newman, '*Cotidie meditare*: Theory and Practice of the
meditatio in Imperial Stoicism', *Aufstieg und Niedergang der
römischen Welt* 2.36.3, Berlin 1989, 1473–1517

M. C. Nussbaum, *The Therapy of Desire: Theory and Practice in
Hellenistic Ethics*, Princeton 1994

J. M. Rist, *Stoic Philosophy*, Cambridge 1969

F. H. Sandbach, *The Stoics*, London 1975

M. Schofield, *The Stoic Idea of the City*, Cambridge 1991

R. W. Sharples, *Stoics, Epicureans and Sceptics: An Introduction to Hellenistic Philosophy*, London 1996

Meditations: Thought, Style

E. Asmis, 'The Stoicism of Marcus Aurelius', *Aufstieg und Niedergang der römischen Welt* 2.36.3, Berlin 1989, 2228–52

P. A. Brunt, 'Marcus Aurelius in his *Meditations*', *Journal of Roman Studies* 64 (1974), 1–20

C. Gill, 'Musonius, Dio, Epictetus, Marcus Aurelius', in C. J. Rowe and M. Schofield (eds), *Cambridge History of Greek and Roman Political Thought*, Cambridge, forthcoming

A. A. Long, 'Epictetus and Marcus Aurelius', in J. Luce (ed.), *Ancient Writers: Greece and Rome vol. 2*, New York 1982, 985–1002

J. M. Rist, 'Are You a Stoic? The Case of Marcus Aurelius', in B. F. Meyer and E. P. Sanders (eds), *Jewish and Christian Self-Definition*, Philadelphia 1982, 23–45, 190–2

R. B. Rutherford, *The Meditations of Marcus Aurelius: A Study*, Oxford 1989 (the only modern book–length study of *Med.* in English, with emphasis on form of *Med.* and on Marcus' intellectual style)

G. R. Stanton, 'The Cosmopolitan Ideas of Epictetus and Marcus Aurelius', *Phronesis* 13 (1968), 183–95

MEDITATIONS

BOOK 1

1.1   From my grandfather* Verus, nobility of character and evenness of temper.

1.2   From the reputation of my father* and what I remember of him, modesty and manliness.

1.3   From my mother,* piety and generosity, and to abstain not only from doing wrong but even from contemplating it; and the simplicity, too, of her way of life, far removed from that of the rich.

1.4   From my great-grandfather,* that I never had to attend the public schools, but had the use of good teachers at home, and to have come to realise that this is a matter on which one should spare no expense.

1.5   From my tutor,* not to have sided with the Greens or the Blues at the races, or the fighters with the light shields or the heavy in the amphitheatre; to endure hardship, and have few needs; to do things for myself and not meddle in the affairs of others; and to turn a deaf ear to slander.

1.6   From Diognetus:* not to become obsessed with trivialities, and not to believe the claims of miracle-mongers and charlatans about incantations and the expulsion of demons and the like; not to engage in quail-fighting or become excited over other pursuits of the kind; to be willing to tolerate plain speaking; to have

Words or phrases followed by * are discussed in the notes (pp. 121–53). Where the chapter number is followed by *, the chapter as a whole is discussed.

become familiar with philosophy, and to have attended the lectures first of Baccheius,* and then of Tandasis and Marcianus; to have written compositions as a boy; to have wished for a plank bed covered only with a skin and for everything else that formed part of the Greek discipline.

1.7   From Rusticus:* I gained the idea that my character was in need of correction and cultivation; and from him I learned not to be led astray into a passion for rhetoric, and not to write treatises on speculative matters, or deliver little moralising homilies, or play the ascetic or the benefactor in a manner calculated to impress; to abstain from oratory, and verse, and fine language, and not to walk around the house in ceremonial clothing, or indulge in other such vanities; to write letters in an unaffected style, as he himself did when he wrote to my mother from Sinuessa; with regard to those who have angered or wronged me, to be easily recalled to my usual frame of mind, and to be easily reconciled as soon as they are willing to make a move in my direction; to read with care and attention, and not be satisfied with a superficial impression; not to agree too quickly with those who talk with a fluent tongue; and finally, it was through him that I came to know the *Discourses* of Epictetus, for he lent me a copy from his own library.

1.8   From Apollonius:* moral freedom, and never to give oneself over to chance; to look to no other guide, even for an instant, than reason alone; to remain ever the same, in the throes of pain, at the loss of a child, or during a lengthy illness; to see clearly from a living example that a person can be extremely energetic and yet relaxed; not to become irritable when expounding a text; and to see in him a man who clearly regarded the skill and fluency that he showed in communicating philosophical doctrines as the least of his gifts; and to learn how one should accept from friends what pass for favours without lowering oneself as a result or showing an insensitive disregard.

1.9   From Sextus:* A kindly disposition, and the example of a household governed by the father of the house; the idea of what it means to live in accordance with nature;* gravity without affectation, and a careful regard for the interests of one's friends; patience towards the unlearned and those whose opinions are not founded on methodical reflection. The example of one who could accommodate himself to all kinds of people, so that not only was his conversation more beguiling than any flattery, but at the same time he exacted the highest respect from those who associated with him. The ability to grasp with precision and to search out and order in a methodical manner the principles necessary to human life. And he never displayed even a sign of anger or of any other passion, but seemed at once to be free from such passions and full of affection for his fellow human beings; and to be ready to praise, without being too demonstrative, and to possess extensive knowledge without making a show of it.

1.10   From Alexander the grammarian:* not to be censorious; and not to reprimand in a captious spirit those who introduce a solecism or some outlandish or discordant expression, but rather to suggest adroitly the very expression which ought to have been used while professing to offer a reply or some further confirmation, or to join in a debate on the matter itself rather than the diction, or by some other tactful procedure which allows the right expression to be suggested in an indirect fashion.

1.11   From Fronto:* to have some conception of the malice, caprice and dissimulation that accompany absolute rule; and that on the whole, those whom we rank as Patricians are somewhat lacking in natural affection.*

1.12   From Alexander the Platonist:* That we should not often or without due necessity either say to anyone or write in a letter, 'I am too busy', nor in this way should we constantly try to evade the obligations imposed on us by our social relationships by pleading the excuse of urgent business.

1.13   From Catulus:* not to disregard a rebuke from a friend, even if his criticism may be unreasonable, but to try to restore him to his usual frame of mind; to offer unstinting praise to one's teachers, as is recorded of Athenodotus and Domitius;* and to show genuine love to one's children.

1.14*   From Severus: love for one's family, for truth, for justice; that through him I came to know Thrasea, Helvidius, Cato, Dio, Brutus, and to conceive the idea of a balanced constitution, and of government founded on equity and freedom of speech, and of a monarchy which values above all things the freedom of the subject; and from him too, a consistent and unfailing respect for philosophy; and a readiness to help others, and open-handed generosity; to be of good heart, and trust in the affection of one's friends; and how he would be completely open with those who incurred his disapproval, and that his friends never had to resort to conjecture about what he wished or did not wish, for it was plain to see.

1.15   From Maximus:* to be master of oneself, and never waver in one's resolve; to be cheerful when ill, or in any other predicament; the example of a character marked by a harmonious blend of graciousness and gravity; to set to work on the task at hand without complaint. And the confidence he inspired in all that what he was saying was just what he thought, and that whatever he did was done with no bad intent; never to be surprised or discontented; and never to act in haste, or hang back, or be at a loss, or be downcast, and never to fawn on others or, on the other hand, be irascible or suspicious. To be beneficent, and ready to forgive, and free from guile; to give the impression of being a man who never deviates from what is right rather than of one who has to be kept on the right path; and how nobody would ever have imagined that Maximus looked down on him, or yet have ventured to suppose that he was a better man than Maximus; and to be of good humour.

1.16   From my adoptive father:* to be gentle, and to hold immovably to judgements arrived at after careful deliberation; to be free of vain conceit with regard to worldly honours; love of work and perseverance; to lend a ready ear to those who have anything to propose for the common benefit; never to be deflected from rewarding each person according to his deserts; to know by experience when to exert oneself and when to relax the pressure; to put a check on pederastic love affairs;* regard for the feelings of others, and how he would not insist that his friends should always attend his table or accompany him on his progresses, and how they would find him ever the same if they had been kept away by other business. At sessions of the Council,* to examine every question with scrupulous care, and to be patient, for it was not his way to cut short any enquiry because he was satisfied with first impressions; to hold on to one's friends, and never be fickle in one's affections, or give way to infatuations; to be self-sufficient in every respect, and show a cheerful face to the world; to look far ahead, and plan even the smallest matters in advance, but not make a song and dance about it. How he put a curb on public acclamations and every kind of flattery during his reign; and the care that he constantly devoted to the needs of the empire, and his prudent stewardship of the public revenues, and his willingness to put up with the criticisms that such economies provoked. With regard to the gods, to be free from superstitious fears; and with regard to men, not to court public favour by seeking to please at any price or pandering to the mob; but sobriety in all things, and firmness, and never a trace of vulgarity or lust for novelty.

The things that contribute to the comfort of life, of which fortune had granted him copious supply, he used without ostentation but also without apology, so as to enjoy them unaffectedly when they were at hand, but to feel no need of them when they were not. No one would have described him as a sophist, a wag or a pedant, but rather as a man of maturity and accomplishment who was inaccessible to flattery and well able to preside over his own affairs and those of others.

In addition to all this, he had a high respect for genuine philosophers,* but towards the other sort he was not unduly disparaging, but neither on the other hand was he readily taken in by them; and further, his approachability and good humour, though not to excess; and how he cared for his body with due moderation without valuing his life at too high a rate or being concerned about his outward appearance, but also without neglecting it, and in such a way that because of his own attentions, he rarely had need of a doctor's help, or medicines or external treatment. And most admirable too was his readiness to give way without jealousy to those who possessed some special ability, such as eloquence or a knowledge of law and custom and the like, and how he did his best to ensure that each of them gained the recognition that he deserved because of his eminence in his particular field; and how he would always act according to the traditions of our forefathers, without making a show of the fact that he was following established tradition. Furthermore, he was not changeable or capricious, but remained faithful to the same places and the same practices; and after severe bouts of headache, he would return to his usual occupations with renewed vigour; and his secrets were not many, but few and far between, and even those were only in connection with affairs of state; and he showed good sense and moderation in the provision of public spectacles, the construction of buildings, the distribution of largesse, and the like, looking only to what ought to be done, and not to the reputation that he would gain for having done it.

It was not his way to take baths at unreasonable hours, and he was not over-fond of building, and he attached little importance to his food, or the fabric and colour of his garments, or the attractiveness of his slaves. His clothing was sent up from his country house at Latium, and most other things from Lanuvium. How he behaved to the tax collector at Tusculum who sought his forgiveness, and his general conduct in such matters. He was never harsh, or implacable, or overbearing, nor, as the saying goes, was he the sort of man who 'gets into a sweat', but everything was planned out in every detail, as if at leisure, and calmly, methodically, vigorously and consistently. What is reported of Socrates* applies just as well to him, that he was equally able to enjoy or to abstain from those things which many are too weak to abstain from and too self-indulgent in enjoying. To have strength and endurance, and to show restraint in either case, is the mark of a man who possesses a perfect and indomitable soul, as was shown by Maximus during his illness.

1.17 From the gods:* to have had good grandparents, good parents, a good sister, good teachers, good companions, relatives and friends, almost without exception; and that with regard to none of them did I ever lapse into any serious offence, although my disposition was such that I might well have behaved in such a manner if circumstances had favoured it; but through the grace of the gods, no conjunction of circumstances ever developed which would have put me to the test. That I was not brought up any longer than I was with my grandfather's concubine,* and that I preserved the flower of my youth and did not play a man's part before the proper season, but even deferred it until somewhat later. That I was placed under a ruler and a father who was able to rid me of all my vanity, and lead me to understand that it is possible to live at court and yet have no need of bodyguards, or embroidered robes, or candelabra and statues and pompous trappings of that kind, but that it is possible for a prince to restrict himself to something very close to the style of a private citizen, without lowering his status as a result or neglecting any of the duties that a ruler must perform on behalf of the public.

To have had such a brother,* whose character was able to stimulate me to cultivate my own nature, and yet at the same time gratify me by his respect and affection; that my children* were not feeble-minded or physically deformed; that I was not more proficient at rhetoric,* poetry and other pursuits in which I might well have become engrossed if I had felt that I was making good progress; that I was not slow to advance my tutors to the honours which they seemed to desire, and that I did not put them off with the hope that, since they were still young, I would do so at a later date; to have come to know Apollonius, Rusticus and Maximus;* to have clearly and frequently envisaged the proper meaning of a life according to nature,* so that, in so far as it depends on the gods and communications, assistance and inspiration from the divine, there is nothing to prevent me from living according to nature right away, although I still fall somewhat short of this by my own fault and because I have failed to heed the reminders and, one might almost say, the instructions of the gods.

That my body has held out for all this time in the midst of such a life as my own; that I never touched Benedicta or Theodotus,* but that even afterwards, when I did fall prey to the passions of love, I was cured of them; that although I was often angry with Rusticus, I never resorted to measures which I would have regretted; that although my mother* was destined to die at an early age, she at least spent her last years with me; that whenever I wanted to help somebody who was short of money or needed assistance in some other respect, I was never told that I lacked the means to do so, and that I for my part never fell into any similar need, so as to require assistance from another; that my wife* is such as she is, so obedient, so affectionate, so simple; that I have been well provided with suitable tutors for my children; that remedies have been granted to me through dreams, especially against blood-spitting and vertigo, and the response of the oracles at Gaieta; that when I conceived a passion for philosophy, I did not fall in with any sophist, nor did I sit down to pore over books or resolve syllogisms or busy myself with speculations about matters in the heavens.*

For all these things require the help of the gods and of fortune.

BOOK 2

Amongst the Quadi on the River Gran[*]

2.1 Say to yourself at break of day, I shall meet with meddling, ungrateful, violent, treacherous, envious, and ungrateful men. All these vices have fallen to them because they have no knowledge of good and bad. But I, who have beheld the nature of the good, and seen that it is the right; and of the bad, and seen that it is the wrong; and of the wrongdoer himself, and seeing that his nature is akin to my own – not because he is of the same blood and seed, but because he shares with me in mind and a portion of the divine – I, then, can neither be harmed by any of these men, nor can I become angry with one who is akin to me, nor can I hate him, for we have come into being to work together, like feet, hands, or eyelids, or the two rows of teeth in our upper and lower jaws. To work against one another is therefore contrary to nature; and to be angry with another and turn away from him is surely to work against him.

2.2[*] This thing, whatever it is, that I am, is mere flesh, and some breath, and the governing faculty. Despise the flesh – mere blood and bones, and a mesh of interwoven nerves and veins and arteries. Consider, too, what kind of a thing your breath is: a stream of air, and not even forever the same, but expelled at each moment and then drawn in anew. So that leaves our third part, the governing faculty. Away with your books, distract yourself no longer, that is no longer permissible. But rather, as if your death were already upon you, think these thoughts: you are an old man, no longer allow this part of you to play the part of a slave, or to be drawn this way and that, like a puppet, by every uncooperative impulse, or to be discontented any longer with what is allotted to it in the present or to feel apprehension at what will be allotted in time to come.

2.3* Providence permeates the works of the gods; and the works of fortune are not dissociated from nature, but intertwined and interwoven with all that is ordered by nature. Everything flows from there; but necessity is implicated too, and the wellbeing of the entire universe of which you are a part. Now for every part of nature, the good is that which universal nature brings, and which serves to sustain that nature; and the universe is sustained not merely by the changes of the elements, but also by the changes of the bodies compounded from them. May these truths suffice for you, and always be your doctrines. As for your thirst for books, be done with it, so that you may not die with complaints on your lips, but with a truly cheerful mind and grateful to the gods with all your heart.

2.4   Remember how long you have been deferring these things, and how many times you have been granted further grace by the gods, and yet you have failed to make use of it. But it is now high time that you realised what kind of a universe this is of which you form a part, and from what governing part of that universe you exist as an emanation; and that your time here is strictly limited, and unless you make use of it to clear the fog from your mind, the moment will be gone, as you are gone, and never be yours again.

2.5   At every hour devote yourself in a resolute spirit, as suits a Roman and a man,* to fulfilling the task in hand with scrupulous and unaffected dignity, and love for others, and independence and justice; and grant yourself a respite from all other preoccupations. And this you will achieve if you perform every action as though it were your last, freed from all lack of purpose and wilful deviation from the rule of reason, and from duplicity, self-seeking, and dissatisfaction with what is allotted to you. You see how few are the things that a person needs to master if he is to live a tranquil and godfearing life; for the gods themselves will demand nothing more from one who observes these precepts.

2.6   You are ill-treating, ill-treating yourself, o my soul; and no occasion will be left for you to do yourself due honour. For everyone's life lasts but a moment, and yours is almost done, and yet you have no respect for yourself, but allow your happiness to depend on what passes in the souls of others.

2.7   Are you distracted in any way by what befalls you from outside? Then give yourself some free time to learn something new and worthwhile, and stop straying from your path. But after that, you must also guard against going astray in the opposite direction; for equally foolish are those who have become wearied of life as a result of their activities and have no aim to which they can direct every impulse and, indeed, every thought.

2.8   Rarely is a person seen to be in a bad way because he has failed to attend to what is passing in the soul of another; but those who fail to pay careful attention to the motions of their own souls are bound to be in a wretched plight.

2.9   Always keep the following points in mind: what the nature of the whole is, and what my own nature is; and how my nature is related to that of the whole, and what kind of a part it is of what kind of a whole; and that no one can prevent you, in all that you do and say, from always being in accordance with that nature of which you are a part.

2.10   Theophrastus* speaks like a true philosopher when he says in his comparison of faults (for one may make such a comparison when speaking in a more or less popular sense) that faults committed through appetite are graver than those committed through anger. For when a person loses his temper, he seems to turn his back on reason with a kind of pain and unconscious wringing of the heart, but when he offends through appetite and is overpowered by pleasure, he somehow seems more licentious and more unmanly in his wrongdoing. Theophrastus was right, then, and was speaking as befits a philosopher, when he maintained that wrongdoing associated with pleasure calls for harsher condemnation than that associated with pain. And generally speaking, in the one case the offender is more like a person who has first been injured by another and has been driven by pain to lose his temper, while in the other, he has been impelled to do wrong as a result of his own inclination, being carried away by appetite to act as he does.

2.11   Let your every action, word and thought be those of one who could depart from life at any moment. But to take your leave of the human race is nothing to be feared, if the gods exist; for they would not involve you in anything bad. If, on the other hand, they do not exist,* or if they have no concern for human affairs, why should I care to go on living in a world devoid of gods or devoid of providence? But they do exist, and they do show concern for human affairs, and they have placed it wholly within the power of man never to fall into genuine evils; and if amongst everything else, anything were bad for us, they would have made provision for that too, to ensure that everyone would have it in his power not to fall victim to it. But if something does not make a person worse in himself, how could it make his life worse? Universal nature would not have allowed this to pass, whether through ignorance, or, if she knew of it, because she lacked the power to guard against it or put it right. She would never, through lack of power or skill, have committed such a grave fault as to allow good and evil to fall to good people and bad alike without distinction. Now death and life, fame and obscurity, wealth and poverty, fall to good and bad in equal measure, being neither honourable nor shameful in themselves; and so it follows that they are neither good nor bad.

2.12 How swiftly all things vanish away, both the bodies themselves in the universe, and the remembrance of them in time; and of what a nature is all that falls beneath our senses, especially the things that entice us with the promise of pleasure, or frighten us with the thought of pain, or are noised abroad through vanity. How cheap it all is, how despicable, sordid, corruptible, dead, must be left to our faculty of reason to determine; and consider too what kind of people these are whose opinions and voices confer renown, and what it means to die, and that if one considers death in isolation, stripping away by rational analysis all the fancies that cluster around it, one will no longer consider it to be anything other than a process of nature, and if somebody is frightened of a process of nature, he is no more than a child; and death, indeed, is not only a process of nature but also beneficial to her. Consider too how man makes contact with god, and through what part of himself, and how that part must be disposed if he is to do so.

2.13 There is nothing more wretched than one who made the circuit of everything and, as the poet says,* 'searches into what lies beneath the earth, and tries to read the secrets of his neighbour's soul', yet fails to perceive that it is enough to hold fast to the guardian-spirit within him* and serve it single-mindedly; and this service is to keep it pure from passion and irresponsibility and discontentment with anything that comes from god or man. For what comes from the gods is worthy of reverence because of their excellence, and what comes from our fellows should be dear to us because we share a common nature, although sometimes, in a sense, it deserves our pity too, because of their ignorance of good and evil – an infirmity no less grave than that which deprives us of the power to distinguish black from white.

2.14* Even if you were due to live three thousand years or ten times as long, you should still remember this, that no one loses any other life than the one that he is living, nor does he live any other than the one that he loses, so the shortest life and the longest amount to the same. For the present is equal for all, and what is passing must be equal also, so what can be lost is shown to be merely a moment; for no one could lose either the past or the future, for how can he be deprived of what he does not possess? So always bear in mind these two points: the one that all things are alike in nature for all eternity and recur in cycles, and it therefore makes no difference whether one beholds the same spectacle for a hundred years or two hundred or for time everlasting; and the other, that the longest-lived and the earliest to die suffer an equal loss; for it is solely of the present moment that each will be deprived, if it is indeed the case that this is all that he has and a person cannot lose what he does not have.

2.15 Everything is what you think it is.* For the words addressed to the Cynic Monimus are clear enough, and clear too the value of what was said, if one accepts its inner meaning, so far as it is true.

2.16* The soul of man does violence to itself above all when it becomes, so far as it can, an abscess and a sort of morbid outgrowth on the universe. For to set your mind against anything that comes to pass is to set yourself apart from nature, which embraces as part of itself the natures of all individual things. Again, it does violence to itself when it turns away from any other person or moves against him with the intention of causing him harm, as is the case with those who lose their temper; and thirdly, when it is overcome by pleasure or pain; and fourthly, when it dissimulates, and says or does anything under false pretences; and fifthly, when failing to direct any act or impulse of its own towards a definite mark, it embarks on anything whatever in an aimless and ill-considered manner, although even the least of its actions should be performed with reference to an end; and the end for rational creatures is this, to conform to the reason and law of the most venerable of cities and constitutions.

2.17[*] In human life, our time is a point, our substance a flux, our senses dull, the fabric of our entire body subject to corruption, our soul ever restless, our destiny beyond divining, and our fame precarious. In a word, all that belongs to the body is a stream in flow, and all that belongs to the soul, mere dream and delusion, and our life is a time of war and an interlude in a foreign land, and our fame thereafter, oblivion. So what can serve as our escort and guide? One thing and one alone, philosophy; and that consists in keeping the guardian-spirit within us inviolate and free from harm, and ever superior to pleasure and pain, and ensuring that it does nothing at random and nothing with false intent or pretence, and that it is not dependent on another's doing or not doing some particular thing, and furthermore that it welcomes whatever happens to it and is allotted to it, as issuing from the source from which it came itself, and above all, that it awaits death with a cheerful mind as being nothing other than the releasing of the elements from which every living creature is compounded. Now if for the elements themselves it is nothing terrible to be constantly changing from one to another, why should we fear the change and dissolution of them all? For this is in accordance with nature; and nothing can be bad that accords with nature.

BOOK 3

Written at Carnuntum[*]

3.1   We must take account not only of the fact that our life is being consumed each day and an ever smaller part of it is left, but also of this, that if one should live for longer, it is by no means clear that one's mind will remain unchanged and still be adequate for the understanding of affairs and for the theoretical reflection that strives after a knowledge of things divine and human. For if a person's mind begins to fail him, his respiration, digestion, power to deal with sense impressions, desire and appetite, and other functions of the kind will not give out; but his ability to make proper use of himself, to determine the components of his duty with accuracy, to analyse what is presented to his senses, to reach a clear judgement on when it is the right moment for him to depart from life,[*] and to attend to all such questions, in which well exercised powers of reasoning are especially required – all of these are extinguished at an earlier stage. We must act with all urgency, then, not only because we are drawing closer to death at every moment, but also because our power to understand things and pay close attention to them gives out before the end.

3.2   Truths such as this should also be carefully noted, that even the by-products of natural processes[*] have a certain charm and attractiveness. Bread, for instance, in the course of its baking, tends to crack open in places, and yet these very cracks, which are, in a sense, offences against the baker's art, somehow appeal to us and, in a peculiar way, promote our appetite for the food. And figs again, when fully ripe, tend to split open; and in olives which are ready to drop, the very fact of their impending decay lends a peculiar beauty to the fruit. And ears of corn bending towards the earth, and the wrinkled brows of a lion, and the foam dripping from the jaws of a wild boar, and many other things are far from beautiful if one views them in isolation, but nevertheless, because they follow from natural processes lend an added beauty to these and so beguile us. So if a person is endowed with sensibility and has a deep enough insight into the workings of the universe, he will find scarcely anything which fails to please him in some way by its presence, even among those which arise as secondary effects. Such a person will view the gaping jaws of wild beasts in their physical reality with no less pleasure than the portrayals of them displayed by painters and sculptors, and he will be able to see in an old woman or old man a special kind of mature beauty, and to look on the youthful charms of his attendants with chaste eyes. And one could cite many similar examples, which will not seem persuasive to everyone, but will only strike home with those who are genuinely familiar with nature and all her works.

3.3* Hippocrates, after curing many an illness, himself fell ill and died. The Chaldaean asrologers predicted many a death, and then they too were overtaken by fate. Alexander, Pompey and Gaius Caesar often razed whole cities to the ground and slaughtered tens of thousands of horsemen and footsoldiers on the battlefield, and yet there came a day when they too departed from life. Heraclitus, after many a learned discourse on how the world would be destroyed by fire, became overfilled with water, and died besmeared with cow-dung. And Democritus was killed by lice, and Socrates by lice of quite another kind. So what does it all amount to? You climbed aboard, you set sail, and now you have come to port. So step ashore! If to another life, there will be no want of gods even in that other world; but if to insentience, you will no longer be exposed to pain and pleasure or be the servant of an earthen vessel which is as much inferior to it as that which serves it surpasses it in value: for the one is mind and guardian-spirit, and the other mud and gore.

3.4 Do not waste what remains of your life in thoughts about others, unless you are doing so with reference to the common good. For you are depriving yourself of the opportunity for some other action [which may be of real benefit],* to imagine instead what so-and-so is doing and to what end, and what he is saying, and thinking, and devising, and other such thoughts which serve only to divert you from paying proper attention to your own governing faculty. Rather, you must exclude from the sequence of your thoughts all that is aimless and random, and, above all, idle curiosity and malice; and you must train yourself only to think such thoughts that if somebody were suddenly to ask you, 'What are you thinking of?', you could reply in all honesty and without hesitation, of this or that, and so make it clear at once from your reply that all within you is simple and kindly, and worthy of a social being who has no thought for pleasure, or luxury in general, or contentiousness of any kind, or envy, or suspicion, or anything else that you would blush to admit if you had it in your mind.

For such a man, who no longer postpones his endeavour to take his place among the best, is indeed a priest and servant of the gods, behaving rightly to the deity stationed within him, which ensures that the mortal being remains unpolluted by pleasures, invulnerable to every pain, untouched by any wrong, insensible of any evil, a wrestler in the greatest contest of all, never to be overthrown by any passion, deeply steeped in justice, welcoming with his whole heart all that comes about and is allotted to him, and never, save under some great necessity and for the good of his fellows, giving thought to what another is saying or doing or thinking. For he devotes himself solely to the realisation of his own duty, and is always mindful of what is assigned to him from the whole; and he fulfils his duty through fine deeds, and is convinced that whatever is allotted to him is good; for the fate assigned to each person accompanies him through life and is only to his benefit.

He remembers, furthermore, that all rational beings are akin, and that while it follows from human nature that he should care for all of his fellows, he should pay heed to the opinion not of all of them, but only of those who live a life that accords with nature. As for those who live otherwise, he is constantly mindful of what they are like, at home and abroad, by night and by day, and what sort of people they mix with; and accordingly, he sets no value on praise from such people, who are not pleasing even to themselves.

3.5   When you act, let it be neither unwillingly, nor selfishly, nor unthinkingly, nor half-heartedly; do not attempt to embellish your thoughts by tricking them out in fine language; avoid excessive talk and superfluous action. Furthermore, let the god within you be the overseer of one who is manly and mature, a statesman, a Roman, and a ruler,* who has taken his post as one who is awaiting the signal for his recall from life and is ready to obey without need of an oath or another man as his witness. And show a cheerful face to the world, and have no need of help from outside or the peace that others confer. In brief, you must stand upright, not be held upright.

3.6 If you can discover in human life anything better than justice, truth, temperance, and courage – in short, than a mind that is contented both with itself, in so far as it ensures that your actions follow the rules of right reason, and with destiny, in what is allotted to you and beyond the sphere of your choice – if, I say, you can see anything better than this, then turn to it with all your heart and profit from this supreme good which you have discovered. But if nothing better is revealed than the guardian-spirit enthroned within you, which has subjected your impulses to its own authority, and scrutinises your thoughts, and, as Socrates used to say,* has withdrawn itself from the enticements of the senses, and submitted itself to the authority of the gods, and devotes itself to the care of others – if you find all else to be trivial and cheap when compared to this, then grant no place to anything else which, if once you turn to it and turn aside from your path, you would no longer be able to pay the highest honour without distraction to the good that is proper to you and truly your own. For it is not right that one should set in competition to the rational and social good anything at all that is foreign to its nature, such as praise from the crowd, position, or wealth, or sensual pleasure. All of these, even if they seem to suit our nature in the short term, suddenly seize control of us and carry us away. For your part, I say, you must in all simplicity and freedom choose what is higher and hold to that. – 'But the higher is that which brings me benefit.' – Well, if it benefits you as a rational creature, keep a firm hold on it; but if it benefits you merely as an animal, acknowledge it, and maintain your judgement without arrogance, only taking care that your examination* is conducted on a secure basis.

3.7 Never prize as advantageous to yourself anything that will compel you some day to break your word, to offend against propriety, to hate, suspect or curse another, to dissemble, or to desire anything that needs to be veiled behind walls and curtains. One who has chosen above all to honour his own intelligence, and consecrates himself to the cult of its excellence, never strikes a theatrical pose, or gives way to complaint, or feels the need of solitude or the companionship of crowds; and most important of all, he will pass his life neither pursuing nor fleeing from anything whatever, and it concerns him not at all whether he will have his soul enclosed in his body for a longer or a shorter space of time. For even if he must depart at once, he will make his departure as easily as he performs any other action that can be accomplished with decency and order, caring for this alone throughout his life, that his mind should never be in any state which is alien to a rational and social being.

3.8   In the mind of one who has been chastened and thoroughly purified, you will find no infected tissue, no contamination, no festering sore beneath the skin; nor is the life of such a person incomplete when fate overtakes him, so that one could say that the actor is leaving the stage before he has completed his role and the play is done. Furthermore, there is nothing servile in him, nothing affected, nor is he dependent on others, nor is he cut off from them, nor is there anything in him which would not bear examining or hides away from the light.

3.9   Venerate your faculty of judgement. For it depends entirely on this that there should never arise in your governing faculty any judgement that fails to accord with nature or with the constitution of a rational being; and it is this that guarantees freedom from hasty judgement, and fellowship with humankind, and obedience to the gods.

3.10   Cast everything else aside, then, and hold to these few truths alone; and remember, furthermore, that each of us lives only in the present, this fleeting moment of time, and that the rest of one's days are either dead and gone or lie in an unknowable future. Human life is thus a little thing, and little too the corner of the earth on which it is lived, and little too even the fame that endures for the longest, and even that is passed on from one poor mortal to another, all of whom will die in no great while, and who have no knowledge even of themselves, let alone of one who has died many long years before.

3.11[*] To the preceding principles, one more should be added: always define or describe whatever presents itself to your mind, so as to see what sort of thing it is when stripped to its essence, as a whole and in its separate parts; and tell yourself its proper name, and the names of the elements from which it was compounded and into which it will finally be resolved. For nothing is so conducive to elevation of mind as to be able to examine methodically and truthfully everything that presents itself in life, and always to view things in such a way as to take account at the same time of what use each thing serves in what kind of a universe, and what value it has in relation to the whole, and what value to man as a citizen of the most exalted of cities, of which all other cities are, as it were, mere households; and what this object which now produces an impression in my mind actually is, and what it is composed of, and how long it will naturally endure; and what virtue is needed to confront it, such as gentleness, courage, sincerity, fidelity, simplicity, self-sufficiency, and the rest. So, as each case presents itself, one must say: this has come from god; this is allotted to me by the spinning and interweaving of the threads of destiny and suchlike coincidence or chance; this comes to me from one of my own kind, my relative, my friend, who yet has no knowledge of what truly accords with his nature. But I am not ignorant of it, and thus I will treat him kindly and justly, as the natural law of fellowship requires, aiming at the same time, however, to assign to him what he deserves in the case of things that are neither good nor bad in themselves.

3.12 If you accomplish the task set before you following right reason and with dedication, steadfastness and good humour, and you never allow secondary issues to distract you, but keep the deity within you pure and upright, as if you might have to surrender it at any moment – if you hold to this, looking for nothing and fleeing from nothing, but satisfied if your present action is in accordance with nature and all that you say and utter accords with the truthfulness of an earlier and purer age, you will live a happy life; and no one can stand in your way.

3.13[*] As doctors always keep their knives and instruments at hand to deal with emergency cases, so you too should keep your doctrines at the ready, to enable you to understand things divine and human, and so to perform every action, even the very smallest, as one who is mindful of the bond that unites the two realms; for you will never act well in any of your dealings with the human unless you refer it to the divine, and conversely in your dealings with the divine.

3.14* Run astray no longer; for you are not likely to read those notebooks of yours, or your accounts of the deeds of the ancient Romans and Greeks, or the extracts from their writings, which you were laying aside for your old age. Hasten, then, towards your goal, and dismissing idle hopes, come to your own rescue, if you have any care for yourself, while it is still possible.

3.15* They have no idea of how much is signified by terms such as stealing, sowing, purchasing, being at peace and seeing what ought to be done; for this is seen not by our eyes, but quite another kind of vision.

3.16* Body, soul, mind: for the body, sense-impressions; for the vital spirit, impulses; for the intellect, judgements. To receive impressions by means of images is something that we share even with cattle; and to be drawn this way and that by the strings of impulse, we share with wild beasts, with effeminates, and with a Phalaris or a Nero; and to have the mind as a guide towards what appear to be duties is something that we share with those who do not believe in the gods, with those who betray their country, with those who will do anything whatever behind locked doors. If you share everything else with those whom I have mentioned, there remains the special characteristic of a good person, namely, to love and welcome all that befalls him and is spun for him as his fate, and not to defile the guardian-spirit seated within his breast, nor to trouble it with a host of fancies, but to preserve it in serenity, following god in an orderly fashion, never uttering a word that is contrary to the truth nor performing an action that is contrary to justice. And if all others refuse to believe that he is living a simple, modest, and cheerful life, he is not angry with any of them nor is he diverted from the path that leads him to life's close, which he must reach as one who is pure, at peace, and ready to depart, consenting to his destiny without need for constraint.

BOOK 4

4.1 When the ruling power within us is in harmony with nature, it confronts what comes to pass in such a way that it always adapts itself with ease to what is practicable and what is granted to it. For it attaches its preference to no specific material; rather, it sets out to attain its primary objects, but not without reservation,* and if it comes up against something else instead, it converts it into material for itself, much as with a fire when it masters the things which fall into it. These would have extinguished a little lamp, but a blazing fire appropriates in an instant all that is heaped on to it, and devours it, making use of this very material to leap ever higher.

4.2 Never embark on an action without a clear end in view, or otherwise than according to one of the principles which perfect the art of living.

4.3 People seek retreats* for themselves in the countryside, by the seashore, in the hills; and you too have made it your habit to yearn for such things with all your heart. But this is altogether unphilosophical, when it is possible for you to retreat into yourself at any hour you please; for nowhere can one retreat into greater calm or freedom from care than within one's own soul, especially when a person has such fine things within him that he has merely to look at them to achieve from that very moment perfect ease of mind (and by ease of mind I mean nothing other than having one's mind in good order). So constantly accord yourself this retreat, and give new life to yourself; but have within you brief and fundamental precepts which will suffice, as soon as you meet with them, to cleanse you from all distress and to send you back without discontent to the life to which you will return.

For what shall arouse your discontent? Human wickedness? Call to mind the doctrine that rational creatures have come into the world for the sake of one another, and that forbearance is a part of justice, and that when people do wrong, they do so involuntarily;* and think of all those who, up to this time, have lived in enmity and suspected, hated and battled with one another, only to be laid out dead and reduced to ashes. Only think of that, and complain no more. But perhaps you are discontented with what is allotted to you from the whole? Then call to mind the alternative, 'either providence or atoms',* and all the proofs that the universe should be regarded as a kind of constitutional state. Or shall the affections of the body still have a hold on you? Reflect that the mind, as soon as it draws in on itself and comes to know its own power, no longer associates itself with the motions, be they rough or smooth, of the breath; and think too of all that you have heard, and have assented to, with regard to pleasure and pain. Or is it a petty desire for fame that draws you from your path? See, then, how swiftly all things fall prey to oblivion, and the abyss of boundless time that stretches before you and behind you, and the hollowness of human applause, and the fickleness and fatuousness of those who make a show of praising you, and the narrowness of the confines in which this comes to pass; for the earth in its entirety is merely a point in space, and how very small is this corner of it in which we have our dwelling. And even here how few there will be, and of what a mean nature, who will sing your praises.

So henceforth, remember to retreat into this little plot of earth which is truly your own, and above all, do not distress or overstrain yourself, but preserve your freedom, and look at things as a man, a human being, a citizen, a mortal creature. And amongst the precepts which you keep most closely at hand for frequent reference, let the following be included: the first, that things of themselves have no hold on the mind, but stand motionless outside it, and all disturbances arise solely from the opinions within us; and the second, that all that you now behold will change in no time whatever and be no more; and constantly reflect on how many such changes you yourself have already witnessed.

'The universe is change, and life mere opinion.'

4.4[*] If mind is common to us all, then so is the reason which makes us rational beings; and if that be so, then so is the reason which prescribes what we should do or not do. If that be so, there is a common law also; if that be so, we are fellow-citizens; and if that be so, the world is a kind of state. For in what other common constitution can we claim that the whole human race participates? And it is from there, from this constitution, that our intelligence and sense of law derive; or else, where could they come from? For as what is earthy in me has been apportioned to me from some earthy element, and what is watery from another element, and what is hot and fiery from yet another specific source – for nothing proceeds from nothing, just as nothing returns to nothing – so our mind also has come from some particular source.

4.5 Death, like birth, is a mystery of nature, the one being the coming together of the same elements that in the other are dispersed into the same; and there is nothing at all in this to cause one any shame, for it conflicts neither with what suits a rational creature nor with the principles of his constitution.

4.6 Given the nature of such people, these things naturally follow, as an inevitable consequence; and one who wants this not to be so would want a fig tree not to have its bitter sap. As a general rule, you should remember this, that in a short span of time both you and he will be dead, and that shortly afterwards not even your names will be left.

4.7 Do away with the judgement, and the notion 'I have been harmed' is done away with; do away with that notion, and the harm itself is gone.

4.8 If something does not make a person worse in himself, neither does it make his life worse, nor does it harm him without or within.

4.9 Necessity demanded that what is naturally beneficent should bring this to pass.

4.10 All that comes to pass, comes to pass justly. You will discover this to be the case, if you look closely. I do not say simply according to the sequence of cause and effect, but according to justice and as if it were assigned by somebody according to the merits of the case. So look carefully, as you have begun, and whatever you do, do it with this in mind, that you should do it as a good person ought, according to the specific conception that you have formed of what it means to be good. And hold to this in all that you undertake.

4.11 Do not view things from the standpoint from which the wrongdoer judges them or would have you judge them, but see them as they truly are.

4.12 You should always be ready to apply these two rules of action, the first, to do nothing other than what the kingly and law-making art ordains for the benefit of humankind, and the second, to be prepared to change your mind if someone is at hand to put you right and guide you away from some groundless opinion. But this change of view must always be based on a conviction that it serves justice or the common benefit; and this or something like it should be the sole reason for your choice, rather than the impression that it would be pleasant or popular.

4.13 You have reason? – Yes, I do. – Then why not use it? For if this performs its function, what else would you have besides?

4.14 You entered the world as a part, and you will vanish into the whole which brought you to birth; or rather, you will be received back into its generative reason through a process of change.

4.15 Many grains of incense cast on the same altar; one falls earlier, another later, but it makes no difference at all.

4.16 Before ten days are over, you will seem a god to those who presently view you as a wild beast or an ape, if only you return to your principles and your reverence for reason.

4.17 Do not act as if you had ten thousand years to live. The inescapable is hanging over your head; while you have life in you, while you still can, make yourself good.

4.18 What ease of mind he gains who casts no eye on what his neighbour says or does or thinks, but looks only to what he himself is doing, to ensure that his own action may be just, and holy, and good in every regard. Do not look round at the black character of another, but run straight towards the finishing line, never glancing to left or right.

4.19   One who feels a passionate desire for posthumous fame fails to recognise that everyone who remembers him will die very swiftly in his turn, and then again the one who takes over from him, until all memory is utterly extinguished as it passes from one person to another and each in succession is lit and then snuffed out. And supposing for the sake of argument that those who will remember are indeed immortal, and the remembrance is immortal, what is that to you? I hardly need say that praise means nothing to the dead; but what does it mean to the living, unless, perhaps, it serves some secondary purpose? For you are rejecting unseasonably the gift that nature grants to you in the present, and are setting your mind on what others may say of you hereafter.

4.20   Everything that is in any way beautiful is beautiful of itself and complete in itself, and praise has no part in it; for nothing comes to be better or worse for being praised. And I say this even of things which are described as beautiful in everyday speech, such as material objects and works of art. As for what is truly beautiful, has it need of anything beyond? Surely not, any more than law does, or truth, or benevolence, or modesty. Which of these is beautiful because it is praised, or becomes any less so if it is criticised? Does an emerald become any worse if nobody praises it? Or gold, ivory, purple, a lyre, a sword, a blossom, or a shrub?

4.21*   If souls continue to exist, how does the air have room for them from all eternity? One would do as well to ask how the earth has room for the bodies of those who have been buried in it for countless ages. The fact is, that just as here below bodies change and decompose after a certain period of time to make room for other dead bodies, so likewise, the souls which pass into the air endure for a certain time, and then change and are diffused, and are burned up when they are taken back into the generative principle of the universe; and in that way they make room for the souls that take their place. Such would be our reply, assuming that souls continue to exist. But we should consider not only the multitude of bodies that are buried in this way, but also the quantities of animals which are eaten each day by ourselves and other creatures. How large a number are consumed and thus, in a way, buried in the bodies of those who feed on them! And yet there is space for them because they are turned into blood, or transformed into air or fire. How are we to find the truth of the matter? By distinguishing the material from the causal.

4.22 Do not stray from your course, but with regard to every impulse deliver what is right, and with regard to every idea that presents itself preserve your power to grasp the truth.

4.23 Everything suits me which suits your designs, o my universe. Nothing is too early or too late for me which is in your own good time. All is fruit for me that your seasons bring, o nature. All proceeds from you, all subsists in you, and to you all things return. The poet says: 'Dear city of Cecrops';* and you, will you not say: 'Dear city of Zeus'?

4.24 Do little, says the sage, if you want contentment of mind. Would it not be better to do what is necessary, and whatever the reason of a naturally sociable creature may demand, and as it demands it? For this will bring not only the contentment of mind that comes from acting aright, but also that which comes from doing little; for considering that the majority of our words and actions are anything but necessary, if a person dispenses with them he will have greater leisure and a less troubled mind. You should also remember to ask yourself on every occasion, 'Is this one of the unnecessary things?' And we should dispense not only with actions which are unnecessary, but also with unnecessary thoughts; for in that way the needless actions which follow in their train will no longer ensue.

4.25 Try living as a good man and see how you fare as one who is well pleased with what is allotted to him from the whole and finds his contentment in his own just conduct and kindly disposition.

4.26 You have seen all that? Now consider this. Do not disturb yourself; strive to be simple. Someone is doing wrong? The wrong is to himself. Something has befallen you? It is well; all that falls to you from the whole was ordained for you from the beginning and spun to be your fate. In short, life is brief; and you should profit from the present with prudence and justice. Be sober and yet relaxed.

4.27* Either a well-ordered universe, or a heterogeneous mass heaped together, which yet forms an order; or can it be that a certain order subsists within yourself, but disorder in the whole, and that too when all things are distinct and yet interfused and bound together by a common sympathy?

4.28   A dark character, an unmanly character, an obstinate character, bestial, brutish, puerile, fatuous, deceitful, scurrilous, mercenary, tyrannical.

4.29* If he is a stranger in the universe, one who has no knowledge of what is in it, he is no less a stranger who has no knowledge of what takes place in it. A fugitive is he who flees from civic reason; a blind man, he who closes the eyes of his mind; a beggar, he who depends on another and does not possess in himself all that is needed for life; an abscess on the body of the universe, he who sets himself apart and cuts himself off from the reason of our common nature because he is dissatisfied with what comes to pass – for the same nature brings this to be that brought you too into being; and a limb severed from human society is he who severs his own soul from the soul of all rational beings, which is but one.

4.30* This man has no tunic, and that no book, and yet they live as philosophers; and here is a third who is naked and says, 'I have no bread, and yet I hold to reason'; and I for my part gain nourishment from my studies and yet I do not hold to it.

4.31   Love the art which you have learned, and take your rest in that; and pass through the rest of your life as one who has entrusted all that he has, with a full heart, to the gods, and makes himself neither a tyrant nor a slave to any man.

4.32* Call to mind, say, the time of Vespasian, and you will see the same old things: people marrying, bringing up children, falling sick, dying, fighting wars, feasting, trading, tilling the land, flattering, putting on airs, suspecting their fellows, hatching plots, praying for the death of others, grumbling at their present lot, falling in love, piling up fortunes, lusting for high office or a crown; and now that life of theirs is utterly dead and nowhere to be seen. And then pass on to the time of Trajan. Once again the same old things; and that life too is dead. Consider likewise the annals of other ages and of entire nations, and see how many people, after their brief exertions, soon fell prey to death and were resolved into their elements. But above all, you should run over in your mind those whom you yourself have known, who, distracted by vain pursuits, have neglected to do what their own constitution demanded, and to hold firm to this and rest content. And here it is essential to remember that the care bestowed on each action should be proportionate to its worth; for then you will not lose heart and give up, if you are not busying yourself with lesser matters to a greater extent than they deserve.

4.33   The everyday expressions of earlier times are now archaic; and likewise, the names of those who were highly acclaimed in earlier ages are now, in a sense, archaic; Camillus, Caeso, Volesus, Dentatus, and a little later, Scipio too and Cato, and then Augustus* also, and then Hadrian and Antoninus. For all things are swift to fade and become mere matter for tales, and swiftly too complete oblivion covers their every trace. And here I am speaking of those who shone forth with a wonderful brightness; as for all the rest, the moment that they breathed their last, they were 'out of sight, out of mind'. And what does it amount to, in any case, this everlasting remembrance? Sheer vanity and nothing more. What, then, is worthy of our striving? This alone, a mind governed by justice, deeds directed to the common good, words that never lie, and a disposition that welcomes all that comes to pass, as necessary, as familiar, as flowing from a like origin and spring.

4.34   Willingly surrender yourself to Clotho, and let her spin the thread of your fate into whatever events she chooses.

4.35   All is ephemeral, both that which remembers and that which is remembered.

4.36   Observe constantly that all things come into being through change, and accustom yourself to the thought that universal nature loves nothing so much as to change the things that are and create new ones in their place. For everything that exists is, in a sense, the seed of what will arise from it, whilst to your way of thinking, the only seeds are those which are cast on to the earth or into a womb; but that is very much a layman's view.

4.37   Your life will soon be over, and you are not yet simple, or unperturbed, or free from the suspicion that things from outside can harm you, nor do you yet believe that wisdom lies in one thing alone, in acting justly.

4.38   Look into their governing faculties, even with those who pass for wise, and see what things they flee from and what they pursue!

4.39   What is bad for yourself lies neither in the governing faculty of another, nor yet in any change and alteration in the things that surround you. Where, then? In that part of you which judges that certain things are evils. So let it pass no judgement, and all is well. Even if its closest companion, your poor body, is cut or cauterised, or festers or decays, let the part of you which forms a judgement about these matters keep its peace none the less; in other words, let it judge nothing to be good or bad if it can fall to a good person or a bad without distinction. For that which falls alike to one whose life is contrary to nature and one whose life accords with nature is itself neither in accordance with nature nor contrary to it.

4.40   Constantly think of the universe as a single living being, comprised of a single substance and a single soul; and how all things issue into the single consciousness of this being, and how it accomplishes all things through a single impulse; and how all things work together to cause all that comes to be, and how intricate and densely woven is the fabric formed by their interweaving.

4.41*   You are a little soul carrying a corpse around, as Epictetus used to say.

4.42   For things to suffer change is no more bad for them than it is good for them to subsist as a consequence of change.

4.43*   There is a stream of things entering into being, and time is a raging torrent; for no sooner does each thing enter our sight than it has been swept away, and another is passing in its place, and that too will be swept away.

4.44   All that comes to pass is as accustomed and familiar as the rose in spring and the fruit in autumn; and so likewise is illness and death and slander and intrigue and all that brings delight or causes distress to the foolish.

4.45   What comes after is always linked by a tie of affinity to what came before; for this is not like the counting out of a series of independent units linked only by the necessary sequence of cause and effect, but a rational conjunction. And as existing realities are harmoniously co-ordinated, so also what comes into being displays no mere succession but a wonderful inward affinity.

4.46* Always remember the saying of Heraclitus, that the death of earth is birth for water, and the death of water is birth for air, and that of air for fire, and conversely. Remember, too, his saying about the man who forgets where his road is leading, and this: 'they are at variance with that with which they have the most constant communion' – the reason that governs the universe; and again, that we should not 'act and speak like those who are asleep' – for even in our sleep we seem to act and speak; and that we should not behave as children do to their parents, that is to say, simply follow what we have been taught.

4.47 If one of the gods informed you, 'You will die tomorrow or, at any rate, the day after tomorrow', you would consider it no great matter whether it were the day after tomorrow rather than tomorrow, unless, indeed, you were an extraordinary coward, for the difference is minimal; so likewise, consider it no great matter whether you will die after many a long year rather than tomorrow.

4.48 Reflect constantly on how many physicians have died after knitting their brows again and again over the beds of the sick; and how many astrologers after foretelling the deaths of others as though death itself were some great thing; and how many philosophers after endless disputes about death and immortality; and how many heroes after slaying a multitude of others; and how many tyrants after exercising their power over life and death with fearful arrogance, as though they themselves would be immortal; and how many entire cities have, if one may use the word, died: Helice, Pompeii, Herculaneum* and others without number. Also call before your mind, one after another, the many whom you yourself have known. This man, after paying his last respects to that, was then laid out himself, and the one who laid him out was laid out in his turn, and all in so short a time. In a word, never cease to observe how evanescent are all things human, and how worthless: today a drop of mucus, and tomorrow a mummy or a pile of ash. So make your way through this brief moment of time as one who is obedient to nature, and accept your end with a cheerful heart, just as an olive might ripen and fall, blessing the earth that bare it and grateful to the tree that gave it growth.

4.49   Be like the headland with wave after wave breaking against it, which yet stands firm* and sees the boiling waters round it fall to rest. 'Unfortunate am I, that this has befallen me.' No, quite the contrary: 'Fortunate am I, that when such a thing has befallen me, I remain undisturbed, neither crushed by the present nor afraid of what is to come.' For such a thing could have befallen anyone, but not everyone would have remained undisturbed in the face of such a blow. So why is this a misfortune rather than something fortunate? Or do you generally say that human misfortune can lie in something other than a deviation from man's true nature? And do you suppose anything to be a deviation from man's nature if it does not conflict with the will of that nature? Well then, you have learned to know that will. Can what has befallen you prevent you in any way from being just, high-minded, self-controlled, prudent, deliberate in your judgement, empty of deceit, self-respecting, free, or from possessing any of the qualities which by their presence make it possible for man's nature to come into its own? So henceforth, in the face of every difficulty that leads you to feel distress, remember to apply this principle: this is no misfortune, but in bearing it nobly there is good fortune.

4.50   An unphilosophical but none the less effective aid to attaining contempt for death is to review in your thoughts those who have clung tenaciously to life. For how are they any better off than those who died a premature death? Somehow or other, in any case, they lie at last beneath the earth, Caedicianus, Fabius, Julianus, Lepidus,* and others like them, who carried so many to their graves and were then carried out to their own; and small, in any event, is the difference, and through what troubles, and with what companions, and in what a body we drag out our lives! So regard it as no great matter. For look at the abyss of time behind you, and the other infinity which stretches before you; in the midst of this, what difference between a child that lives for three days and a Nestor who lives for three generations?

4.51   Always run by the shortest route; and the shortest is that which follows nature, and leads us to say and do everything in the soundest fashion. For such a plan of action delivers us from trouble and conflict, and from every artifice and affectation.

5.1   Early in the morning, when you find it so hard to get up, have these thoughts ready at hand: 'I am rising to do the work of a human being. Why, then, am I so irritable if I am going out to do what I was born to do and what I was brought into this world for? Or was I created for this, to lie in bed and warm myself under the bedclothes?' – Well, it is certainly more pleasant. – So were you born for pleasure or, in general, for feeling, or for action? Do you not see how the little plants, the little birds, the ants, the spiders, the bees, each do their own work and play their part in the proper running of the universe? And will you, then, for your part, refuse to do the work of a human being? Will you not hasten to do what your nature requires of you?' – Yes, but one also needs one's rest. – Quite so, but nature has set limits on that, as she has on eating and drinking, and yet you are going beyond those limits, and beyond what is sufficient. But when it comes to your actions, that is no longer the case, but there you stop short of what you could do. The truth is, you have no love for yourself; or otherwise, you would love both your own nature and all that your nature wills. Others who love their own crafts wear themselves to the bone as they work away at them without pausing to wash or feed; but you hold your own nature in less honour than the engraver his metal-work, the dancer his dancing, the miser his money, or the glory-hunter his scrap of fame. And yet these people, when the fit takes them, would sooner do without food or sleep rather than fail to make progress in the things that they care about, while you for your part fancy that actions that serve the common good are of lesser value and less deserving of effort.

5.2   How easy it is to repel and wipe away every disturbing or unbefitting thought, and recover at once a perfect calm.

5.3   Consider every word and deed that accords with nature to be worthy of you, and do not allow yourself to be turned aside by the criticisms and talk that may follow, but if anything is rightly said or done, do not consider that you deserve anything less. For those others have their own inner guide and follow their own impulses. Do not look around at them, but keep to a straight course, following your own nature and universal nature; for the path of both is but a single path.

5.4   I proceed along the path laid down by nature until the day arrives for me to fall and take my rest, yielding my last breath to the air from which I daily draw it in, and falling to that earth from which my father drew his seed, my mother her blood, and my nurse her milk, and from which day by day these many years I have gained my food and drink; the earth that bears me as I tread over it and misuse it to so many ends.

5.5   They cannot admire you for the sharpness of your mind. – So be it, but there is much else of which you cannot say, 'I have no gift for that'. So display the qualities that are wholly within your power, sincerity, dignity, endurance, disdain for sensual pleasure, satisfaction with your lot, contentment with little, kindness, freedom, frugality, avoidance of idle chatter, and elevation of mind. Do you not see how many fine qualities you are already able to display, for which you can offer no excuse of want of natural talent or lack of aptitude? And yet of your own free will you still fall short of your proper level. Or are you compelled to grumble, to be grasping, to flatter others, to heap scorn on your poor body, to be ingratiating, and boastful, and restless in your mind, because you were created without the necessary gifts? No, by the gods, you could have been delivered from all of this long ago, and then have been open to only the one charge, if indeed that, of being somewhat slow in your mind and slow in the uptake; and even in that regard you should exercise yourself, instead of neglecting your faults and taking comfort in your dullness.

5.6   It is the way of one person, when he has done someone a good turn, to count as a matter of course on being repaid in kind. Another is not as quick to do so, but all the same, in his own mind, he regards the beneficiary as being in his debt, and he is conscious of what he has done. A third is, in a sense, not even conscious of what he has done; he is rather like a vine which has produced its grapes, and seeks for no further reward once it has borne its proper fruit, as with a horse when it has run its race, or a dog when it has followed its trail, or a bee when it has made its honey. And so such a person, when he has done a good deed, does not cry it abroad, but passes straight on to the next, as the vine yields new clusters of grapes when the season comes around. 'So one should be one of these people who act in this way without, as it were, being aware of it?' To be sure. 'But surely that is precisely what he should be aware of? For it is the mark, they say, of a social being to perceive that he is acting to the good of society, and, by Zeus, to wish that his neighbours should perceive it too!' What you say is true enough, but you are misreading the present argument; and because of that, you will be one of those people whom I mentioned earlier. For they too are led astray by reasoning which has a certain plausibility. But if you make an effort to understand what I really meant, you should have no fear that on that account you will neglect any act which serves the common good.

5.7   A prayer of the Athenians: 'Rain, rain, dear Zeus, on the ploughlands and plains of Attica'. We should either pray in this simple and artless fashion, or not pray at all.

5.8   As people say, 'Asclepius* has prescribed horse riding for this person, or cold baths, or walking barefoot', so we might also say, 'Universal nature has prescribed sickness for this person, or disablement, or loss, or something else of the kind.' Now in the first case, the expression 'prescribe' means something like 'he laid this down for him as appropriate to his health'; and in the latter what 'fits' each person has been laid down for him as being in some way appropriate to his destiny. For when we say that these things 'fit' us, we are talking like the masons when they say that squared blocks fit in walls or pyramids, because they fit in with one another in a particular structural arrangement. Now there is a single harmony that embraces all things, and just as all bodies combine together to make up this single great body, the universe, so likewise, all individual causes combine together to make up the single great cause known as destiny. And that even wholly uneducated people understand what I am saying here is shown when they say, 'Fate brought it on him'; for if it was brought on him, this means that it was prescribed for him. So let us accept what fate prescribes as we accept what Asclepius prescribes for us. For there is surely much in these which is none too agreeable, but we welcome them in the hope of regaining our health. You should regard the realisation and fulfilment of what seems good to universal nature in much the same light as the securing of your health, and so come to welcome whatever comes to us, even if it appears somewhat unpalatable, because it contributes to this great end, the health of the universe and the well-being and well-doing of Zeus. For he would not have brought it on anyone if it were not to the benefit of the whole, any more than any nature you care to mention brings on anything which is against the interest of that which is governed by it. There are thus two reasons why you should be contented with whatever befalls you, firstly, that it was for you that it came about, and it was prescribed for you and stands in a special relationship to you as something that was spun into your destiny from the beginning and issues from the most venerable of causes, and secondly, that for the power which governs the whole, that which comes to each of us individually contributes to its own well-being and perfection, and, by Zeus, its very continuance. For the perfection of the whole suffers a mutilation if you cut off even the smallest particle from the coherence and continuity of its causes no less than of its parts; and you break it off, so far as you can, whenever you are discontented, and, in a certain sense, you destroy it.

5.9   You should not be disgusted, or lose heart, or give up if you are not wholly successful in accomplishing every action according to correct principles, but when you are thwarted, return to the fray, and be well contented if for the most part your actions are worthier of human nature. Love that to which you are returning, and come back to philosophy not as to a schoolteacher, but as those with sore eyes turn to a sponge and white of egg, and another patient to a poultice, and another to fomentations. For in that way, you will not merely make a show of obeying reason, but you will find your rest in it. And remember this, that philosophy wishes nothing other than what your nature wishes, whereas you were wishing for something else which is not in accordance with nature. Now what could be more delightful than to follow nature?

And is it not on account of such delight that vulgar pleasures seduce us? Well, see whether elevation of mind, freedom, simplicity, goodness of heart, and piety afford you greater delight. For what is more delightful than wisdom itself, when you consider how sure of touch and how happy in all its undertakings is the faculty of understanding and knowledge?

5.10* Realities are concealed, so to say, behind such a veil that not a few philosophers, and those of no mean quality, have supposed them to be wholly beyond our comprehension, while even the Stoics themselves find them hard to comprehend; and every assent to sense impressions is subject to alteration – for where are we to find a person who is never subject to error? Now pass on to the sensible objects themselves: how ephemeral they are, how cheap, how liable to become the property of an effeminate, a prostitute, or a robber! Turn next to the characters of your associates, of whom even the most agreeable are hard to endure, not to mention the fact that it is not at all easy even to bear with oneself. In the midst of all this murk and filth, this unending flux of substance and time, and of movement and things that are moved, what there could be that deserves our respect or is worthy in any way of serious pursuit I cannot even conceive. On the contrary, one should content oneself with the expectation of one's natural dissolution, and not be aggrieved at the delay, but put one's trust in these two thoughts alone, firstly that nothing will befall me which is not in accordance with the nature of the whole, and secondly, that it is in my power never to do anything which is contrary to the deity and guardian-spirit within me; for no one can force me to disobey its will.

5.11   'To what purpose, then, am I presently using my soul?' Ask yourself this question at every moment, and examine yourself as follows: what is the present content of the part of me which is commonly called the governing faculty? And whose soul do I have at present? That of a child? That of an adolescent? That of a woman, of a tyrant, of a domestic animal, of a wild beast?

5.12* You can gain an idea of the nature of the things that pass for good amongst the mass of people from the following observations. If a person were to conceive the existence of genuine goods, like wisdom, temperance, justice and courage, he would not be able, with the idea of these in his mind, to listen any longer to the old verses about the man who is 'so well endowed with good things'; for it would be quite inappropriate. But if, on the contrary, he first pictures in his mind the things that appear good to the mass of people, he will lend a willing ear to the saying from the comic poets and readily accept it as a fitting remark. In this way we see that even the average person feels the difference; or otherwise, the joke would not cause offence and be repudiated in the first case, and yet, when applied to wealth and the blessings associated with luxury and fame, be accepted as a telling and witty observation. Go on, then, and ask whether we should prize and accept as good those things with regard to which, when we have formed an idea of them in our mind, we could fittingly remark of their possessor that because he is so richly endowed with them, 'he has nowhere where he can shit.'

5.13   I am composed of the material and the formal;* and neither of these will perish into nothingness, just as neither arose from nothingness. Thus every part of me will be appointed by change to a new station as some part of the universe, and that again will be changed to form another part of the universe, and so on to infinity. It was through a similar process of change that I too came to exist, and my parents before me, and so again to infinity in the other direction (for nothing prevents us from using such language, even if the administration of the universe is organised into a succession of finite periods).

5.14   Reason and the art of reasoning are capacities which are sufficient for themselves and their own works. They start, then, from their own specific principle and make their way to the goal set before them; and that is why actions founded on reason are called 'right acts', to indicate that they follow the right path.

5.15   A human being should count none of those things as his own which do not fall to him in his nature as a human being. For they are not required of him, nor does human nature promise them, nor do they contribute to the perfection of that nature. Accordingly, the human end cannot lie in them, and neither, to be sure, can its correlative, the good. Furthermore, if any of these were proper to human beings, it would not be fitting for them to spurn them or hold out against them, nor would a person who ensured that he had no need of them be deserving of praise, nor would one who was sparing in his enjoyment of any of them be a good person, if it were really the case that these were good things. But as it is, the more a person deprives himself of these or others like them, and the better he bears it when he is deprived of them by another, the better he is as a human being.

5.16 As are your regular impressions, so will your mind be also; for the soul takes it colouring from its impressions. Dye it, then, with a succession of impressions like these: where it is possible to live, there it is also possible to live well; now it is possible to live at court, so it must also be possible to live well at court.* Or again: to that for the sake of which each being has been constituted and for which it was made, to that it strives; now in what it strives towards, there resides its end; and where its end lies, there also lies its specific advantage and good. It follows that the good of a rational being must be fellowship with others; for it has long been proved that we were born for fellowship. Or is it not clear that inferior beings were made for the sake of the superior, and superior beings for the sake of one another? Now animate beings are superior to the inanimate, and rational beings to those which are merely animate.

5.17 To pursue the impossible is madness; now it is impossible that people of bad character should abstain from such behaviour.

5.18 Nothing happens to anyone that he is not fitted by nature to bear. The same things happen to another, and either because he fails to realise that they have happened, or because he wants to display his strength of mind, he stands firm and remains unaffected. Is it not extraordinary that ignorance and self-conceit should prove more powerful than wisdom?

5.19 Things as such have not the slightest hold on our soul, nor do they have access to the soul, nor can they alter it or move it; but the soul alone alters and moves itself, and ensures that whatever is submitted to it conforms to the judgements of which it considers itself worthy.

5.20* From one point of view, human beings are the beings who are closest to us, in so far as we must do good to our fellows and show them forbearance; but in so far as any of them stand in the way of our closest duties, a human being then comes to be one of the things that are indifferent to me, no less than the sun, or the wind, or a wild beast. Now these may hinder one or other of my actions, but they are not hindrances to my impulses or my disposition, because I have the power to act under reservation and turn circumstances to my own advantage. For the mind adapts and converts everything that impedes its activities into something that advances its purpose, and a hindrance to its action becomes an aid, and an obstacle on its path helps it on its way.

5.21 Revere the highest power in the universe, the power that makes use of all things and presides over all. And likewise, revere the highest power in yourself: and this power is of one kind with the other. For in yourself too, this is what makes use of all else, and your life is governed by it.

5.22 What causes no harm to the city causes no harm to the citizen. Every time that the idea occurs to you that you have been harmed, apply this rule, 'if the community is not harmed by this, neither am I'. But if the community really is harmed, do not be angry with the person who is responsible, but show him what he has failed to see.

5.23 Reflect often on the rapidity with which all that exists and is coming to be is swept past us and disappears from sight. For substance is like a river in perpetual flow, and its activities are ever changing, and its causes infinite in their variations, and hardly anything at all stands still; and ever at our side is the immeasurable span of the past and the yawning gulf of the future, in which all things vanish away. Then how is he not a fool who in the midst of all this is puffed up with pride, or tormented, or bewails his lot as though his troubles would endure for any great while?

5.24 Think of substance in its entirety, of which you have the smallest of shares; and of time in its entirety, of which a brief and momentary span has been assigned to you; and of the works of destiny, and how very small is your part in them.

5.25 Another does me wrong? Let him look to that; he has his own disposition, and his actions are his own. For my part, I presently have what universal nature wills that I should have, and I am doing what my own nature wills that I should do.

5.26* Ensure that the governing and pre-eminent part of your soul remains indifferent to every movement, smooth or violent, in your flesh, and let it not combine with them, but circumscribe itself, and restrict these affections to the members of the body. But when they communicate themselves to the mind by virtue of that other sympathy, as must occur in a unified organism, you should not attempt to resist the sensation, which is only natural, but ensure that the governing faculty does not add to it from itself by judging it to be good or bad.

5.27 Live at one with the gods. And he is living with the gods who constantly displays to them a soul that is satisfied with the lot assigned to it and obedient to the will of the guardian-spirit which Zeus has granted to each of us as a portion of his own being to serve as our overseer and guide; and this guardian-spirit is the mind and reason of each one of us.

5.28 You are angry with a man if he smells of stale sweat, or has bad breath? What good will it do you? He has such a mouth, he has such armpits; and being as they are, such exhalations are bound to arise from them. 'Yes, but the man is endowed with reason, and if he would only think, he could see why he is out of line.' Gracious me, you have reason too, so set his powers of reason to work by making use of your own! Show him his fault, call it to his attention; for if he listens, you will cure him, and there will be no need for anger.

Neither a play-actor nor a prostitute.

5.29 You can live here on earth as you intend to live once you have departed. But if others do not allow it, then depart from life even now, but do so in the conviction that you are suffering no evil. Smoke fills the room, and I leave it: why think it any great matter? But while no such reason causes me to leave, I remain a free agent and none shall prevent me from doing what I will: and my will is to act according to the nature of a rational and sociable creature.

5.30 The mind of the whole is concerned for the good of all. At any event, it has made the lower for the sake of the higher, and adapted the higher to one another. You can see how it has subordinated, co-ordinated, and assigned to each the lot that is owing to it and brought the ruling beings into good accord with one another.

5.31   Up until now, how have you behaved towards the gods, your parents, brother, wife, children, teachers, tutors, friends, relatives, servants? Have you acted to all of them hitherto as the saying demands, 'neither doing to anyone nor saying anything except what is right'? And remember all that you have passed through and what you have found the strength to endure; and that the story of your life is almost told and your service accomplished; and how many noble spectacles you have beheld, how many pleasures and pains you have viewed with disdain, how many ambitions you have disregarded; and to how many inconsiderate people you have shown consideration.

5.32   Why do ignorant and uncultivated souls trouble one that is cultivated and knowledgeable? So what is a cultivated and knowledgeable soul? That which knows the beginning and end and the reason that interpenetrates all substance and, through all eternity, governs the whole from one appointed cycle to the next.

5.33   Soon, very soon, you will be ashes or a skeleton, and simply a name, or not even that; and a name itself is an empty sound and an echo. All that is highly prized in life is hollow, putrid, and trivial; puppies snapping at one another, little children bickering, and laughing, and then all at once in tears. And Faith, Modesty, Justice and Truth have fled away 'from the broad-pathed earth up to high Olympus'.* What is there, then, that still holds you back in the world below? The objects of sense are forever in change with never a stay, and our senses are dull and easily deceived by false impressions, and our poor soul* itself is an exhalation from our blood, and glory in such a world as this is utterly vain. So what is one to do? Wait with a good grace, either to be extinguished or to depart* to another place; and until that moment arrives what should suffice? What else than to worship and praise the gods, and do good to your fellows, and bear with them and show forbearance; but as to all that lies within the limits of mere flesh and breath, to remember that this is neither your own nor within your own control.

5.34   You can ensure that your life always follows a happy course if you are able to follow the right path, and hold to what is right in all your thoughts and deeds. For these two properties are shared by the souls of god and man alike, and of every rational creature: not to be subject to hindrance from another, and to find one's good in a just disposition and righteous action and to make that the limit of one's desire.

5.35   If this is neither an evil of mine nor anything that follows from an evil of mine, and the common good is not harmed by it, why am I troubled because of it? And what harm does it bring to the common good?

5.36*   Do not allow yourself to be wholly carried away by your imagination, but come to their aid as best you can and as they deserve, even if what they have lost is of no inherent value. You should not imagine, however, that any real harm is involved; for that is an unhealthy habit. Rather, you must act like the old man [in the play], who, when he went away, would ask for his foster-child's top without losing sight of the fact that it was merely a top. So follow a similar course in the present case also. [And yet you are giving vent to your sympathies in this theatrical fashion;] tell me, man, have you forgotten what these things really were? – 'Yes, but they were of great importance to those who have lost them.' – Is that a reason why you should join them in their folly?

5.37   'Once there was a time, wherever they caught me, when I was one who was blessed by good fortune.' But the person who is blessed by good fortune is the one who has assigned a good lot to himself; and a good lot consists of this, good dispositions of the soul, good impulses, good actions.

BOOK 6

6.1   The substance of the whole is compliant and malleable, and the reason that governs it has nothing within itself which could cause it to bring about anything bad; for it has no evil in itself, nor does it do any wrong, nor is anything injured by it; and all things come into being and are accomplished according to its will.

6.2   Let it make no difference to you whether you are shivering or warm if only you are doing your duty, or whether you are overtired or have had sufficient sleep, or are greeted with disparagement or praise, or are passing away, or are busy at something else. For even the act of dying is one of the acts of our life; and so in that too, it is enough to make good use of what the moment brings.

6.3   Look to the inner nature of things; and in each instance, let neither its specific quality nor its worth escape you.

6.4*   All existing things will change very swiftly, and will either be turned to a vapour, if it be true that all substance is one, or else be scattered abroad.

6.5   The reason that governs all things knows its own disposition, and what it creates, and in what material.

6.6   The noblest way to avenge yourself is not to become as they are.

6.7   Take your delight and find your rest in one thing alone: to pass from one action that serves the good of your fellows to the next, keeping god in your thoughts.

6.8   The governing faculty is that which arouses itself, and adapts itself, making itself as it wishes itself to be, and making whatever happens to it seem to itself as it wishes it to be.

6.9   All things are accomplished in every case in accordance with the nature of the whole; for they could hardly be accomplished according to any other nature, whether embracing the universe from outside, or contained within it, or existing independently outside it.

6.10*   Either a hotchpotch and the entangling of atoms and their dispersal, or unity, order, and providence. If the first thought is true, why should I even wish to linger in such a random assemblage and chaotic disarray? Why should I be concerned about anything else than how one day I shall 'turn again to earth'? And why, indeed, should that trouble me? For dispersal will be my lot whatever I do. But if the latter thought be true, I submit reverently, I stand secure, I place my trust in the power that governs all.

6.11   When the force of circumstances causes you, in some sense, to lose your equilibrium, return to yourself with all speed, and never lose the rhythm for any longer than you must; for you will be more in control of the measure if you return to it again and again.

6.12   If you had a stepmother and a mother at the same time, you would fulfil your obligations to your stepmother, but for all that you would be constantly returning to your mother; and that is your present situation with regard to the court and philosophy. So return to philosophy as often as you can, and take your rest in her; for it is through her that life at court seems bearable to you, and you bearable to your court.

6.13   When you have savouries and fine dishes set before you, you will gain an idea of their nature if you tell yourself that this is the corpse of a fish, and that the corpse of a bird or a pig; or again, that wine is merely grape-juice, and this purple robe some sheep's wool dipped in the blood of a shellfish; and as for sexual intercourse, it is the friction of a piece of gut and, following a sort of convulsion, the expulsion of some mucus. Thoughts such as these reach through to the things themselves and strike to the heart of them, allowing us to see them as they truly are. So follow this practice throughout your life, and where things seem most worthy of your approval, lay them naked,* and see how cheap they are, and strip them of the pretences of which they are so vain. For pride is an ever-subtle deceiver, and it is just when you are most confident that you are engaged on serious matters that it most surely beguiles you. Consider, for instance, what Crates said about Xenocrates himself in this regard.

6.14[*] Most of the things which ordinary people admire may be referred to the broad category of things that are held together by physical cohesion, as with stones and timber, or by organic growth, as with figs, vines and olives; and those which are admired by people of somewhat greater discrimination to things which are held together by animal soul, as with flocks and herds; and those which are admired by people of still greater refinement to things which are held together by rational soul, not, however, that which is rational in the fullest sense, but merely in so far as it possesses a technical skill or some other instrumental capacity. But he who prizes the soul in so far as it is fully rational and is concerned for society will no longer turn his mind to all the rest, but strives above all to ensure that his own soul remains rational and sociable in itself and in its activity and co-operates to that end with those who are of like nature.

6.15[*] Some things are hastening to come into being, and others to be no more; and of that which is coming to be, some part is already extinct. Flux and transformation are forever renewing the world, as the ever-flowing stream of time makes boundless eternity forever young. So in this torrent, in which one can find no stay, which of the things that go rushing past should one value at any great price? It is as though one began to lose one's heart to a little sparrow flitting by, and no sooner has one done so than it has vanished from sight. Indeed, the very life of every one of us is like an exhalation from our blood or inhalation from the atmosphere; for such as it is to draw a breath of air into your lungs and then surrender it, so it is to surrender your power of respiration as a whole, which you acquired but yesterday or the day before at the time of your birth, and are now surrendering to the source from which you first drew it.

6.16 That neither to transpire like plants, nor to breathe like cattle and wild beasts, nor to receive sense-impressions, nor to be pulled around like puppets by our impulses, nor to gather together in herds, nor to feed ourselves, is anything of real value; indeed, the last corresponds to the process by which we expel the waste-products from our food. In that case, what should we value? That people should clap when we appear? No indeed. Then there is no value either in being greeted by clapping tongues (for praise from the crowd is simply the clapping of tongues). So you have now disposed of glory too; what does that leave that is truly of value? In my view, to act or abstain from action as our own constitution requires, the end to which all arts and professions are directed. For every art aims at this, that what it produces should be suited to the purpose for which it has been produced; that is what the gardener who tends the vines and the horse-breeder or dog-trainer seek to achieve. And the training and education of children, to what end do they aspire? It is there, then, that true value should be sought; and if you succeed in this you will no longer seek any other good. Will you not cease to value many other things besides? Otherwise you will be neither free, nor self-sufficient, nor beyond the reach of passion; for you are bound to be envious and jealous, and suspicious of those who can deprive you of the objects of your desire, and to scheme against those who possess what you value. All in all, one who feels a need for any of these things is sure to be in a constant turmoil, and what is more, he must often find fault even with the gods. But if you respect and honour your own understanding, you will make yourself pleasing in your own eyes, and be in harmony with your fellows, and in accord with the gods; that is to say, you will have nothing but praise for all that they dispense and have ordained.

6.17　Up, down, and round about are the courses of the elements. But the movement of virtue follows none of these courses: it is something more divine, and goes happily on its way along a path not easily discerned.

6.18　What curious behaviour! They have nothing good to say of those who live in their own time and share their lives, and yet they themselves are greatly concerned that they should be well spoken of by those who will live after them, whom they have never seen and never will see. This is much the same as if you were aggrieved because those who lived before you never spoke in praise of you.

6.19　Do not suppose that, if you find something hard to achieve, it is beyond human capacity; rather, if something is possible and appropriate for man, assume that it must also be within your own reach.

6.20   During exercises in the gymnasium, someone may have scratched us with his nails or have collided with us and struck us a blow with his head, but, for all that, we do not mark him down as a bad character, or take it amiss, or view him with suspicion afterwards as one who wishes us ill. To be sure, we remain on our guard, but not in a hostile spirit or with undue suspicion; we simply try to avoid him in an amicable fashion. So let us behave in much the same way in other areas of life: let us make many allowances for those who are, so to speak, our fellow-competitors. For it is possible, as I have said, to avoid them, and yet to view them with neither suspicion nor hatred.

6.21   If anyone can give me good reason to think that I am going astray in my thoughts or my actions, I will gladly change my ways. For I seek the truth, which has never caused harm to anyone; no, the person who is harmed is one who persists in his self-deception and ignorance.

6.22   I attend to my own duty, and other things do not distract me; for they are either lifeless, or devoid of reason, or have gone astray and have no knowledge of their path.

6.23   Towards irrational creatures and material things in general, act in a generous and liberal manner, because you have reason and they have none; but towards human beings, because they have reason, you must also behave in a neighbourly manner; and in all things call on the help of the gods. And let it make no difference to you how long you will be doing this; for even three hours lived in such a fashion is time enough.

6.24*   Alexander the Great and his stable boy were brought to a level in death; for they were either taken back into the same generative principle of the universe or were scattered impartially into atoms.

6.25   Consider how many things, in body and soul alike, are coming to pass in each of us in the same brief moment of time; and then you will not be surprised that many more things – indeed, all that comes to be in the one and all which we call the universe – should exist there at one and the same time.

6.26   If someone were to ask you, 'How is the name Antoninus written?', would you spell out each of the letters in an emphatic tone? And then if those around you were angry, would you be angry in return? Or would you not proceed to count out each of the letters in a quiet manner, passing from one to the next? You should remember, then, that in life too, every duty is composed of a number of separate elements. These you must observe, without allowing yourself to be disturbed, and if others become annoyed with you, do not be annoyed in return, but bring the task that lies before you to a methodical conclusion.

6.27   How cruel it is not to allow people to strive after what they regard as suitable and beneficial to themselves. And yet, in a sense, you are withdrawing their right to do so whenever you are angered by their bad behaviour. For it is surely the case that they are simply drawn towards what they consider to be suitable and beneficial to themselves. – 'Yes, but they are wrong to think that.' – Well, instruct them, then, and show them the truth, without losing your temper.

6.28   Death is a rest from the solicitations of sense, and from impulse which pulls us around like a puppet, and from the vagaries of discursive thought, and from our service to the flesh.

6.29   How shameful it is that, in this life, when your body does not give up the struggle, your soul should do so first.

6.30*   Take care that you are not turned into a Caesar, that you are not stained with the purple; for such things do come about. Keep yourself simple, then, and good, sincere, dignified, free from affectation, a friend to justice, reverent towards the gods, affectionate, and firm in the performance of your duties. Struggle to remain such a man as philosophy wished to make you. Honour the gods, protect your fellows. Life is short; and our earthly existence yields but a single harvest, a holy disposition and acts that serve the common good. Be in everything a true disciple of Antoninus: imitate his energy in acting as reason demands, his unchanging equanimity, his piety, the serenity of his expression, the sweetness of his character, his freedom from vanity, and his eagerness to get to the heart of matters. And remember how he would never dismiss a matter until he had examined it carefully and clearly understood it; and how he would put up with people who reproach him unjustly, and never responded in kind; how he never acted in haste, and refused to listen to slander; and how acute he was in appraising people's characters and actions, and how he was never one to carp, or to be easily flustered, or over-suspicious, or pretentious; how it took little to satisfy him, in his lodgings for instance, or his dress, his food, his attendants; how hard-working he was, and how patient; how he would stay at his post from morning till night, and because of his frugal diet would not even need to relieve himself except at his accustomed hour; his firmness and consistency in friendship; how he would tolerate frank opposition to his views and was pleased if somebody could point to a better course; and what reverence he showed to the gods without a trace of superstition. Follow his example, then, so that you may have as clear a conscience as he when your final hour arrives.

6.31   Become sober again, call yourself back, and when you have roused yourself from your sleep and realised that these were mere dreams that were troubling you, look at these things, now that you are awake again, as you looked at those.

6.32* I consist of a body and a soul. Now to the body all things are indifferent; for it is unable to differentiate between them. And to the mind, all that forms no part of its own activity is indifferent, and all that belongs to its own activity is within its own control. But even in relation to that, it is concerned only with the present; for its future and past activities are themselves indifferent at that moment.

6.33   Neither pain to the hand nor pain to the foot is contrary to nature, as long as the foot is doing the work of a foot or the hand the work of a hand. So for a human being likewise, as a human being, pain is not contrary to nature, as long as he is doing the work of a human being; and if it is not unnatural for him, neither is it an evil for him.

6.34   Just think where robbers, effeminates, parricides and despots find their pleasures.

6.35   Do you not see how common craftsmen, although willing to accommodate themselves to laymen to a certain extent, hold fast all the same to the principles of their crafts, and cannot bear to depart from them? Is it not strange, then, that architects and doctors should regard the principles of their crafts with higher respect than man does the principle that governs his life, the reason which he shares in common with the gods?

6.36   Asia and Europe are mere corners of the universe; and by that measure, every ocean is a drop of water, and Mount Athos* is a clod of earth; and the whole of present time is but a point in eternity. All is paltry, ever mutable, swift to vanish. All things flow from there, arising directly from that common governing principle, or else as a secondary effect. Thus even the gaping jaws of a lion, and poison, and every noxious thing, from a thistle to a quagmire, are by-products* of what is sublime and noble. Do not suppose, then, that these are alien to what you revere, but direct your thoughts to the common source of all things.

6.37   One who has seen the present world has seen all that ever has been from time everlasting and all that ever will be into eternity; for all things are ever alike in their kind and their form.

6.38   Reflect again and again on how all things in the universe are bound up together and interrelated. For all things, in a sense, are mutually intertwined, and by virtue of that all are dear to one another; for one thing follows duly upon another because of the tonic movement and the common breath that pervades throughout and the unity of all substance.

6.39   Adapt yourself to the circumstances in which your lot has cast you; and love these people among whom your lot has fallen, but love them in all sincerity.

6.40   Every instrument, tool and utensil is in a good way if it performs the task for which it was fashioned; and here, it should be noted, the maker is separate from what he has made. But where things are co-ordinated by nature, the part that made them lies within them and remains there; and for that reason, you should revere it the more, and believe that if you live and act according to its will, all will proceed for you according to your mind's desire; as likewise, in the universe, all proceeds according to the mind of the whole.

6.41   If you regard anything which is independent of your will as good or bad for yourself, it will necessarily follow that if you fail to escape such an evil or attain such a good, you will cast blame on the gods and hate the people who are responsible for your failing in the one or the other respect, or whom you suspect will be the cause of your failure in the future; and, in truth, we commit many injustices because we attach a value to such things. But if we judge that alone to be good or evil which lies within our own power, we will no longer have occasion to find fault with the gods or assume a hostile attitude to our fellow men.

6.42　We are all working together to a single end, some of us knowingly and with understanding, and others without knowing what they do, in just the same way as those who are asleep, for even they, as Heraclitus,* I think, remarks, are workers and fellow-workers in what comes to pass in the universe. Some help in one way, others in another, and even, in full measure, he who finds fault with what is coming to pass, and tries to resist or suppress it; for the universe has need even of people like that. It remains for you, then, to decide on which side you will be placing yourself; for he who governs all things will make good use of you in any event, and will welcome you to a place amongst his collaborators and fellow-workers. But take care that you assume no such role as that mean and ridiculous verse in the play which Chrysippus mentions.*

6.43　Does the sun undertake to do the work of the rain? Or Asclepius* the duties of the goddess who brings the harvest?* And what of each particular star? Are they not all different, and yet working together to a single end?

6.44*　If the gods have taken counsel about me and what must befall me, they have taken good counsel; for a god who makes ill-advised decisions can scarcely be imagined, and what motive could possibly impel them to do me harm? For what advantage would that bring either to themselves or to the common good, which is their primary concern? But if they have taken no counsel about me as an individual, they will in any event have taken counsel about the common good, and whatever comes about as a consequence of that I am bound to welcome and acquiesce in. But if we imagine that they take counsel about nothing at all – which would be would be an impiety to believe, or else let us no longer sacrifice to them, or pray to them, or swear by them, or do any other of the things that we do in the belief that the gods are close by and dwelling amongst us – but if we imagine, I say, that they take no counsel about our affairs, it is still possible for me to take counsel about myself, and it is for me to consider where my own benefit lies. And the benefit of every being lies in what accords with its own constitution and nature. Now my nature is that of a rational and sociable being. As Antoninus,* my city and fatherland is Rome; as a human being, it is the universe; so what brings benefits to these is the sole good for me.

6.45* All that happens to the individual is to the benefit of the whole; and that should be sufficient. But if you look carefully, you will on the whole observe this further point, that what benefits one person also brings benefits to others. In this case, however, the word 'benefit' should be understood in its everyday sense, as applied to things which are neither good nor bad in themselves.

6.46* Just as you are sickened by the displays in the amphitheatre and such places, because the same scenes are forever repeated and the monotony makes the spectacle irksome, so you should feel also about life as a whole; for all things, high and low, are ever the same and arise from the same. For how long, then?

6.47* Think without cease of the men of all kinds, of all manner of occupations and of every conceivable race, who have passed away; and do so until you come down to Philistion, Phoebus and Origanion. And then pass on to other groups in turn. We too must remove to that other world where so many powerful orators, so many grave philosophers – Heraclitus, Pythagoras, Socrates – and so many heroes of old and commanders and kings of later ages have preceded us, as have Eudoxus, Hipparchus and Archimedes besides, and other acute minds, noble spirits, lovers of toil, men of wide ability, and indomitable characters like Menippus and many another like him, who have scoffed at the transient and perishable nature of human life itself. Of all of these, reflect on this, that they were laid in the dust long ago. Why should that be terrible for them? Or for those whose very names have passed from our memory? In this world there is only one thing of real value, to pass our days in truth and justice, and yet be gracious to those who are false and unjust.

6.48 When you want to gladden your heart, think of the good qualities of those around you; the energy of one, for instance, the modesty of another, the generosity of a third, and some other quality in another. For there is nothing more heartening than the images of the virtues displayed in the characters of those around us, and assembled together, so far as possible, in close array. So be sure to keep them ever at hand.

6.49   You are not aggrieved, surely, because you weigh only so many pounds and not three hundred? Then why be aggrieved that you will live only a certain number of years and no longer? For as you are content with the portion of matter assigned to you, so be contented also with the time.

6.50*   Try to persuade them, but act even if they themselves are unwilling, when the principles of justice demand it. Should anyone, however, use force to block your way, have recourse instead to equanimity and refusal to yield to distress, and so use the setback to display another virtue. Remember, moreover, that your original impulse was not unconditional, and you were not aiming at the impossible. At what, then? Simply to exercise an impulse subject to certain conditions. And this you have achieved; just what we have proposed to ourselves comes to pass.

6.51   The glory-hunter holds that his own good lies in the activity of others, and the pleasure-seeker that it lies in his own sensations; but one who has understanding holds that it lies in his own actions.

6.52   It is possible to form no opinion on this matter and not be troubled in one's mind; for things themselves are not of such a nature that they can create judgements within us.

6.53   Acquire the habit of attending carefully to what is being said by another, and of entering, so far as possible, into the mind of the speaker.

6.54   What brings no benefit to the hive brings none to the bee.

6.55   If the crew spoke ill of the captain or the patients of the doctor, would they have anything else in view than how the man in question could ensure the safety of his crew or the health of his patients?

6.56   How many who entered the world with me have already taken their leave!

6.57*   To those suffering from jaundice, honey seems bitter; to those suffering from rabies, water is an object of terror; to young children, a ball is a thing of beauty. Why, then, am I angry? Or do you fancy that false opinions have less power over people than bile over the jaundiced or the toxin over those bitten by a rabid dog?

6.58 None can prevent you from living according to the rule of your own nature; and nothing can befall you which is contrary to the rule of universal nature.

6.59 What kind of people are they, those whom they wish to please; and to what ends, and through what actions? How swiftly unending time will cover all things, and how much it has covered already!

BOOK 7

7.1   What is vice? It is something that you have often seen. And with regard to everything that comes to pass, be ready to apply this thought, 'This is something that you have often seen.' For everywhere, high and low, you will find the same old things, the things which fill the histories of old and of ages since and of recent times, and fill our cities and our households even now. There is nothing new; everything is long familiar, and swift to pass.

7.2   Your principles have life in them. For how can they perish, unless the thoughts that correspond to them are extinguished? And it is up to you to be constantly fanning them into new flame. I am able, on this matter, to form the opinion that I ought; and if I am able to do so, why am I troubled? Things that lie outside my mind have no hold whatever over my mind. Learn this and you are well set up. To recover your life is within your power; simply view things again as once you viewed them, for your revival rests in that.

7.3*   The idle pageantry of a procession, plays on the stage, flocks and herds, the clashing of spears, a bone tossed to puppies, a scrap of bread cast into a fishpond, the wretched labours of overladen ants, the scurryings of startled mice, puppets pulled about on their strings. You must take your place, then, in the midst of all this, with a good grace and without assuming a scornful air; and yet, at the same time, keep in mind that a person's worth is measured by the worth of what he has set his heart on.

7.4   In conversation, one should attend closely to what is being said, and in every impulse, attend to what arises from it; in the latter case, to see from the first what end it has in view, and in the former, to keep a careful watch on what people are meaning to say.

7.5   Is my understanding equal to this or not? If it is, I apply it to the task in hand as an instrument granted to me by universal nature; but if it is not, I either relinquish the task to someone who is better able to accomplish it, if that accords with my duty in every other respect, or else I perform it myself as best I can, calling on the assistance of one who is able, with the aid of my own governing faculty, to effect what is presently seasonable and advantageous to the community. For all that I do, whether on my own or assisted by another, should be directed to this single end, the common benefit and harmony.

7.6   How many whose praises were once widely sung are now consigned to oblivion; and how many who sang their praises are now departed and gone.

7.7   Think it no shame to be helped by another; for you have to accomplish the duty that falls to you, like a soldier at the storming of a rampart. Now what if you were lame and unable to scale the battlements by your own efforts, but were able to do so with the help of another?

7.8   Do not allow the future to trouble your mind; for you will come to it, if come you must, bringing with you the same reason that you now apply to the affairs of the present.

7.9   All things are interwoven, and the bond that unites them is sacred, and hardly anything is alien to any other, for they have been ranged together and are jointly ordered to form a common universe. For there is one universe made up of all that is, and one god who pervades all things, and one substance and one law, and one reason common to all intelligent creatures, and one truth, if indeed there is one perfection for all creatures who are of the same stock and partake of the same reason.

7.10   Everything material disappears very swiftly into the universal substance, and swiftly too every cause is reabsorbed into the universal reason, and very swiftly the memory of everything is buried in eternity.

7.11   For a rational creature, to act according to nature and to act according to reason is one and the same.

7.12*   Stand upright, or be set upright.

7.13   Just as with the limbs of the body in individual organisms, rational beings likewise in their separate bodies are constituted to work in conjunction. The thought of this will strike you more forcibly if you say to yourself again and again, 'I am a limb (*melos*) of the common body formed by rational beings.' If, however, by changing a single letter, you call yourself a part (*meros*), you have not learned to love your fellows with all your heart, nor do you yet rejoice in doing good for its own sake; for you are still doing it merely as a duty, and not yet in the conviction that you are thus doing good to yourself.

7.14   Let anything from outside that so wishes befall the parts of me which can be affected by its incidence; for it is up to them, if that is their will, to make their complaint. But I myself, if I do not suppose that anything bad has happened to me, have yet to suffer any harm; and it is open to me not to make that supposition.

7.15*   Whatever another may do or say, I for my part must be a good man; it is just as if an emerald – or some gold or purple – should say again and again, 'Whatever another may do or say, I for my part must be an emerald and preserve my native hue.'

7.16   Our governing faculty never disturbs its own peace; I mean, it never arouses fear in itself, or desire. But if someone else can arouse fear in it or cause it pain, let him do so, for on its own account it will not exercise its judgement in such a way as to deliver itself to such feelings. Let the body take care, if it can, that it should suffer no hurt; and let the soul, which can come to know pain and distress, speak out if it suffers any such thing; but that which judges these matters overall will suffer nothing at all, for it is not its way to make such a judgement. In itself the governing faculty wants for nothing, unless it creates the want for itself, and likewise, it is not subject to disturbance or hindrance, unless it disturbs or hinders itself.

7.17*   Happiness (*eudaimonia*) is a good guardian-spirit (*daimon*), or govening faculty within. What, then, are you doing here, impression? Go away in the name of the gods, just as you came; for I have no need of you. But you have come according to your age-old habit. I am not angry with you: only, go away!

7.18   Is one afraid of change? Why, what can take place without change? And what is nearer and dearer to universal nature? Can you yourself take a hot bath unless the firewood suffers change? Can you be fed unless your food suffers change? Can anything else of value be accomplished without change? And do you not see, then, that change in yourself is of a similar nature, and similarly necessary to universal nature?

7.19　All bodies sweep through the substance of the whole as through a winter torrent; all are of one nature with the whole and work with it, as our limbs work with one another. How many a Chrysippus, how many a Socrates, how many an Epictetus has time already engulfed. And may that thought strike you with regard to everyone whatever and every single thing.

7.20　One thing alone troubles me, that I for my part may do something which the constitution of man does not wish, or otherwise than it wishes it, or which it does not wish at this present moment.

7.21　Close is the time when you will forget all things; and close, too, the time when all will forget you.

7.22　It is a special characteristic of man to love even those who stumble. And this love is realised as soon as the thought strikes you that these are your relations and do wrong through ignorance[*] and against their will; and that in no time at all both you and the wrongdoer will be dead, and above all, that he has caused you no harm, for he has not caused your governing faculty to become worse than it was before.

7.23　From the substance of the whole, as if from wax, universal nature moulds first a little horse, and then, melting it down again, uses its material to make a little tree, and then a human being, and then something else again; and each of these endures for only a very short time. But it is nothing terrible for a casket to be broken up, as it was nothing terrible for it to be put together.

7.24　An angry expression on one's face is utterly contrary to nature, and if it often reappears, the grace begins to die from one's face, until, in the end, it is wholly extinguished, and can never be rekindled . . . Try to grasp this specific point, that this is contrary to reason; for if our very awareness of doing wrong is lost, what is left to make life worth living?

7.25 All that you now behold will be changed in no time at all by nature which governs the whole, and from its substance she will make new things, and from their substance new things again, to keep the universe forever young.

7.26 Whenever somebody wrongs you, ask yourself at once, 'What conception of good and evil led him to commit such a wrong?' And when you have seen that, you will pity him, and feel neither surprise nor anger.* For you yourself still hold the same opinion about what is good as he does, or another not unlike it; and you are thus obliged to forgive him. Or if you no longer suppose that things of that kind are good or bad in themselves, you will find it easier to show kindness to one who is still in the dark.

7.27 Do not think of things which are absent as though they were already at hand, but pick out the most pleasant from those which you presently have, and with these before you, reflect on how greatly you would have wished for them if they were not already here. At the same time, however, take good care that you do not fall into the habit of overvaluing them because you are so pleased to have them, so that you would be upset if you no longer had them at some future time.

7.28 Retire into yourself. The rational governing faculty is of such a nature that it finds its contentment in its own just conduct and the serenity that it gains from it.

7.29 Wipe out impression. No longer allow your passions to pull you around like a puppet.* Confine your attention to the present time. Learn to recognise what is happening to yourself or another. Divide and analyse every given object into the material and the causal.* Give thought to your last hour. Let the wrong committed by another remain where it first arose.

7.30 Apply your thoughts to what is being said. Let your mind enter into what is coming to pass and what is causing it to be.

7.31 Hearten yourself with simplicity and modesty and indifference towards all that lies between virtue and vice. Love the human race. Follow god.
  Democritus* says that 'all is convention, and only the elements truly exist'. It is enough to remember that [it is not actually the case that] all things are merely conventional; in fact very little is.

7.32*   On death: Either dispersal, if we are merely atoms; or if we form a unity, extinction or passage to another place.

7.33   On pain: If it is unbearable, it carries us off; if it persists, it can be endured. The mind, too, can preserve its calm by withdrawing itself, and the governing faculty comes to no harm; as for the parts that are harmed by pain, let them declare it, they are able to.

7.34   On fame: Look at the minds [of those who aspire to it] and see what they are like, and the sort of things that they flee from and those that they pursue. And reflect, too, that just as sand dunes are always drifting over one another and concealing what came before, so in life also, what comes earlier is very swiftly hidden by all that piles up afterwards.

7.35*   'Do you suppose that human life can seem any great matter to a man of elevated mind who has embraced the whole of time and the whole of reality in his thoughts?' 'Quite impossible', he replied. 'So to such a person not even death will seem anything terrible?' 'Not in the least.'

7.36*   'It is a king's part to do good and be ill spoken of.'

7.37   How shameful that when the face assumes a fitting expression and agreeable aspect at the bidding of the mind, the mind itself should not adopt such an expression and aspect at its own bidding.

7.38*   'Be not angry with outward events,
           For they care nothing for it.'

7.39*   'To the immortal gods and to ourselves may you bring joy.'

7.40*   'Our lives are reaped like ripened ears of corn,
           And as one comes to be, another is no more.'

7.41*   'If the gods have neglected myself and my sons,
           This too has its reason.'

7.42*   'For fortune is with me and the right.'

7.43*   'Join them not in their laments and feel no excitation.'

7.44*   'But to such a person I could justly reply, "You are mistaken, my friend, if you suppose that a man who is worth anything at all ought to weigh up his chances of living and dying, rather than looking in every action to this single point, whether what he is doing is just or unjust, and the act of a good or a bad man." '

7.45* 'For this, men of Athens, is the truth of the matter: wherever a man has stationed himself, whether he believed it to be best or was posted there by his commander, there, I believe, he ought to remain and face the danger, taking into account neither death nor any other thing apart from dishonour.'

7.46* 'But consider, my good sir, whether the noble and the good may not lie in something other than saving one's life and being saved. Perhaps a man who is worthy of the name should put aside this question of how long he will live, and not cling to life, but entrust these matters to god, believing what old wives say, that "no one can escape his destiny", and turn his attention to this instead, to how he can live the best life possible in the time that is granted to him.'

7.47 Watch the stars in their courses as though you were accompanying them on their way, and reflect perpetually on how the elements are constantly changing from one to another; for the thought of these things purifies us from the defilement of our earthly existence.

7.48 One who would converse on humankind should look on all things earthly as though from some point far above, upon herds, armies, and agriculture, marriages and divorces, birth and death, the clamour of the law courts, deserted wastes, alien peoples of every kind, feasts, lamentations and traffickings, this intermixture of everything and order conjured from opposites.

7.49 Cast your eye on the past: such shifts in the pattern of rule. And it is also possible to foresee the future. For its nature will be just the same, and there is no possibility of its deviating from the present rhythm of events. So it is all the same whether you study human life for forty years or ten thousand; for what more can you expect to see?

7.50*   'What springs from the earth to earth returns,
            But that which springs from a heavenly seed
            Returns again to the heavens above.'

Or this: an unloosing of the forces that bind the atoms and a consequent dispersal of the senseless elements.

7.51*   'With meats and drinks and magic spells
        To turn aside the stream and hold death at bay.'

        'When a storm from the gods blows down upon us,
        Man must toil and endure and not complain.'

7.52* 'Better at throwing his opponent.' Yes, but not more devoted to the common good, or more modest, or more skilful in meeting the moment, or more forgiving of the oversights of his neighbours.

7.53   Where a task can be accomplished in accordance with the reason that the gods and human beings hold in common, there is nothing to fear; for where we can obtain benefit by action which follows its proper course and accords with our constitution, there is no occasion for harm to be anticipated.

7.54   Everywhere and all the time it lies within your power to be reverently contented with your present lot, to behave justly to your present neighbours, and to deal skilfully with your present impressions so that nothing may steal into your mind which you have not adequately grasped.

7.55   Do not turn aside to look into the governing faculties of others, but look straight ahead to where nature is leading you, both universal nature through what befalls you, and your own nature through what you must do on your own account. Now each being must act as its constitution requires; and while the other creatures are constituted for the sake of the rational – just as in every other case the lower exists for the sake of the higher – rational beings exist for the sake of one another. Thus the leading principle in the constitution of man is concern for the good of others, and the second, resistance to the passions of the body; for rational and intelligent movement has this special characteristic, that it delimits itself and never allows itself to be overcome by movements arising from sense and impulse; for the latter belong to our animal nature, but the movement of intelligence demands supreme authority and not to be overpowered by these lower movements, and with good reason too, because it was formed by nature to apply them to its own ends. The third principle in the constitution of a rational being is to be neither hasty in its judgements nor easily deceived. So let your governing faculty proceed directly on its way, holding firm to these three principles, and it will come into its own.

7.56 As if you had died and your life had extended only to this present moment, you must use the surplus that is granted to you to live henceforth according to nature.

7.57 Love only that which falls to you and is spun as the thread of your destiny; for what could be better suited to you?

7.58 In the face of everything that befalls you, keep before your eyes those who, when the same things befell them, were at once distressed, bewildered, and resentful. And where are they now? Nowhere! Well then, do you want to be as they were? Why not leave these shifting humours to others to change and be changed, and concentrate wholly on how you are to make the best use of whatever befalls you? For then you will turn it to good account, and it will serve as material for you. Only pay attention, and resolve to present a fair aspect to yourself in all that you do; and keep in mind these two points, that how you act is of moral significance, and that the material on which you act is neither good nor bad in itself.

7.59 Dig within; for within you lies the fountain of good, and it can always be gushing forth if only you always dig.

7.60* One's body too should hold firm and not be allowed to droop, whether in motion or at rest; for what the mind achieves for the face, by ensuring that it preserves an intelligent and decorous expression, should be required likewise of the body as a whole. But all of this should be attended to without affectation.

7.61 The art of living is more like the wrestler's art than the dancer's in this regard, that it must stand ready and firm to meet whatever besets it, even when unforeseen.

7.62 You should constantly consider what sort of people these are whose testimony you are wishing to acquire, and what ruling principles they have. For if you look into the sources of their judgements and impulses, you will not blame them when they stumble involuntarily, nor will you seek their witness on your behalf.

7.63* 'No soul', he said, 'is willingly deprived of the truth'; and
the same applies to justice too, and temperance, and benevolence,
and everything of the kind. It is most necessary that you should
constantly keep this in mind, for you will then be gentler towards
everyone.

7.64* In the presence of every pain have this thought at hand,
that there is nothing shameful in this nor does it make our
governing intellect worse than it was; for neither in so far as it is
rational nor in so far as it is concerned for the common good does
pain cause it any harm. With regard to most pains, furthermore,
let this saying of Epicurus come to your aid, that 'pain is neither
unendurable nor everlasting, if you keep its limits in mind and do
not add to it through your own imagination'. And remember this
too, that many disagreeable things are really just the same as pain
although we do not perceive them to be, such as drowsiness, or
the oppression that we feel in hot weather, or loss of appetite. So
when something like this is beginning to distress you, say to
yourself, 'You are giving way to pain.'

7.65 See that you never feel towards misanthropes as such
people feel towards the human race.

7.66* How do we know that Telauges was not superior in
character to Socrates? For it is not enough that Socrates died a
more glorious death, or that he showed greater skill in his
arguments with the sophists, or greater endurance when he stood
outside through the whole of a frosty night, or that when he
received the order to arrest the man from Salamis, he thought it
nobler to refuse, and that he strutted through the streets with his
nose in the air (though in regard to this one might feel
considerable doubt as to whether it is true). No, what we ought to
be examining is this, what kind of soul Socrates had, and whether
he could be content to be just towards his fellows and pious
toward the gods, without being aggrieved to no purpose by
human wickedness or ever becoming the slave of another man's
ignorance, or regarding anything that was allotted to him from the
whole as alien to himself, or abiding it as something intolerable, or
submitting his mind to the seductive influence of the passions of
the flesh.

7.67 Nature* has not blended your soul and body so closely together in the compound being that she does not allow you to circumscribe yourself and ensure that what is yours is subject to yourself. Always keep this in mind, and also this further point, that happiness in life depends on very few conditions; and just because you have resigned any hope of excelling in dialectic and natural philosophy,* do not on that account despair of becoming a free man, and one who is modest, concerned for his fellows, and obedient to god; for it is possible to become a wholly god-like man and yet be recognised by nobody.

7.68 Live your whole life through free from all constraint and with the utmost joy in your heart, even if all others are crying out against you with whatever charges they please, even if wild beasts are rending the poor limbs of this lump of clay that has congealed around you. For what in all of this can prevent your mind from preserving its calm, and passing true judgement on what surrounds it, and being ready to make right use of what is submitted to it, so that Judgement can say to what it encounters, 'This is what you are in your true nature even if opinion makes you seem otherwise', and Use can say to what is presented to it, 'It is you that I was seeking; for to me, what is present is always material for rational and civic virtue, and, in general, the workmanship of man or god'; for all that comes to pass is well suited to god or man, and is neither strange nor difficult to handle, but familiar and easy to work upon.

7.69 Perfection of character requires this, that you should live each day as though it were your last, and be neither excitable, nor lethargic, nor duplicitous.

7.70 The gods, who live forever, do not take it amiss that through such endless ages they will constantly have to put up with so many people of such a despicable character; and what is more, they even take care of them in all manner of different ways. So will you, who will cease to exist so very soon, give up the struggle, and that when you too are one of those despicable beings?

7.71 It is absurd not to try to escape from one's own wickedness, which is possible, but equally absurd to try to escape from that of others, which is impossible.

7.72   Whatever the rational and social faculty finds to be neither intelligent nor social, it judges with good reason to be beneath itself.

7.73   Whenever you have done a good deed and another has gained some good from it, why do you seek a third reward in addition, as foolish people do, to become known for having done good, or to be granted the same in return?

7.74   No one grows tired of receiving benefits, and to bestow benefits is to act according to nature; so never grow tired of receiving benefits by bestowing benefits on others.

7.75* Universal nature set out to create a universe; and now it is either the case that all that comes to be does so as a necessary consequence of that, or else even the most important things, to which the governing faculty of the universe directs its own efforts, lie outside the rule of reason. Remember this, and you will face many a trouble with a calmer mind.

BOOK 8

8.1* This thought too will help to free you from vanity, that it is now beyond your power to have lived your whole life, or at least the time since you were young, as a philosopher; for you have made it plain to many people, including yourself, that you fall far short of philosophy. And thus you are tarnished, and it is no longer easy for you to win the reputation of being a philosopher; and your calling counts against it. So if you have truly seen how the matter lies, put aside all concern about what others will think of you, and be satisfied if you live the rest of your life, be it long or short, as your nature wills. Reflect, then, on what it wills, and let nothing else distract you; for you know by experience how many byways you have strayed along without ever discovering the good life. It lay neither in subtleties of argument, nor in riches, nor in glory, nor in sensual pleasure, nor anywhere at all; so where does it lie? In doing what human nature requires. And how is one to do that? By having principles to govern every impulse and action. And what principles are those? Those concerned with good and bad, which tell us that nothing is good for man except what makes him just and temperate, brave and free, and that nothing is bad except what gives rise to the opposing vices.

8.2 On the occasion of every action, ask yourself this: How will this affect me? Shall I have cause to repent of it? A short while, and I shall be dead, and all will be gone. What more need I ask for, if my present action is that of an intelligent and sociable being and of one who is subject to the same laws as god himself?

8.3 What are Alexander, Caesar and Pompey when compared to Diogenes,* Heraclitus and Socrates? For these latter viewed all things in terms of both matter and cause, and their governing faculties were self-determined. As to the others, consider how many cares they had, and of how much they were the slaves!

8.4   Even if you burst with rage, they will do the same things none the less for that.

8.5   First of all, be untroubled in your mind; for all things come about as universal nature would have them, and in a short while you will be no one and nowhere, as are Hadrian and Augustus. And next, keep your eyes fixed on the matter in hand and see it as it really is, remembering that it is your duty to be a good person, and that whatever human nature demands, you must fulfil without the slightest deviation and in the manner that seems most just to you; only do so with kindness and modesty, and without false pretences.

8.6   The work of universal nature is this, to remove what is here to there, to transform it, and to take it from there and convey it elsewhere. All is change, yet not in such a way that we need fear anything new; all things are familiar, but their allotment is also equitable.

8.7*   Every nature is contented when things go well for it; and things go well for a rational nature when it never gives its assent to a false or doubtful impression, and directs its impulses only to actions which further the common good, and limits its desires and aversions only to things which are within its power, and welcomes all that is assigned to it by universal nature. For it is a part of universal nature, just as a leaf's nature is part of a plant's nature, with this difference, however, that the leaf's nature is part of a nature which is devoid of sentience and reason and is susceptible to hindrance, whereas human nature is part of a nature which is not subject to hindrance and is intelligent and just, in so far as it assigns to every being, equally and in proportion to its worth, its share of time, substance, cause, activity, and the contingent. What you must look to, however, is not whether you will find one thing equal to another in every respect, but whether what is assigned to one thing, taken overall, is equal to the sum of what is assigned to another.

8.8   You are unable to read? But you are able to curb your arrogance, you are able to prevail over pleasures and pains, you are able to rise above a petty desire for glory, and you are capable not only of keeping yourself from becoming angry with foolish and ungrateful people, but what is more, of taking pains on their behalf.

8.9   Let no one, from this time on, hear you disparaging life at court; and may you not even hear yourself.

8.10   Regret is a kind of self-reproach for having let something useful pass you by. Now the good is necessarily a useful thing, and something that a truly good person should make his special concern; but no such person would feel regret at having let a pleasure pass him by; so pleasure should be regarded as neither useful nor good.

8.11*   The object in question, what is it in itself, in its own constitution? What is its substance and material, and its formal cause? What part does it play in the world? And how long does it subsist?

8.12   When you find it hard to rise from your sleep, remind yourself that the fulfilment of your social duties accords with the requirements of your constitution and of human nature, whilst sleep is something that you share in common with animals devoid of reason. Now for every creature, what accords with its nature is more fittingly its own and more appropriate to it, and, one might say, more agreeable.

8.13*   Continually and, if possible, with regard to every mental impression, apply your knowledge of nature, of the passions, and of dialectic.

8.14   With everyone you meet, begin at once by asking yourself, 'What ideas does this person hold on human goods and ills?' For if he holds particular views on pleasure and pain and the causes of each, and on reputation and disrepute, and life and death, it will not seem extraordinary or strange to me if he acts in some particular way, and I shall remember that he is constrained to act as he does.

8.15   Bear in mind that, as it would be absurd to be surprised that a fig tree produces figs, it is just as absurd to be surprised that the world gives birth to the fruits which it bears by its very nature; and likewise, it would be a poor thing for a physician or ship-master to be surprised if a patient developed a fever or an adverse wind began to blow.

8.16* Remember that to change your mind and follow somebody who puts you on the right course is nonetheless a free action; for it is your own action, effected in accordance with your own impulse and judgement, and, indeed, your own reason.

8.17 If the choice rests with you, why are you doing this? If it rests with another, who are you to blame? The atoms, or the gods? Either would be madness. You should cast blame on nobody. For if you can, you should put the person right; or if you are unable to, at least put the matter itself right; and if even that is beyond you, what more will you achieve by casting blame? For nothing should be done without an end in view.

8.18 What has died does not fall out of the universe; and if it remains here, it is also transformed here and resolved into its constituent parts, which are the elements of the universe and of yourself. And these elements themselves are transformed and utter no complaint.

8.19* Everything, such as a horse, say, or a vine, has come into being for a purpose; and why should you wonder at that? The Sun himself would say, 'I was born to perform a function', and so would the rest of the gods. And you, then, what were you born for? To enjoy yourself? See if that thought bears examination!

8.20 Nature has looked to each thing's ending no less than its beginning and its course in between, as does a boy who throws a ball into the air. What good is there for the ball in rising up or harm in falling down and even striking the ground? What good is there for the bubble in being blown or harm in being burst? And the same applies to a lamp.

8.21 Turn it inside out, and see what sort of thing it is, and what becomes of it when it grows old, or falls sick, or succumbs to vice. Short is the life of both praiser and praised, and of the one who remembers and the one who is remembered; and this comes about in just a corner of one region of the world, and not even there are all at one, nor indeed is anyone at one with himself; and the earth as a whole is but a point* in the universe.

8.22 Attend to the matter in question, or the activity, or the doctrine, or the meaning of the words.

It is right that you should suffer this; for you would rather become good tomorrow than be so today.

8.23 I am performing an action? Then I do it with reference to the good of humankind. Something happens to me? Then I accept it, with reference to the gods and the universal source from which all things arise and become intertwined.

8.24* Just as it seems to you when you take your bath − oil, sweat, filth, greasy water, all quite vile − such is every part of life and every given thing.

8.25* Lucilla buried Verus, and Lucilla's turn came next; Secunda buried Maximus, and Secunda's turn came next; Epitynchanus buried Diotimus, and his own turn came next; Antoninus buried Faustina, and his own turn came next. And so it goes on, ever the same: Celer buried Hadrian, and Celer's turn came next. Those sharp-witted men, who could see into the future or were puffed up with pride, where are they now? Sharp-witted men like Charax and Demetrius and Eudaimon, and many another like them? All creatures of a day, and dead long ago; some not remembered even for a passing moment, others becoming the stuff of legend, and others again fading from legend at this very time. So remember this, that either this compound which makes you up must be dispersed, or else your breath of life must be extinguished or be removed from here and stationed somewhere else.

8.26 A human being finds his delight in doing what is proper to a human being; and what is proper to him is to show goodwill to his own kind, to scorn the movements of the senses, to distinguish reliable impressions, and to reflect on universal nature and all that comes to pass according to her will.

8.27 We have three relationships: the first to the vessel that encloses us, the second to the divine cause,* the source of all that befalls every being, and the third to those who live alongside us.

8.28 Pain is an evil either to the body − and if that be so, let the body itself declare it − or to the soul; but the soul has the power to preserve its own serenity and calm, and to refuse to accept that pain is an evil. For every judgement, impulse, desire, or aversion arises from within us, and nothing evil can enter in.

8.29   Wipe out vain impressions by continually telling yourself, 'It now rests with me to make sure that no wickedness, or appetite, or disquiet should exist within my soul; but rather, by looking to the true nature of all things, I should employ each of them according to its worth.' Be ever mindful of this power that nature has granted to you.

8.30*   Speak both in the Senate and to anyone whatever in a decorous manner, without affectation. Use words that have nothing false in them.

8.31   The court of Augustus – his wife and daughter, his descendants and forebears, his sister, and Agrippa,* his relatives, associates and friends, Areios, Maecenas,* his doctors, his sacrificial priests – an entire court, all of it dead. And then pass on to other courts and their death, and then the death not of individuals but of whole families, as with that of Pompey. And that inscription which you see on tombs, 'The Last of his Line' – think of the lengths to which his ancestors would have gone to leave behind an heir, and then it must come about that someone should be the last: here again a whole family and all of it dead.

8.32   You must fashion your life one action at a time, and if each attains its own end as far as it can, be satisfied with that; and that it should attain its end is something in which no other person can hinder you. 'But some obstacle from outside may stand in my way.' None at least that can prevent you from acting justly, temperately, and with prudence. 'But perhaps my activities will be hindered in some other respect.' Yes, but if you accept the obstacle itself with a good grace, and redirect your efforts in a sensible manner to what is practicable, a new action is immediately substituted which accords with the course of action of which we are speaking.

8.33   Accept without arrogance, relinquish without demur.

8.34   If you have ever seen a severed hand or foot, or a head which has been cut off, lying at some distance from the rest of the body, you will have some idea of what a person makes of himself, as far as he can, when he is unwilling to consent to what comes to pass and cuts himself off from others or when he acts against the common interest. By so doing, you have, as it were, cast yourself loose from the natural unity; for you were born to be a part of it, and now you have cut yourself off. But you have this rare privilege, that it is possible for you to make yourself a part of that unity once again. To no other part has god granted this, to come together again with the whole after it has been severed and cut away; but observe the kindness with which he has honoured man, for he has put it in his power not to be broken away from the whole in the first place, and then, if he has been, to come back again and be reunited, and recover his place as a part.

8.35 Just as every rational creature is granted the rest of its powers by universal nature, so we have received this power too from her; and just as she turns to her own purposes whatever resists or opposes her, and assigns it to its place in the order of destiny, so also can the rational creature turn every hindrance into material for itself, and employ it on whatever purpose it has engaged upon.

8.36 Do not disturb yourself by picturing your life as a whole; do not assemble in your mind the many and varied troubles which have come to you in the past and will come again in the future, but ask yourself with regard to every present trouble: 'What is there in this which is unbearable and beyond endurance?' You would be ashamed to confess it! And then remind yourself that it is not the future or what has passed by that afflicts you, but always the present, and the power of this is much diminished if you take it in isolation, and call your mind to task if it thinks that it cannot stand up to it when taken on its own.

8.37 Pantheia or Pergamos,* are they sitting by the coffin of Verus? Or Chabrias or Diotimus* by that of Hadrian? How absurd! And even if they were, would the dead be aware of it? And if they became aware of it, would it bring them any pleasure? And if it brought them pleasure, would their mourners be immortal? Or were they not fated like others first to become old women and old men, and then to die? So what would the dead do afterwards, when their mourners had passed away? Nothing here but a stink of decay and matted blood on a winding-sheet.

8.38   If you can see clearly, then look [and judge according to your best judgement; if you cannot, choose the wisest man as your adviser].

8.39   In the constitution of a rational creature I see no virtue that pits itself against justice; but I see one that pits itself against pleasure – self-control.

8.40   If you suppress your opinion on what seems to cause you pain, you yourself will be in perfect safety. – 'What is your "self"?' – Reason. – 'But I am not reason!' – So be it. In that case, may reason itself cause no pain to itself, and if some other part of you is in a bad way, let it form its own opinion on the matter!

8.41   Any hindrance to sense perception is detrimental to animal nature, as likewise is any hindrance to impulse. And something else again will be liable to hinder, and be detrimental to, the constitution of a plant. Accordingly, anything that hinders intelligence is detrimental to an intelligent nature. Now apply all this to yourself. Have pain or pleasure taken hold of you? Your senses must look to that. Did something stand in the way of your impulse? If you exercised your impulse without reservation the hindrance will at once be detrimental to you as a rational being, but if you accepted our common lot, you have yet to be harmed or hindered. As to the operations of your intellect, no other person is in a position to hinder them; for neither fire, nor steel, nor a tyrant, nor abuse, can affect the mind in any way. When it has become a 'well-rounded sphere',* it always remains so.

8.42   It ill befits me to cause myself pain, for I have never willingly caused pain to another.

8.43   One thing gives delight to one person, and another thing to another; and my delight is to keep my governing faculty unimpaired, and not turn my back on any human being or on anything that befalls humankind, but look on all things with a kindly eye, and welcome and make use of each according to its worth.

8.44   See that you accord this present time to yourself. Those who would rather seek after fame in time to come fail to consider that people then will be just the same as these are now whom they find such a burden, and no less mortal. But after all, what is it to you that they should re-echo your name in such tones, or hold such an opinion about you?

8.45   Take me up and cast me down wherever you will; for there too I shall keep the guardian-spirit within me in good humour, that is to say, well contented if in itself and its activity it is faithful to the requirements of its own constitution.

Is this really of such value that on account of it my soul* should be in such a plight and fall beneath itself, humiliated, a prey to desire, fettered and all of a fright? And could you find anything that is worth such a price?

8.46   Nothing can befall any human being, which is not an accident natural to man, nor to an ox which is not natural to oxen, nor to a vine which is not natural to vines, nor to a stone which is not proper to a stone. So if there falls to each only what is both customary and natural, why should you be aggrieved? For universal nature never brings you anything which you are unfitted to bear.

8.47   If you suffer distress because of some external cause, it is not the thing itself that troubles you but your judgement on it, and it is within your power to cancel that judgement at any moment. But if what distresses you is something that lies in your own character, who is to prevent you from correcting your principles? And likewise, if you are distressed because you are failing to accomplish some particular action which strikes you as sound, why do you not persist in the action rather than yield to the distress? – 'But something too strong for me is blocking my way.' – Then you should not be distressed, because the responsibility for your failure to act does not rest with you. – 'But my life is not worth living if this act is left undone.' – Then depart from life with generous feelings in your heart, dying in the same spirit as one who achieves his purpose, and with goodwill, too, to what has stood in your way.

8.48   Remember that your governing faculty becomes invincible when it withdraws into itself and rests content with itself, doing nothing other than what it wishes, even where its refusal to act is based on no reasonable ground; and how much more contented it will be, then, when it founds its decision on reason and careful reflection. By virtue of this, a mind free from passions is a mighty citadel;* for man has no stronghold more secure to which he can retreat and remain unassailable ever after. One who has failed to see this is merely ignorant, but one who has seen it and fails to take refuge is beyond the aid of fortune.

8.49* Say nothing more to yourself than what the first impressions report. You have been told that some person is speaking ill of you? That is what you have been told: as for the further point, that he has harmed you, that you have not been told. I see that my little child is ill? I see just that; I do not see that his life is at risk. And so, in this way, always keep to first impressions and add nothing of your own from within, and then nothing bad will befall you. Or rather, add that you are well acquainted with everything that comes to pass in the world.

8.50   The cucumber is bitter? Cast it aside. There are brambles in the path? Step out of the way. That will suffice, and you need not ask in addition, 'Why did such things ever come into the world?' For anyone who has made a study of nature would laugh at you, just as a carpenter or shoemaker would laugh at you if you criticised them because you could see in their workshop the shavings or parings from what they were working on. To be sure, they have somewhere where they can dispose of their scraps, whilst universal nature has nothing outside herself, but the extraordinary thing about nature's craftsmanship is that, having established her own limits, she transforms into herself everything within her that seems to be decaying and growing old and useless, and out of these very things creates other new things in their place, so that she needs neither additional substance from outside nor anywhere else to dispose of decaying material. And thus she is well satisfied with her own space, her own material, and her own handicraft.

8.51   Be neither dilatory in your actions, nor disorganised in your conversation, nor rambling in your thoughts; ensure that your soul, in brief, neither contracts into itself nor wells over, and that your life is not so busy that you have no time for yourself. 'They kill you, cut you up, pursue you with curses.' And how does that prevent your mind from remaining pure, balanced, temperate, and just? It is as if someone were standing by a sweet clear-flowing spring* and hurling curses at it: but for all that, it never stops brimming over with water good to drink, and if he throws mud into it, or dung, it will swiftly disperse it and wash it away, and suffer no defilement. How, then, are you to have an ever-flowing spring in you, and not a pool of standing water? If you hold firm to freedom at every hour, along with kindness, simplicity and reverence.

8.52   He who does not know what the universe is, does not know where he is. He who does not know the purpose of its existence knows neither who he is nor what the universe is. He who fails in any of these questions could not even tell why he himself was born. So what do you make of a man who shuns or pursues the praise of those who offer their applause, and yet are unaware of where or whom they are?

8.53   Do you want praise from a man who curses himself three times an hour? Do you want to please a man who is unable to please himself? Or can a man be said to please himself who repents of nearly everything that he does?

8.54* No longer, through your breathing, merely share in the air that surrounds you, but also henceforth, through your thinking, share in the mind that embraces all things. For the power of the mind is diffused throughout and makes itself available everywhere to one who is able to take it in to no less an extent than the power of the air to one who is able to breathe it in.

8.55   Taken generally, evil does no harm to the universe, and in each particular case, it does no harm to another, but only to the person who has been granted the power to be delivered from it as soon as he himself makes that choice.

8.56   To my own will, the will of my neighbour is as much a matter of indifference as his breath and his flesh. For even though we exist primarily for the sake of one another, it is still the case that the governing faculty of each individual has its own independent authority. Otherwise the evil of my neighbour would become an evil for myself too, and that was not god's will, so that my ill fortune should not be dependent on any other than myself.

8.57   The light of the sun seems to be poured down, and to be poured, indeed, in every direction, but not poured away; for this pouring is an extension, and that is why the sun's beams are called 'rays'(*aktines*), because they are extended (*ekteinesthai*).* And what kind of thing a ray is you can readily see if you look at sunlight entering a darkened room through a narrow opening. For it stretches out in a straight line and comes to rest, so to speak, on any solid body that intercepts it, cutting off the air that lies beyond; and there it rests, neither slipping off nor falling down. The pouring forth and diffusion of our understanding should follow a comparable pattern, and in no way be a pouring away, but rather, an extension; and it should not make a forcible or violent impact on the obstacles that it meets with nor sink down, but stand firm and illuminate the object that receives it; for that which fails to welcome it will deprive itself of its light.

8.58   One who is afraid of death fears either an absence of consciousness or its alteration. But if consciousness is no longer present, you will no longer be conscious of any evil; and if you come to have a slightly altered consciousness, you will merely be a living creature of another kind, and you will not have ceased to live.

8.59   Human beings are here for the sake of one another; either instruct them, then, or put up with them.

8.60   An arrow moves in one way, the mind in another. And yet the mind, when it takes good care and concentrates on the question in hand, is no less direct in its flight and sure in hitting its mark.

8.61   Enter into the governing faculty of everyone, and let everyone else enter into your own.

9.1[*] Whoever commits injustice acts irreverently; for since universal nature has created rational creatures for the sake of one another, to benefit their fellows according to their deserts and in no wise to do them harm, it is plain that one who offends against her will is guilty of irreverence towards the most venerable of gods. And furthermore, one who lies is guilty of irreverence towards the same god; for she is also called Truth, and is the first cause of all truths. So one who lies intentionally is guilty of impiety, in so far as he commits wrong through deception; and one who lies unintentionally is also impious, in so far as he is out of tune with universal nature, and gives rise to disorder by entering into conflict with the natural order of the universe. For one who embarks of his own accord on a course which leads him to oppose the truth does enter into such a conflict, because he has received the necessary aptitudes from nature but has so neglected them that he is no longer capable of distinguishing falsehood from truth.

Again, one who pursues pleasure as good and tries to avoid pain as an evil is acting irreverently; for it is inevitable that such a person must often find fault with universal nature for assigning something to good people or bad which is contrary to their deserts, because it is so often the case that the bad devote themselves to pleasure and secure the things that give rise to it whilst the good encounter pain and what gives rise to that.

And furthermore, one who is afraid of pain is sure to be afraid at times of things which come to pass in the universe, and that is already an impiety; and one who pursues pleasure will not abstain from injustice, and that is a manifest impiety. But towards those things with regard to which universal nature is neutral (for she would not have created both opposites unless she was neutral with regard to both), it is necessary that those who wish to follow nature and be of one mind with her should also adopt a neutral attitude. Accordingly, anyone who is not himself neutral towards pleasure and pain, or life and death, or reputation and disrepute, to which universal nature adopts a neutral attitude, commits a manifest impiety.

And when I say that universal nature employs these things in a neutral manner, I mean that, through the natural sequence of cause and effect, they happen indifferently to all that comes into being and whose existence is consequent upon a primeval impulse of providence, by which it set out from a first beginning to create the present order of things, having conceived certain principles of all that was to be, and assigned powers to generate the necessary substances and transformations and successions.

9.2   It would have been the mark of a better and a wiser man to depart from the human race without having had any taste of falsehood, dissimulation, luxury and pride; but the next best course is to breathe your last when you have at least become sated with such things. Or do you prefer to settle down with vice, and has experience not yet persuaded you to flee from this pestilence? For corruption of the mind is a far graver pestilence than any comparable distemper and alteration in the air which surrounds us; for the one is a plague* to living creatures as mere animals, and the other to human beings in their nature as human beings.

9.3   Do not despise death, but welcome it gladly, for this too is amongst the things which nature wishes. For as are youth and old age, growth and maturity, the appearance of teeth and whiskers and white hairs, and conception, pregnancy, and childbirth, and all the other natural functions which the seasons of life bring around, so too is its very dissolution. It is the part, then, of one who is trained to reason, not to be casual in his approach to death, and neither to reject it violently nor treat it with disdain, but to await its coming as one of life's natural functions; and as you now await the time when your unborn child will be delivered from the womb of your wife, so await the hour when your soul will break free of its bodily shell. But if, in addition, you would like an unphilosophical rule which appeals to the heart, nothing will make you more cheerful in the face of death than to consider the things from which you are about to be parted, and the sort of characters with whom your soul will no longer be entangled. For although you should in no way be repelled by them, but rather take care of them and bear with them gently, you should nevertheless bear in mind that death will not part you from people who share the same principles as yourself; for this alone, if anything, could draw you back and detain you in life, that you would be allowed to live with people who had adopted the same principles as yourself. But as things are, you see how utterly wearisome is the discord of the life that you share with them, and you are moved to say, 'Come quickly, death, or one of these days I too may forget myself.'

9.4   Whoever does wrong, wrongs himself; whoever acts unjustly, acts unjustly towards himself, because he makes himself bad.

9.5   A person often acts unjustly by what he fails to do, and not only by what he does.

9.6   It is sufficient that your present judgement should grasp its object, that your present action should be directed to the common good, that your present disposition should be well satisfied with all that befalls it from a cause outside itself.

9.7   Efface imagination; put a curb on impulse; quench desire; ensure that your governing faculty stays in its own control.

9.8   One animal soul is distributed amongst irrational creatures, and one rational soul has been divided among rational creatures; just as there is one earth for all things formed from earth, and there is one light by which we all see and one air from which we all breathe, we who have sight and life.

9.9*   All things that share in a common element strive to rejoin their kind. All that is earthy inclines towards earth, and all that is watery flows together, as does all of an aerial nature, so that barriers and the use of force are needed to hold them apart. Fire, indeed, tends to rise towards the elemental fire [which surrounds the universe], but it is so eager to blaze up in combination with all fire here below that every material that is a little on the dry side is easily kindled because it has less of the matter mixed in with it that serves to hinder ignition. So likewise, all that shares in the common nature of mind strives with as great an eagerness, or indeed greater, toward what is akin to itself; for in proportion to its superiority to all other things, it is the more eager to mix and coalesce with its own kind.

Accordingly, there could be found from the beginning amongst irrational creatures, swarms, flocks, birds caring for their young, and associations founded on something resembling love; for already, at this level, there are souls, and in higher forms of life the power of mutual attraction was found to be more intense than it was in plants or minerals or timber. Amongst irrational creatures political communities could be found, and friendships, households, assemblies, and treaties and truces in time of war. And amongst beings which are higher still, there existed a sort of union in separation, as is the case with the stars. Thus ascent towards the higher was able to create a sympathetic connection even between bodies which remain apart.

And now see what happens at the present day; for nowadays only the intelligent creatures have forgotten this eagerness and inclination to come together, and it is here alone that one fails to find this confluence of like with like. But for all their efforts to flee this union, they are held together nonetheless, such is the power of nature. Look carefully and you will see what I mean; for you will sooner find something earthy which has no contact with anything earthy than a human being who is wholly severed from humankind.

9.10   They all bear fruit – humanity, and god, and the universe; each in due season bears its fruit. But if custom has come to apply the word, in its strict sense, to the fruit of the vine and suchlike, it matters not a bit. Reason too has its fruit, both for the whole and for itself; and from it are born other things of like nature to reason itself.

9.11   If you can, show them the error of their ways; but if you cannot, remember that kindness was granted to you for this. The gods themselves are kind to such people, and even help them to certain ends, to health, to wealth, to reputation, such is their benevolence. And you could do so too; or tell me this, who is standing in your way?

9.12   Labour, not as one who is miserable, nor as one who wishes to be pitied or admired, but direct your will to one thing alone, to set to work or take your rest as the reason of the city requires.

9.13   Today I escaped the power of circumstance, or rather I cast all circumstance out; for it was not outside me, but within me, in my judgements.

9.14   All things are ever the same, familiar in experience, ephemeral in time, foul in their matter; all is just the same now as it was in the days of those whom we have consigned to the dust.

9.15   Things stand outside the doors of our soul, keeping themselves to themselves, neither knowing nor stating anything about themselves. So what is it that states a judgement about them? Our governing faculty.

9.16   It is not in feeling but in action that the good of a rational social being lies; just as his virtue or wickedness lies not in feeling but in action.

9.17   For the stone thrown into the air, it is no bad thing to fall down again, as it was no good thing to rise up.

9.18   Penetrate within them, into their ruling faculties, and you will see what judges you are afraid of, and what manner of judges they are with regard to themselves.

9.19   All is in the course of change; and you yourself are constantly changing and, in a sense, decaying; and so too is the entire universe.

9.20*   The wrongdoing of another should be left with its author.

9.21   The ending of an activity, the cessation of an impulse or opinion, and, so to speak, its death, is no evil. Pass now to the various stages of life – childhood, adolescence, the years of one's prime, and old age. There too each change is a death; is there anything to fear in that? And turn now to the life that you lived under your grandfather, and then under your mother, and then under your adoptive father. There again you will find many losses, alterations, and cessations; so ask yourself again: was there anything to fear in that? So correspondingly, there is nothing to fear in the termination, cessation and change of your entire life.

9.22   Make haste to look into your own governing faculty, and that of the universe, and that of your neighbour. Into your own, to ensure that your mind holds to justice; into that of the universe, to remind yourself of what whole you form a part; into that of your neighbour, to know whether ignorance or judgement rules, and to recognise at the same time that his mind is of one nature with your own.

9.23   Since you yourself are one of the parts which serve to perfect a social system, let your every action contribute to the perfecting of social life. Any action of yours, then, which has no reference, whether direct or indirect, to these social ends, tears your life apart, prevents it from being at one, and creates division, as does the citizen in a state who for his own part cuts himself off from the concord of his fellows.

9.24*   Children's wrangles and pranks, and 'little souls carrying their corpses around', so that the journey to the land of the dead appears the more vividly before one's eyes.

9.25*   For each object, look to the nature of its cause, and consider that in isolation from its material; and then determine how long, at most, the object can subsist according to its specific nature.

9.26   You have endured a thousand miseries because you are not content to have your governing faculty play the part that it was formed to play. Surely that should be enough!

9.27   When another blames or hates you or people give voice to such feelings, look to their souls, enter into them, and see what sort of people they are. You will then see that there is no need for you to tear yourself apart so they that they will come to form this or that opinion of you. Nevertheless, you must show goodwill to them; for by nature, you and they are friends. And the gods themselves lend them every aid, through dreams and oracles,* if only to gain the things on which their hearts are set.

9.28   The revolutions of the universe are ever the same, upwards and downwards, from age to age. Either the mind of the whole takes a specific initiative on each occasion – and if that is so, you must welcome what it initiates – or else it took a single initiative at the beginning, and everything else has followed from that. As to the whole, if it is god, all is well; but if it is governed by chance, you should not on that account allow yourself to be governed by chance. In a little while, earth will cover us all; and then that too will change, and what arises from that will change and change to eternity, and that again to eternity. One who reflects on these repeated waves of change and transformation and how swiftly they ensue will feel nothing but contempt for all that is mortal.

9.29* The world-cause is a rushing torrent; it carries all things in its stream. How paltry are these creatures who turn to public affairs and, as they fondly imagine, act a philosopher's part; like snotty children, one and all! Tell me, man, what are you to do? Do what nature demands of you at this very moment. So set to work, if you are able, and do not look around you to see if anyone will notice. You should not hope for Plato's ideal state, but be satisfied to make even the smallest advance, and regard such an outcome as nothing contemptible. For who can change the convictions of others? And without that change of conviction, what else is there than the slavery of men who grumble away while making a show of obedience? Go on, then, and talk to me of Alexander and Philip and Demetrius. If they saw what universal nature wishes and trained themselves accordingly, I will follow them; but if they merely strutted around like stage heroes, no one has condemned me to imitate them. The work of philosophy is simple and modest; do not seduce me into vain ostentation.

9.30 Look down from a height on the countless herds of men, and their countless rituals, and their manifold voyagings through storm and calm, and the many different beings who are born, live together, and are gone. Imagine, too, the life lived by others long ago, and the life that will be lived after your departure, and the life that is being lived at this very moment amongst alien peoples; and how many are not even aware of your name, and how many will soon forget it, and how many who now, perhaps, are praising you will very soon be deriding you; and reflect that neither remembrance nor fame nor anything else whatever is worth a passing thought.

9.31 Imperturbability in the face of what comes to pass from a source outside yourself; and justice in actions that proceed from a cause within yourself; that is to say, impulses and actions which find their end in the very exercise of social duty because, for you, that is in accordance with nature.

9.32   You have the power to rid yourself of many superfluous troubles which exist only in your own imagination; and you will then create ample room for yourself to embrace the whole universe in your thoughts and encompass everlasting time, and to reflect on the rapid change in every part of every particular thing, and the briefness of the span of time between birth and dissolution, and how vast is the expanse of time that stretches before our birth and how equally boundless the time that will follow our dissolution.

9.33   All that you now behold will swiftly pass away, and those who have seen it passing will swiftly pass in their turn, and he who dies in extreme old age will be brought to a level with one who has died before his time.

9.34   What governing faculties these people have, and to what unworthy ends they have directed their efforts, and for what unworthy reasons they bestow their love and esteem! Imagine here that you were viewing their souls in their naked state.* When they suppose that their criticisms harm or their praises bring benefit, what utter presumption!

9.35   Loss is nothing other than change; and change is the delight of universal nature, according to whose will all things come to pass. From time everlasting they have come to pass in like fashion, and into eternity others again will pass in a similar way. So why do you say that everything has always come about badly and will always continue to do so, and that among such a host of gods no power, it would seem, was ever found to put this right, but the world is condemned to remain forever in the grip of unintermitting evil?

9.36*   How putrid is the matter which underlies everything. Water, dust, bones, stench! Again, fine marbles are calluses of the earth, and gold and silver its sediments, and our garments matted hairs, and the purple, blood from a shellfish. Even our breath is something similar and changes from this to that.

9.37   Enough of all this pitiful way of life, this whining and apishness. Why are you troubled? What is new in all this? What is there to surprise you? Is it the causal aspect of things? Consider that. The material? Then consider that. Apart from these, there is nothing. But it is now high time, in your relations with the gods, that you became a simpler and a worthier man. It makes no difference whether you look into these matters for a hundred years, or for three.

9.38   If he did wrong, the ill lies with him; but perhaps he did not.

9.39*   It is either the case that everything proceeds from a single intelligent source, as in a single body, and the part should not find fault with what is brought to pass in the interest of the whole, or else there are simply atoms and nothing other than a random commingling and dispersal. Why, then, are you troubled? Say to your governing faculty: Are you dead, have you gone to ruin, have you become a wild beast, or a play-actor, are you running with the herd, are you feeding with it?

9.40   The gods either lack power or they have power. Now if they are powerless, why do you pray to them? But if they have power, why do you not pray to them to grant you the ability neither to fear any of these things nor to desire them, nor to be distressed by them, rather than praying that some of them should fall to you and others not? For surely, if the gods have any power to help human beings, they can help them in this. But perhaps you will object, 'They have placed this in my own power.' Well then, would it not be better to make use of what lies within your power as suits a free man rather than to strain for what lies beyond it in a servile and abject fashion? In any case, who told you that the gods do not assist us even in things that lie within our power? Begin at least to pray so, and you will see. That man prays, 'May I come to sleep with that woman', but you, 'May I be delivered from my desire to sleep with her'. Another prays, 'May I be rid of this man', but you, 'May I no longer wish to be rid of him'. Or another, 'May I not lose my little child', but you, 'May I not be afraid of losing him'. In a word, turn your prayers round in such a way, and see what comes of it.

9.41*   Epicurus says, 'When I was ill, my conversation was not devoted to the sufferings of my body, nor', he says, 'did I chatter about such matters to those who visited me but I continued to discuss the main elements of natural philosophy as before, and this point especially, how it is that the mind, while being aware of the agitations in our poor flesh, is unperturbed and preserves its specific good. Nor (he says) did I allow the doctors to assume grand airs, as though they were engaged in something important, but my life proceeded as well and happily as ever.' So act as he did when you are ill, if you should be ill, and in any other predicament; for never to abandon philosophy in the face of anything whatever that may befall you, and not to chatter with the ignorant and those who have no understanding of nature, are principles which are common to every school. Concentrate alone on what you are presently doing, and on the instrument by which you are doing it.

9.42* Whenever you are shocked by anyone's shameless behaviour, ask yourself at once, 'Is it then possible that there should be no shameless people in this world?' It is quite impossible. So you should not demand the impossible: this person is one of those shameless people who must necessarily exist in the world. And keep this argument at hand for when you meet a rogue, a deceiver, or any other kind of villain; for as soon as you remind yourself that the class of such people cannot fail to exist, you will view them more kindly as individuals. It is also helpful to reflect at once on this further point: what virtue has nature granted to us to meet the wrong in question? For she has granted us gentleness to use against the unfeeling, and in every other case, another such antidote; and generally speaking, it is within your power to show someone who has gone astray the error of his ways (for every wrongdoer is one who has missed the goal set down for him and thus has gone astray). Besides, what harm have you suffered? For you will find that none of these people with whom you are so angry has done anything of such a nature that your mind will be made any worse; and it is in your mind that what is truly bad for you and harmful has its whole existence. Is it really such a bad or extraordinary thing that one who is ignorant should act according to his ignorance? See whether you yourself are not to blame, for failing to see that this person would commit this fault. For by virtue of your reason, you had the resources to conclude that this would probably be the case and yet it escaped you, and you are surprised that he committed the fault.

But above all, when you condemn somebody for disloyalty or ingratitude, turn your attention to yourself; for the fault is clearly your own, whether for trusting that a man of such a character would keep his word, or for the fact that when you bestowed a favour, you did not grant it unconditionally and in the belief that you would immediately reap your full reward from the very action itself. For tell me, man, when you have done a good turn, what more do you want? Is it not enough that in doing this, you have acted according to your own nature, that you should go on to seek a reward for it? It is just as if the eye sought compensation for seeing, or the feet for walking. For as these were made to perform a particular function, and by performing it according to their own constitution, gain in full what is due to them, so likewise, man is formed by nature to benefit others, and when he has performed some benevolent action or accomplished anything else that contributes to the common good, he has done what he was constituted for, and has what is properly his.

BOOK 10

10.1[*] Will there come a day, my soul, when you are good, and simple, and at one, and clearer to see than the body which envelops you? Some day, will you enjoy a loving and affectionate disposition? Some day, will you be satisfied and want for nothing, yearning for nothing, and coveting nothing, animate or inanimate, to cater to your pleasures? And not wish for more time, to enjoy them for a longer period, or a more pleasing place, or country, or climate, or more agreeable company? Or will you be contented instead with your present circumstances and delighted with everything around you, and convince yourself that all that you have comes to you from the gods, and that all is well for you and will be well that is pleasing to them and that they shall grant hereafter for the sustenance of the perfect living being, the good and the just and the beautiful, which generates, upholds and embraces all things, and takes them into itself when they are dissolved to allow others of like nature to come into being? Will there ever come a day when you are fit to dwell in the common city of gods and mortals so as neither to bring any complaint against them nor to incur their condemnation?

10.2 Observe what your nature requires of you, in so far as you are merely governed by physical nature, and then do it and accede willingly, if your nature as a living creature will suffer no impairment. Next you must observe what your nature as a living creature requires of you, and accept that fully, if your nature as a rational living creature will suffer no impairment. Now every rational being is, by virtue of its rationality, also a social being. So apply these rules, and trouble yourself no further.

10.3   Everything that happens either happens in such a way that you are fitted by nature to bear it or in such a way that you are not. If, then, it comes about in such a way that you are fitted by nature to bear it, make no complaint, but bear it as your nature enables you to do; but if it comes about in such a way that you are not fitted by nature to bear it, again you should make no complaint, for it will soon be the end of you. Remember, however, that you are fitted by nature to bear everything that you can render bearable and endurable through the exercise of your judgement, by suggesting the idea to yourself that your interest or your duty demands it.

10.4   If he goes wrong, instruct him in a kindly manner, show him what he failed to see; but if you are unable to, blame only yourself, or not even yourself.

10.5   Whatever happens to you was pre-ordained for you from time everlasting, and from eternity the web of causation was weaving together your own existence and this that befalls you.

10.6*   Whether there are merely atoms or a universal nature, let it be postulated first that I am a part of the whole which is governed by nature, and secondly, that I am bound by a tie of kinship to other parts of the same nature as myself. If I keep those thoughts in mind, I shall never, in so far as I am a part, be discontented with anything allotted to me from the whole, for nothing which benefits the whole brings harm to the part. For the whole contains nothing that is not to its own good, and while this is a characteristic that all natures share in common, universal nature has this further characteristic, that there is no cause outside itself which could compel it to generate anything harmful to itself. If I remember, then, that I am a part of such a whole, I shall be well contented with all that comes to pass; and in so far as I am bound by a tie of kinship to other parts of the same nature as myself, I will never act against the common interest, but rather, I will take proper account of my fellows, and direct every impulse to the common benefit and turn it away from anything that runs counter to it. And when this is duly accomplished, my life must necessarily follow a happy course, just as you would observe that any citizen's life proceeds happily on its course when he makes his way through it performing actions which benefit his fellow-citizens and he welcomes whatever his city assigns to him.

10.7 Every part of the whole, everything that is naturally contained in the universe, must necessarily perish (if the word is understood here in the sense of 'suffer change'). Now if this were naturally a bad thing for the parts as well as a necessity, the world would not be well administered, considering that all its parts are subject to change and have been constituted to perish in a variety of ways. Could it be that nature herself would have undertaken to bring evil to her own parts, and made them such that they were not only liable to fall into a bad state but necessarily would fall into it? Or could this have come about without her being aware of it? Both proposals are equally incredible.

But what if we put nature to one side, and explain matters by saying that all this is naturally so? Even in that case, it would be absurd to maintain that the parts of the whole are naturally subject to change, and yet at the same time be surprised or aggrieved at such change as if something unnatural were coming to pass, especially when every object at its dissolution is merely resolved into the elements of which it is composed. For this occurs through the dispersal of the elements from which it was compounded or through a transformation of the solid into the earthy, and the spiritual into the airy, so that these two are re-absorbed into the reason of the whole, whether the universe is consumed periodically by fire* or renews itself eternally by constant permutations.

And do not imagine that what is solid or of the nature of vital spirit in your present composition dates to the time of your birth. For all this was taken in only yesterday or the day before as an influx from food-stuffs or the air breathed in. It is this, then, which it has taken in which changes, and not that which your mother gave birth to. And even if it is granted that your changing body is very closely bound up with your individuality, there is nothing in that, I think, which contradicts my present argument.

10.8* When you have given yourself these titles, good, modest, truthful, prudent, sympathetic, high-minded, make sure that you never exchange them for others; and if you should ever lose these titles, return to them with all speed. Remember, moreover, that 'prudence' should suggest to you the attention needed to apprehend each object with due accuracy, and freedom from negligence; 'sympathy', the willing acceptance of all that is allotted to you by universal nature; and 'high-mindedness' the elevation of the thinking part of you above the smooth or violent agitations of the flesh, and above a petty desire for fame, and the fear of death, and everything else of that kind. For to continue to be as you have been hitherto, and suffer the lacerations and defilements of such a way of life, is the part of one who is utterly insensitive and clings to mere existence, like the half-devoured beast-fighters in the arena* who, covered as they are with wounds and gore, beg nonetheless to be kept alive until the morrow to be flung in just the same state to the same claws and teeth.

Embark, then, on these few titles, and if you can abide in them, abide as one who has made his passage to the Isles of the Blest;* but if you feel that you are falling away and losing your hold, then withdraw undismayed to some corner where you can recover your grip, or even depart from life altogether, not in anger, but simply, freely, and modestly, having accomplished at least one fine action in your life, to have taken leave of it in such a fashion. When it comes, however, to remembering these titles, it will help you greatly if you are ever mindful of the gods and remember that it is not flattery that they desire, but that all rational beings should strive to resemble them, and that as the fig tree does the work of a fig tree, the dog the work of a dog, and the bee the work of a bee, so should a human being do the work of a human being.

10.9   Cheap comedy, war, excitement, lethargy, servitude – day by day these will wipe away those sacred principles of yours, which your studies of nature have led you to conceive and which you fail to heed. In all that you undertake, you must look on things and act in such a way that at the same time you ensure that the duties imposed on you by circumstances are accomplished and your powers of thought are fully exercised, and that the self-confidence which arises from a proper understanding of each particular thing is maintained with discretion, but without concealment. When will you find your delight in simplicity? in gravity? in knowing the nature of each particular thing, and the place that it occupies in the universe, and how long it naturally persists, and of what elements it is composed, and who can possess it, and who can bestow it or take it away?

10.10   A spider is proud when it has caught a fly, and one man when he has caught a little hare, another a little fish in his net,

another boars, another bears, and another, some Sarmatians.*
Now if you look into their judgements, are these not simply
robbers?

10.11   Acquire a method* to examine systematically how all
things are transformed from one to another, and direct your
attention constantly to this area of study, and exercise yourself in
it, for nothing is so conducive to elevation of mind. Such a person
has stripped away his body, and reflecting that in no time at all he
will have to leave all this behind and depart from the company of
men, he offers himself up without reservation to justice in what he
himself brings to pass, and to universal nature in all that comes to
pass in any other way. As to what others may say or think of him
or do against him, he gives that not a thought, but is satisfied if he
can achieve these two things, to act justly in what he is presently
doing, and to welcome what is presently assigned to him. And he
has put aside every distraction and care, and has no other desire
than to hold to the straight path according to the law, and by
holding to it, to follow god.

10.12   What need is there for conjecture when it is within your
power* to consider what ought to be done, and if you see the
proper course, to follow it with a cheerful heart and never a
backward glance? Or if you fail to see it, to suspend your
judgement,* and consult your ablest advisers; or if something
further should stand in the way of that, to move forward with due
care as far as your present resources allow, holding firm to
whatever seems just? For there is nothing better than the
attainment of justice, since the only true failure is to fail in that.

   Leisurely, yet quick to act, joyous, yet self-composed, is one
who follows reason in all things.

10.13   The moment you awaken from your sleep, ask yourself
this question: Will it make any difference to me if another
reproaches me for actions which were just and right? It will make
no difference at all. Or have you forgotten what these people who
assume grand airs when praising or blaming others are like in their
beds or at table, and what deeds they commit, and what sort of
things they flee from and what they pursue, and how they thieve
and plunder not with their hands and feet, but with the most
precious part of themselves, the part in which there emerges, if

only a person wishes it, faith and modesty, truth and law, and a good guardian-spirit within.

10.14   To nature who bestows all things and takes them all back, a person of true culture and modesty will say: 'Give what it pleases you to give, and take what it pleases you to take'; and say so in no defiant spirit, but as one who only obeys her designs and thinks nothing but good of her.

10.15   Small is the span of time now left to you. Live as on a mountain top; for what matter whether you live here or there, if everywhere you live in this great city of the universe? Let people see, let them study, a true man who lives according to nature. If they cannot bear with him, let them kill him! For it were better to die than to live such lives as theirs.

10.16   No more of all this talk about what a good man should be, but simply be one!

10.17   Continually picture to yourself the whole of time and the whole of substance, and reflect that every particular part of them, when measured against substance overall, is but a fig-seed, and when measured against time, but the single turn of a drill.

10.18   Look carefully at every existing thing and reflect that its dissolution is already under way and it is in the course of change and, as it were, of decay or dispersal, or is dying in whatever way its nature appoints.

10.19   Think what they are like when they eat, sleep, copulate, relieve themselves, and so forth; and then when they play the lord and master and give themselves such airs or give way to anger and criticise others from a height. And yet but a short time before, how many masters they were slaving for, and with what ends in view; and in no time at all, they will be reduced to a similar state.

10.20   What universal nature brings to each thing is to the benefit of that thing, and to its benefit at just the time that she brings it.

10.21   'The earth loves showers, and the holy ether loves [to fall in showers].' And the universe loves to create whatever is to be; so I will say to the universe, 'Your love is my love too.' Is that not also implied in the expression,* 'This loves to come about'?

10.22   Either you continue to live in this world, and you are used to that by now; or else you take yourself out of it, and that by your own desire; or else you die, and your service is completed. There is no other alternative; so be cheerful, then.

10.23   Always be clear about this, that the countryside there is no different from any other, and that all things here are just as they would be on the summit of a hill, or by the seashore, or wherever you choose. For you will find that Plato's words are wholly to the point: 'penned in a sheepfold on the mountain and milking his bleating flocks'.*

10.24   What does my governing faculty mean to me, and what use am I presently making of it, and to what end am I employing it? Is it devoid of reason? Is it detached and severed from sociability? Or is it so fused and blended with my poor flesh as to move at one with it?

10.25   One who flees from his master is a runaway slave; now the law is our master, and one who departs from it is therefore a runaway slave. And likewise one who, yielding to grief, anger or fear, wishes that something had not come about, or were not coming about, or should not come about, of what has been ordained by the power which governs all things; for that too is law, assigning to each of us what is due to him; and one who yields to fear or distress or anger is therefore a runaway slave.

10.26   A man spills his seed into a womb, and passes on his way; and then another cause takes it up, and works on it, and creates a newborn child. What a thing from such a start! And again, the body passes some food down its throat, and another cause takes it up and creates sensation and impulse, and in a word, life and strength, and what other wonders too! Picture, then, these things that come about in such concealment, and see the power behind them, as we see the power that causes things to fall down or rise up, not indeed with our eyes, but none the less clearly for that.

10.27   Constantly reflect on how all that comes about at present came about just the same in days gone by, and reflect that it will continue to do so in the future; and set before your eyes whole dramas and scenes ever alike in their nature which you have known from your own experience or the records of earlier ages, the whole court of Hadrian, say, or Antoninus, the whole court of Philip, or Alexander, or Croesus;* for in every case the play was the same, and only the actors were different.

10.28* Look on anyone who is pained or discontented at anything that comes to pass as being like a little pig kicking and screaming at the sacrifice. So also is one who alone* on his bed silently laments the chains that hold us down. Reflect, too, that it is granted to a rational creature alone to yield of his own free will to what must come about; as for merely yielding to it, that is a necessity for all.

10.29 As you engage in each particular action, stop and ask yourself this question: Is death something terrible because I would be deprived of this?

10.30* When you are shocked at another's wrongdoing, pass on at once to consider what faults you are committing on your own account; as when you judge, for instance, that money is a good, or pleasure, fame and the like. For if you turn your mind to this, you will soon forget your anger, because it will occur to you at the same time that the other person is acting under compulsion – for what else can he do? [So bear with him;] or else, if you can, free him from this compulsion.

10.31* When you see Satyrion, Eutyches or Hymen, bring to mind a follower of Socrates, and when you see Eutychion or Silvanus, think of Euphrates, and when you see Tropaeophorus, think of Alciphron, when you see Severus, think of Crito or Xenophon, and when you consider yourself, think of one of the Caesars, and in every case, follow a similar procedure. And then allow this thought to strike you: 'Where are they now? Nowhere, or nowhere that we can say.' For in this way you will constantly observe that all things human are mere smoke and nothingness; and all the more so, if you call to mind that what has once changed will never exist again throughout unending time. Why, then, are you troubled? Why are you not content to pass your brief existence in a suitable manner? What material and what a field of action you are running away from! What is all this except a training ground for a reason which has examined with accuracy and scientific care all that life embraces?

Wait, then, until you have assimilated these truths too, as a robust stomach assimilates every kind of food and a blazing fire turns whatever you cast into it into flame and light.

10.32   Let it be impossible for anyone to say of you truthfully that you are not sincere, that you are not a good man; rather let him be a liar who supposes any such thing of you. And this is wholly within your power: for what can prevent you from being good and sincere? Only, you must resolve to live no longer unless you are such a person; for it is not reason's will that you should continue to live if you are not so.

10.33*   Given the material that is granted to you, what is the soundest thing that can be done or said? For whatever it may be, it is in your power to do or say it, and you should not try to excuse yourself by saying that you are being prevented. You will never stop complaining until the time comes when to use the material that is submitted and falls to you means just the same to you as sensual indulgence means to the pleasure-seeker. For you should regard as an enjoyment all that you are able to accomplish in accordance with your own nature; and everywhere that is within your reach. Now it is not granted to a cylinder to realise its own form of movement on every occasion, nor to water, nor to fire, nor to anything else which is governed by nature or irrational soul; for there is much that prevents them and stands in their way. But mind and reason can find their way through every obstacle as their nature and their will dictate. Set before your eyes this ease with which reason can make its way through everything (as fire moves upwards, or a stone downwards, or a cylinder down an incline) and look for nothing beyond; for all other obstacles either relate to that corpse, our body, or else cannot break us or do us any harm whatever without the decision and assent of reason itself. Otherwise the person affected would at once become bad. In all other created things, at any rate, wherever any of them is visited by any evil, that which suffers it becomes worse as a result; whereas here, if one may say so, a human being becomes better and more praiseworthy by making proper use of whatever befalls him. And you should remember in general that nothing harms one who is by nature a citizen which does not harm the city, and that nothing harms the city which does not harm the law; and of these things which we call misfortunes, not one of them harms the law; and accordingly, because it causes no harm to the law, it brings no harm to the city or the citizen.

10.34* For one who has been bitten by true principles, the briefest and most commonplace saying will be sufficient to remind him that he must be free from sorrow and fear. For instance:

> 'Leaves that the wind scatters to the ground,
> Such are the generations of men.'*

And what are your children but leaves, and leaves too these people who acclaim you with such conviction and sing your praises, or, on the contrary, curse you, or reproach you in secret and gibe at your expense; and leaves likewise those who will transmit your fame when you are gone. For all of these 'arrive with the spring', and then the wind brings them down, and the forest puts forth others in their place. This fleeting existence is the common lot of all things, and yet you pursue and flee each thing as though it will last forever. A little while, and you will close your eyes; and he who carried you to your grave will soon be lamented by another.

10.35 A healthy eye should look at all that can be seen and not say, 'I want green things alone', for that is the mark of a diseased eye. And a healthy sense of hearing or smell should be ready for all that can be heard or smelled; and a healthy stomach should accept every food, as a mill accepts everything which it was constructed to grind. Accordingly, a healthy mind should be ready for all that comes about; but the mind which cries 'Let my children be safe and sound!', or 'Let everyone praise me whatever I do!' is like an eye that seeks only for green, or teeth for what is tender.

10.36 No one is so blessed by fortune that there will not be some people standing by his death-bed who will welcome the evil that is coming to him. Suppose that he was serious-minded and wise;* there is sure to be someone there at the last who will say of him, 'What a relief to be finally freed from this schoolmaster; not that he was ever harsh with any of us, but I could sense that he was silently condemning us.' So much for the serious man; but in our own case how many other things there are which would make many people glad to see the end of us. So when you come to die, you will keep this in mind, and your departure will be easier if you argue to yourself, 'I am leaving the kind of life in which even those who were close to me, for whom I toiled, prayed, and took so much care, even they want to see the end of me, hoping, it would seem, to win some relief as a result of my death.' So why should anyone hold out for a longer stay in this world? You must not, however, on that account, depart thinking any less kindly of them, but preserve your true character as one who is friendly, well-disposed, and gracious. And again, do not depart as if you were being dragged away, but rather, you should withdraw from them as one who is dying a happy death as his soul slips painlessly from his body. For it was nature who bound you to them and made you at one with them, but now she is severing the knot. I am severed, indeed, from those who are my family and friends, but without a struggle and without constraint. For this too is one of the things which nature ordains.

10.37　Acquire the habit with regard to every action, so far as possible, performed by someone else, of inquiring within yourself, 'What is his aim in performing this action?' But begin with yourself, and examine yourself first of all.

10.38*　Remember that the power that pulls our strings is that which is hidden within us: that is the source of our action, and our life, and that, if one may say so, is the person himself. When picturing its nature, never confuse it with the fleshly vessel that encloses it or these organs moulded around us; for these are mere instruments like an axe, differing only in this, that they are attached to us as part of ourselves. For in truth, these parts are of no more value without the cause that set them to work or brings them to rest than the shuttle to the weaver, or the pen to the writer, or the whip to the charioteer.

BOOK 11

11.1   The properties of the rational soul are these: it sees itself, it articulates itself, it shapes itself according to its will, it reaps for itself the fruits which it bears (in contrast to the fruits of plants and their counterparts in the animal kingdom, which are harvested by others), and it achieves its proper end, wherever the boundaries of its life may be set; for in that respect it is unlike a dance or a play or the like, in which the whole action is rendered imperfect if anything cuts it short. Rather, in every part of the whole, and wherever its end overtakes it, it realises what it has proposed to itself fully and completely, so that it can say, 'All that is mine, I have'. And what is more, it traverses the whole universe and the void which encircles it and surveys its form, and reaches out into the endlessness of infinite time, and comprehends and reflects upon the periodical rebirth of the whole, and perceives that those who will come after us will see nothing new, just as those who came before us saw nothing more, but that in a sense a forty-year-old, if he has a modicum of understanding, has seen all that has been and all that ever will be because it is ever the same. A property, too, of the rational soul, is love of one's neighbour, and truthfulness, and modesty, and to regard nothing as of higher value than itself (which is also a property of law, and there is thus no difference between right reason and the reason that underlies justice).

11.2   You will feel contempt for the delights of song, and also for dancing and wrestling, if you analyse the melodious strain into its individual notes, and ask yourself with regard to each, 'Would this be enough to overcome me?' You would be surely be ashamed to admit it, as you would with dancing too, if you followed an equivalent course with regard to each movement or posture, and likewise with wrestling. In general, then, except with regard to virtue and all that arises from it, remember to pass to the component parts,* and by this analysis learn to feel contempt for them; and also apply this procedure to your life as a whole.

11.3   How excellent is the soul which is ready, if the need arises, to be released from the body at any moment, whether to be extinguished or dispersed, or to continue its existence. But this readiness must spring from a specific judgement, rather than mere contrariness as with the Christians,* and should be considered, and grave, and, if you want to convince others too, be free of any trace of theatrical bravado.

11.4   Have I done something useful to my fellows? Then I have already profited. May you keep this thought ever at hand and never cease from such action.

11.5*   What is your profession? To be a good person. And how is this to be achieved, except on the basis of theoretical principles, some relating to universal nature and others to man's specific constitution.

11.6*   In the first place tragedies were brought on the stage, to remind us of what comes to pass in life, and that it is natural that such things should come about, and that what enchants you on the stage should not distress you on the greater stage of life. For it can be seen that such events must necessarily run such a course, and that even those who cry, 'Ah, Cithaeron!', must still endure them. The tragic poets have also provided some helpful sayings. This, for instance, is particularly good: 'If the gods have abandoned me and my children, this too has its reason', and again: 'Be not angry with outward events', and this: 'Our lives must be reaped like ripe ears of corn', and many another like them.

   After Tragedy, the Old Comedy was brought on to the stage; it was marked by an instructive freedom of language, and through its very outspokenness it performed no small service in reminding us to beware of arrogance. And such liberties were also adopted by Diogenes, with a similar end in view.

   After this, one should consider what Middle Comedy was like, and then why New Comedy was introduced, and how it gradually declined into an ingenious imitative art. That these authors too have provided some helpful sayings is commonly recognised; but considering its general approach, what was poetry and drama of this kind really aiming to achieve?

11.7* With what clarity it strikes you that no other calling in life so favours the practice of philosophy as that in which you now find yourself.

11.8* It is impossible to cut a branch from its neighbour unless you cut it from the tree as a whole; and likewise, a human being cut off from a single one of his fellows has dropped out of the community as a whole. Now in the case of the branch, someone else cuts it off, but a human being cuts himself off from his neighbour of his own accord, when he comes to hate him and turns his back on him; and he fails to see that by doing this, he has cut himself off from society as a whole. There remains, however, this great gift from Zeus, who first organised human society, that we have the power to come together again with our neighbour, and again become an integral part of the whole. But if this process of separation is often repeated, it becomes difficult for the part that withdraws to reunite with the others and recover its place. And as a general rule, the branch that grew with the tree from the beginning and shared in its life by remaining at one with it is not at all the same as that which has been grafted on to it again after being cut off, whatever the gardeners may tell you. Grow on the same tree with them, but do not share their principles.

11.9 Those who stand in your way as you advance along the path of right reason will never be able to divert you from sound action; so let them be no more successful in making you renounce your kindliness towards them. Rather, you should keep a careful watch on both points alike, that you remain steadfast in your judgement and your action, but also that you are gentle towards those who attempt to hinder you or aggravate you in any other way. For it would be a sign of weakness to be harsh with them, just as it would be to turn aside from your course of action and give way as a result of fear; for both are equally deserters, the coward who yields to fear and the man who is estranged from one who was formed by nature to be his relative and friend.

11.10 'In no case is nature inferior to art';* for the arts merely imitate natural things. And if that is so, the nature which is the most perfect and comprehensive of all cannot be deficient in technical proficiency. Now all the arts create the lower for the sake of the higher, so universal nature surely does the same. And this accounts for the origin of justice, and it is from justice that all the other virtues spring; for justice will not be maintained if we value indifferent objects, or are readily deceived, and hasty in our judgement, and lacking in constancy.

11.11　　They do not come to you, the objects whose pursuit or avoidance causes you such disquiet, but in a certain sense you go to them; so if you will only let your judgement about them remain at rest, they too will remain unmoved, and you will be seen neither to pursue them nor to avoid them.

11.12　　The sphere* of the soul is faithful to its form when it neither reaches out towards anything outside itself nor contracts inwards, and when it is neither dispersed abroad nor dies down, but shines forth with a steady light by which it beholds the truth of all things and the truth within itself.

11.13　　Will someone feel contempt for me? Let him look to that. But I for my part will look to this, that I may not be discovered doing or saying anything which is worthy of contempt. Will someone hate me? Let him look to that. But I will be kind and good-natured to everyone, and ready to show this particular person the nature of his error, not in a reproachful spirit, nor as if I were making a display of my forbearance, but sincerely and kind-heartedly, like the great Phocion* (if he really meant what he said). For that is how one should be within one's heart, to show oneself to the gods as one who is neither disposed to be angry at anything nor to make any complaint. For what harm can come to you if you are presently doing what is appropriate to your nature, and you welcome what is presently seasonable for universal nature, as a man who is supremely anxious that by one means or another the common benefit should be brought to fruition?

11.14　　They despise one another, yet they fawn on one another; they want to climb over one another, yet they grovel to one another.

11.15*　　How corrupt and two-faced is one who claims, 'I intend to be fair and honest in my dealings with you.' What are you up to, my friend? There is really no need for this preamble. The matter will soon become plain. It should be written on your face, it should ring out immediately in your voice, and shine out at once in your eyes, as the beloved at once knows everything about his lovers from the manner of their glance. A good and honest man should be so right through, like one who smells like a goat, so that anyone who comes near him is immediately aware of it whether he wishes it or not. But the mere pretence of simplicity is like an open blade. There is nothing more odious than the friendship of the wolf for the lamb; avoid this above all. A good, straightforward and kindly man reveals these qualities in his eyes, and they will not escape you.

11.16   Always live the finest of lives; and the power to do so lies in one's soul, if one is indifferent to things indifferent. And a person will be indifferent if he examines each of them as a whole and in its separate parts, and bears in mind that none of them creates any opinion in us about itself nor does it make any move towards us, but all of them remain motionless and it is we who create judgements about them and, so to say, inscribe them on our minds (although it is possible for us not to inscribe them, and if we do so unawares, we can immediately wipe them off again). Bear in mind, too, that we will have to attend to these matters for only a short while, and then our life will be over. And after all, what trouble can they bring? If they are in accordance with nature, rejoice in them, and let them be no hardship to you; and if they are contrary to nature, seek for what your own nature requires and strive towards that, inglorious though it may be; for everyone can be pardoned for seeking his own good.

11.17   Consider each thing's origin, and what materials make it up, and what it is changing into, and what it will be like after it has changed, and that it will come to no harm as a result.

11.18*   First, consider how you stand in relation to them, and how we were born to help one another, and, from a different angle, how I was born to preside over them, as the ram over his flock, or the bull over his herd. And then go back to first principles: if all things are not mere atoms, nature must be the power that governs the whole, and if that be so, lower things exist for the sake of the higher, and the higher for one another.

  Secondly, what kind of beings they are, at table, in bed, or elsewhere; above all, what compulsions they are subject to because of their opinions, and what pride they take in these very acts.

Thirdly, that if they are acting rightly in what they do, there is no reason for you to be angry, but if they are acting wrongly, it is plain that they are doing so involuntarily and through ignorance. For as no soul is ever willingly deprived of the truth, so neither is it willingly deprived of the capacity to deal with each person as he deserves. At any rate, people are upset if they hear themselves spoken of as unjust, callous, avaricious, or in a word, as people who offend against their neighbours.

Fourthly, that you for your own part also commit many wrongs, and are just the same as they are; and that even if you do refrain from certain kinds of wrongdoing, you have at least the inclination to commit such wrongs, even if cowardice, or concern for your reputation, or some other vice of that kind, saves you from actually committing them.

Fifthly, that you cannot even be certain that what they are doing is wrong; for many actions are undertaken for some ulterior purpose, and as a general rule, one must find out a great deal before one can deliver a properly founded judgement on the actions of others.

Sixthly, when you are annoyed beyond measure and losing all patience, remember that human life lasts but a moment, and that in a short while we shall all have been laid to rest.

Seventhly, that it is not people's actions that trouble us (for they are a matter for their own governing faculties) but the opinions that we form on those actions. So eliminate your judgement that this or that is of harm to you, make up your mind to discard that opinion, and your anger will be at an end. And how are you to do this? By reflecting that wrong done to you by another is nothing shameful to yourself; for unless action of which one should be ashamed is the only true evil, it would follow that you too must commit many wrongs and become a robber and one who will stop at nothing.

Eighthly, that the anger and distress that we feel at such behaviour bring us more suffering than the very things that give rise to that anger and distress.

Ninthly, that kindness is invincible, if it be sincere and not hypocritical or a mere façade. For what can the most insulting of people do to you if you are consistently kind to him, and, when the occasion allows, mildly advise him and quietly put him on the proper course at the very time when he is attempting to do you a mischief. 'No, my son, we were born for something other than this; it is not I who am harmed, it is you, my son, who are causing harm to yourself.' And show him tactfully, in general terms, that this is so, and that not even bees behave in such a fashion nor any other creature of a gregarious nature. But you must do so in no sarcastic or reproachful spirit, but affectionately and with a heart free from rancour, and not as if you were lecturing him like a schoolmaster, or trying to impress the bystanders, but as one person to another even if others should happen to be present.

Remember these nine rules as if you had received them as a gift from the Muses, and begin at last to be a human being, while you still have life in you. And you should be as careful not to flatter people as you are careful not to become angry with them, because both faults are against the common interest and lead to harm. And when you do become angry, be ready to apply this thought, that to fly into a passion is not a sign of manliness, but rather, to be kind and gentle, for in so far as these qualities are more human, they are also more manly; and it is the man who possesses such virtues who has strength, nerve, and fortitude, and not one who is ill-humoured and discontented; for the nearer a man comes in his mind to impassibility, the nearer he comes to strength, and as grief is a mark of weakness, so is anger too, for those who yield to either have been wounded and have surrendered to the enemy.

And if you will, accept this tenth gift from Apollo, the leader of the Muses, namely, that it is sheer madness to expect the bad to do no wrong; for that is to wish for the impossible. But to allow that they should do wrong to others, yet demand that they should do no wrong to yourself, is senseless and tyrannical.

11.19   There are four principal lapses of the governing faculty which you must guard against at all times, and, whenever they are detected, wholly extirpate, reminding yourself with regard to each: this idea is not necessary; this other leads to a loosening of social ties; or again, what you are about to say does not come from your heart (and to say something that does not come from your heart you must consider to be altogether out of place). And the fourth lapse which should cause you to reproach yourself is this, that the more divine part* of you has been overpowered and has succumbed to what is inferior and perishable in you, your body and its gross pleasures.

11.20*   Although the elements of breath and fire which enter into your composition have a natural tendency to rise upwards, they are nevertheless obedient to the ordering of the whole, and are held fast here on earth within your composite being. And likewise all the earthy elements in you and the watery, although they incline downwards, are yet held up and maintain a position which is not natural to them. Thus even the elements obey the whole, and when they have been assigned to a particular post, remain there by compulsion until the signal sounds from there for their subsequent release. So is it not strange, then, that the intelligent part of you alone should be recalcitrant and discontented with its position? Yet no constraint is imposed on it, but only what accords with its nature, and for all that, it refuses to comply and takes the opposite course. For to move towards unjust and dissolute behaviour, and sorrow, anger, and fear, is nothing other than to cut oneself off from nature. And whenever your governing faculty complains at anything that comes to pass, at that moment too it deserts its proper station; for it was created for holiness and service to the gods no less than for justice to man. For these affections too have to do with good fellowship, and, indeed, are of higher dignity than the practice of justice.

11.21   'He whose aim in life is not always one and the same cannot himself remain one and the same throughout his life.'* This saying is defective, unless you specify in addition what the nature of this aim should be. For as the mass of people are not of the same opinion on all the things that, in one way or another, are held to be good, but only on certain of them, namely, those that relate to the common good, the aim that we set for ourselves should therefore be the common and civic good. For he who directs every impulse of his own towards this end will be consistent in his actions and, by virtue of that, remain ever the same in himself.

11.22*   The mountain mouse and the town mouse, and the alarm and agitation of the latter.

11.23* Socrates used to call the opinions of the masses *Lamiae* – bogeys to frighten children.

11.24 At their festivals, the Spartans would place seats in the shade for their visitors, while they themselves would sit down wherever they could.

11.25 The excuse that Socrates sent to Perdiccas* for refusing to come to his court, 'I want to escape the most wretched of deaths', in other words, I want to receive no benefits when I am in no position to return them.

11.26* The writings of the Epicureans lay down this precept, that one should constantly call to mind the example of one of the ancient sages who lived a life of virtue.

11.27* The Pythagoreans said that, first thing in the morning, we should look up at the sky, to remind ourselves of beings who forever accomplish their work according to the same laws and in the same fashion, and of their orderliness, purity, and nakedness; for nothing veils a star.

11.28 Think of Socrates* dressed only in a loincloth when Xanthippe had taken his cloak and gone outside; and what he said to his friends when they were shocked and drew back at seeing him dressed in such a fashion.

11.29 In writing and reading, you cannot be the instructor before you have been instructed. How much more so in the art of living!

11.30* 'You were born a slave, you have no voice.'

11.31* ' – and my heart laughed within me.'

11.32* 'They will heap reproaches on virtue, uttering
                                    wounding words.'

11.33* It takes a madman to seek a fig in winter; and such is one who seeks for his child when he is no longer granted to him.

11.34* Epictetus used to say that when you kiss your child you should say silently to yourself, 'Tomorrow, perhaps, you will meet your death.' – But those are words of ill omen. – 'Not at all,' he replied, 'nothing can be ill-omened that points to a natural process; or else it would be ill-omened to talk of the grain being harvested.'

11.35* The green grape, the ripe cluster, the dried raisin; at every point a change, not into non-existence, but into what is yet to be.

11.36* No one can rob us of our will, said Epictetus.

11.37* He said too that we 'must find an art of assent, and in the sphere of our impulses, take good care that they are exercised subject to reservation, and that they take account of the common interest, and that they are proportionate to the worth of their object; and we should abstain wholly from immoderate desire, and not try to avoid anything that is not subject to our control.'

11.38* 'So the dispute', he said, 'is over no slight matter, but whether we are to be mad or sane.'

11.39* Socrates used to say, 'What do you want? To have the souls of rational or irrational beings?' 'Of rational beings.' 'And of what kind of rational beings, those that are sound or depraved?' 'Those that are sound.' 'Then why are you not seeking for them?' 'Because we have them.' 'Then why all this fighting and quarrelling?'

12.1 All the things which you hope to attain by a circuitous route, you can secure at this moment, if you do not deny them to yourself; I mean, if you leave all the past behind you and entrust the future to providence, and concerning yourself with the present alone, guide it to holiness and justice; to holiness so that you may love what is allotted to you, for nature brought it to you, and you to it; and to justice, so that you may speak the truth freely and without equivocation, and conform in your actions to what is lawful and equitable. And do not allow yourself to be hindered by another's evil, or opinion, or words, and still less, the sensations of the flesh that has congealed around you (for the part that suffers the ill must see to that). If then, when the time for your departure draws near, you have put all else behind you and you honour your governing faculty alone and what is divine within you, and if what you hold in fear is not that some day you will cease to live, but rather that you may never begin to live according to nature, you will be a person who is worthy of the universe that brought you to birth, and you will no longer be a stranger in your native land, wondering at what happens day after day as if it were beyond foreseeing, and in thrall to one thing and the next.

12.2* God views the governing faculty of each one of us stripped of its material casing and the husk and dross that envelops it; for with his mind alone, he touches only on what has emanated and been drawn into us from himself. And if you make it your habit to do this, you will rid yourself of the many distractions that beset you; for one who disregards the poor flesh that envelops him will surely waste no time in gaping after fine clothes and housing, and glory, and all such externals and make-believe.

12.3   There are three things of which you are composed: body,
breath, and mind.* Of these, the first two are your own in so far as
it is your duty to take care of them; but only the third is your own
in the full sense. So if you will put away from yourself – that is to
say, from your mind – all that others do or say, and all that you
yourself have done or said, and all that troubles you with regard to
the future, and all that belonging to the body which envelops you
and the breath conjoined with it is attached to you independently
of your will, and all that the vortex whirling around outside you
sweeps in its wake, so that the power of your mind, thus delivered
from the bonds of fate, may live a pure and unfettered life alone
with itself, doing what is just, desiring what comes to pass, and
saying what is true – if, I say, you will put away from your
governing faculty all that accretes to it from the affections of the
body, and all that lies in the future or in time gone by, and make
yourself, in Empedocles' words, 'a well-rounded sphere rejoicing
in the solitude around it', and strive to live only the life that is
your own, that is to say, your present life, then you will be able to
pass at least the time that is left to you until you die in calm and
kindliness, and as one who is at peace with the guardian-spirit that
dwells within him.

12.4   I have often marvelled at how everyone loves himself
above all others, yet places less value on his own opinion of
himself than that of everyone else. At all events, if a god or some
wise teacher presented himself and told him not to entertain any
thought or idea in his mind without stating it aloud as soon as he
had conceived it, he would not abide it for even a single day. So
much greater is our respect for what our neighbours think of us
than what we think of ourselves!

12.5*   How can it be that the gods, who have ordered all things
well and with goodwill towards the human race, have overlooked this single point, that some people, and those too of the
finest character, – who have, so to speak, established the closest
agreements with the divine, and by holy deeds and sacred rites
have become most intimately engaged with it – should, once
they have died, never return to life, but be utterly extinguished?
If this is indeed the case, you may be sure of this, that if it ought
to have been otherwise, the gods would have made it so; for if

that had been just, it would also have been feasible, and if it had been in accordance with nature, nature would have brought it about. So from the fact that it is not so, if indeed it is not, you may be well assured that it ought not to have been so. For you yourself can see that by delving into this matter, you are debating a point of justice with god. Now we should not be arguing in such a way with the gods unless they were perfectly good and just; and if that is the case, they would not have allowed anything in the ordering of the universe to be unjustly and irrationally neglected.

12.6   Practise even at the things which you have lost all hope of achieving. For the left hand, though inefficient at everything else through lack of practice, is more powerful than the right when it comes to gripping the bridle; for it has had good practice at that.

12.7   Consider what you should be like in both body and soul when death overtakes you, and the brevity of life, and the abyss of time that yawns behind it and before it, and the fragility of everything material.

12.8   Look at the underlying causes of things, stripped of their covering; and consider what your actions are aiming at, and what pain, pleasure, death, and fame truly are, and who is really to blame if a person is disturbed within, and how no one can be obstructed by another, and that everything turns on opinion.

12.9   In the application of one's principles, one should resemble a boxer, and not a gladiator. For the gladiator lays aside the sword which he uses and then takes it up again, but the boxer always has his fist and simply needs to clench it.

12.10*   See things in their true nature, analysing them into matter, cause and relation.

12.11   How great a power human beings have to do nothing other than what god will applaud, and to welcome all that the gods may assign to them.

12.12   For what comes about in accordance with nature, the gods are not to be blamed, for they do no wrong willingly or unwillingly; nor are human beings, for they do no wrong, unless against their will; so no one is to be blamed.

12.13   How ridiculous and what a stranger in the world is one who is surprised at anything whatever that comes to pass in life.

12.14*   Either an ineluctable destiny and an order that none may overstep, or a providence that can be appeased, or an ungoverned confusion subject to nothing but chance. If, then, an insurmountable necessity, why struggle against it? If a providence that allows itself to be appeased, make yourself worthy of aid from the divine. And if a confusion without a governor, be glad that in the midst of such heavy seas you yourself have a guiding intellect within you, and if the billows sweep you away, let them sweep away your poor flesh, and breath, and all the rest; for your mind they shall never sweep away.

12.15   If the light of the lamp shines forth without ever losing its radiance until it is extinguished, shall truth, justice and temperance be extinguished in yourself before you reach your end?

12.16   When you gain the impression that somebody has done wrong, ask yourself this, 'How can I be sure that this really was wrong?' And even if he did do wrong, how do I know that he has not condemned himself for it, and is thus like one who is tearing at his own face? One who would wish the wicked not to do wrong is like one who wants a fig tree not to produce bitter juice in its fruit, or babies not to cry, or horses not to neigh, or anything else which cannot be otherwise than it is. Now what else can a person do, if he has such a character? So if you have the spirit for it, cure his character.

12.17   If something is not right, do not do it, if something is not true, do not say it; for you should keep your impulses under your own control.

12.18*   Always look to the whole and consider exactly what it is which is creating an impression in your mind, and unfold its nature by analysing it into its cause, its matter, its relation, and its natural duration, within which it must cease to be.

12.19   Realise at last that you have something more powerful and more divine within you than the things which give rise to your passions and set you moving like a puppet. What is your mind taken up with at the present moment? Is it not fear? suspicion? appetite? or something else of that kind?

12.20[*] Firstly, never act at random and without clear reference to an end; and secondly, refer your action to no other end than the common good.

12.21 In no great while you will be no one and nowhere, and nothing that you now behold will be in existence, nor will anyone now alive. For it is in the nature of all things to change, and transform, and perish, so that others may arise in their turn.

12.22 All turns on judgement, and that rests with you. So when you will, pluck out the judgement, and then, as though you had passed the headland, the sea is calm, and all is still, and there is not a wave in the bay.

12.23 Any particular activity, whatever it may be, which comes to an end at its proper time, suffers no evil because it has come to an end; nor has the person who performed the action suffered any evil merely because his action has come to an end. So correspondingly, the aggregate of all actions which constitutes a human life suffers no evil merely because it has come to an end, if it has done so at the proper time, nor has the one who terminates the series at the proper time been harshly dealt with. But the due time and limit is laid down by nature, sometimes by our individual nature, as in old age, but in any event by universal nature, who by the constant changing of her parts keeps the whole universe forever young and in the vigour of its prime. Now what is advantageous to the whole is always entirely good and seasonable; so it follows that for each individual, the cessation of his life is nothing bad or dishonourable, for it is neither subject to his own choice nor contrary to the common benefit; rather, it is good, because it is seasonable for the universe, and brings benefit to it as it is benefited by it. For thus he is truly god-borne who is borne along the same path as god and moves in his thoughts towards the same ends.

12.24[*] You should always keep these three thoughts at hand: firstly, with regard to your actions, that you must never act without a definite aim, or otherwise than Justice herself would have acted; and bear in mind that whatever befalls you from outside is due either to chance or to providence, and that one should neither blame chance nor bring accusations against providence. Secondly, remember what manner of a being each of us is from his conception to his first breath, and from his first breath until he surrenders his soul, and from what elements he is composed and into what elements he will be dissolved. And thirdly, if you were suddenly raised aloft and looked on human affairs from above in all their diversity, with what contempt you would view them, seeing at the same time what a host of beings live all around in the air and the ether, and that however often you were raised aloft, you would behold the same things, one kind of thing unchanging in form, the other brief in duration – and it is in these that you set your pride!

12.25   Cast out the judgement, and then you are saved. So what is preventing you from casting it out?

12.26   Whenever you take exception to something, you have forgotten that all things come to pass in accordance with the nature of the whole, and that the wrong committed is another's, not your own, and that everything that comes about always did and always will come about in such a way and is doing so everywhere at this present moment; and you have forgotten how close is the kinship which unites each human being to the human race as a whole, for it arises not from blood or seed but from our common share in reason. You have forgotten, moreover, that the intellect of each of us is a god and has flowed from there,* and that nothing is our very own, but that our child, our body, our very breath have come to us from there, and that all turns on judgement; and that the life of every one of us is confined to the present moment and this is all that we have.

12.27*   Let your thoughts constantly dwell on those who have been greatly aggrieved at something that came to pass, and those who have achieved the heights of fame, or affliction, or enmity, or any other kind of fortune; and then ask yourself, 'What has become of it all?' Smoke and ashes and merely a tale, or not even so much as a tale. Also give thought to everything such as this, Fabius Catullinus in the country, Lusius Lupus in his gardens, Stertinius at Baiae, Tiberius at Capri, and Velius Rufus, and, in general, the pursuit of any obsession accompanied by conceit; and how cheap is all that man strains for, and how much worthier it is of one who aspires to wisdom to show himself in all simplicity, in relation to the material that is granted to him, as just, temperate and obedient to the gods; for the pride that prides itself on its freedom from pride is the most objectionable pride of all.

12.28   To those who ask, 'Where have you seen the gods, or what evidence do you have of their existence, that you worship them so devoutly?', I reply first of all that they are in fact visible to our eyes,* and secondly, that I have not seen my own soul, and yet I pay it due honour. So likewise with the gods; from what I experience of their power at every moment of my life, I ascertain that they exist and I pay them due reverence.

12.29   Our security in life is to see each thing as it is in its full nature, in both its material and its causal aspect; and to do what is right and speak what is true with all our heart. What remains but to enjoy one's life, linking one good act to another, so that not even the smallest space is ever left between?

12.30*   There is one light of the sun, even though it is interrupted by walls, and mountains, and countless obstacles besides. There is one common substance, even though it is divided into countless individual bodies, each with its own particular qualities. There is one soul, even though it is divided amongst countless natures, each with its own limitations. There is one intelligent soul, though it may appear to be divided. Now of the things which we have mentioned, the other parts, such as breath and material objects, are insentient and have no fellowship with one another; yet even these are held together by the principle of unity and the gravitation which draws things to their like. But it is a peculiar property of mind that it tends towards what is akin to it and combines with it, and the feeling of common fellowship suffers no division.

12.31   What is it that you seek? The mere continuance of your life? To experience sensation, then, and impulse? To grow, and cease from growing? To make use of your tongue, and your mind? And what is there in that which strikes you as worth desiring? But if all these things are worthy of contempt, take the final step, and follow reason, follow god. But to value those other things militates against that, or to be distressed at the thought that you will be robbed of them by death.

12.32   How small a fraction of infinite and unfathomable time has been assigned to each of us. For all too swiftly it is swallowed up in eternity. And how small a part of universal substance. How small a part of universal soul. And how small is this clod of earth that you are creeping over when set against the earth as a whole. Bearing all of this in mind, imagine nothing to be of any great moment apart from this, that you should act as your own nature directs, and love what universal nature brings.

12.33   How is your governing faculty employing itself? For everything rests on that. All else, be it within your control or beyond it, is merely dead matter and smoke.

12.34*   What should rouse us most strongly to feel contempt for death is the fact that even those who judge pleasure to be good and pain to be bad have despised it nonetheless.

12.35   One to whom that alone is good which comes in good season, to whom it is all the same whether he performs a greater or a lesser number of actions according to right reason, to whom it makes no difference whether he looks upon the world for a longer or a shorter period – to such a person not even death can hold any terror.

12.36*   Where is the hardship, then, if it is no tyrant or unjust judge who sends you out of the city, but nature who brought you in? It is just as if the director of a show, after first engaging an actor, were dismissing him from the stage. 'But I haven't played all five acts, but only three.' Very well; but in life three acts can amount to a play. For the one who determines when it is complete is he who once arranged for your composition and now arranges for your dissolution, while you for your part are responsible for neither. So make your departure with a good grace, as he who is releasing you shows a good grace.

NOTES

The *Meditations* (*Med.*) are referred to by book and chapter alone. Key words and phrases from the translation are picked out by italics; italics are also used for transliterated Greek terms. References to the Introduction (Introd.) are to the numbered paragraphs. For scholarly works referred to by author and date alone, see Bibliography. LS = Long and Sedley (1987); numbers and letters refer to sections and passages not pages, unless stated. All dates are AD unless otherwise specified. Further short notes are given by R. B. Rutherford in his edition of Farquharson's translation of *Med.* (1989); Farquharson's edition (1944) comments on the overall content of each chapter in vol. 1, and on the Greek in vol. 2.

BOOK 1

This book, alone in the work, is systematically arranged, as a record of his debts to other people (and to the gods, 1.17), which have helped to promote the ethical and philosophical development that is the main theme of *Med.* (see Introd. 5–6). With each comment, 'From . . . ', we need to supply the idea, 'I have learned to value the following quality' or 'I have received the following benefit'.

1.1
grandfather: Marcus Annius Verus, a distinguished Roman politician of Spanish origin, relative of the emperor Hadrian, who adopted Marcus after his father's death in Marcus' childhood.

1.2
father: also called Marcus Annius Verus, died probably in 124.

1.3

mother: Domitilla Lucilla, a rich and educated woman who brought Marcus up after his father's death.

1.4

great-grandfather: on his mother's side, Lucius Catilius Severus.

1.5

tutor: unnamed, presumably a slave, unlike the distinguished scholars mentioned later. Competitions between rival racing chariot-teams (*Greens* and *Blues*) and gladiators (fighting either with light shields or heavy) aroused huge public enthusiasm; this enthusiam was criticised by Stoics such as Seneca and Epictetus.

1.6

Diognetus: Marcus' painting instructor; *Baccheius*: a Platonic philosopher (the other two named are not known).

1.7

Quintus Junius *Rusticus*, distinguished politican, consul for the second time in 162, descended from Quintus Arulenus Junius Rusticus, a politician and adherent of Stoicism who opposed the emperor Domitian and was executed for this in 93. (For Marcus' admiration for Stoic 'martyrs' of this type, see note on 1.14.) Since Epictetus was a key influence on *Med.* (Introd. 7–8), Rusticus evidently played an important role in turning Marcus to Stoic philosophy; see also 1.17.

1.8

Apollonius of Chalcedon, Stoic philosopher and 'sophist' (orator and teacher of oratory), here presented very positively, but described in other sources as pretentious.

1.9

Sextus of Chaeronea (in Boeotia, central Greece), Platonist philosophy teacher, nephew of Plutarch, a famous intellectual and biographer; *live in accordance with nature*: central ideal of Stoic ethics; see Introd. 6 and LS 63 B–C.

1.10

Alexander the grammarian: from Cotiaeum in Syria, expert on literature, especially Homer; also taught the famous sophist Aelius Aristides.

1.11

Fronto taught Marcus oratory (style and expression); some of the correspondence between the two men survives, showing that they were good friends; the point that Roman nobles (*Patricians*) are generally lacking in *natural affection* appears in the correspondence (1.280, 2.154 in Haines edn). For translation, see C. R. Haines, ed., *Marcus Cornelius Fronto*, Loeb Classical Library, 2 vols. (Cambridge, Mass. 1919–20); also a selection translated by R. B. Rutherford in Farquharson (1989) .

1.12

Alexander the Platonist: a philosopher and orator from Seleucia (in modern Turkey) who became Marcus' Greek secretary.

1.13

Catulus: Cinna Catulus, possibly a Stoic, otherwise unknown; *Athenodotus*: a Stoic and former tutor of Fronto; *Domitius*: unknown.

1.14

Severus: consul 146, whose son married Marcus' eldest daughter. *Thrasea* etc.: famous examples of people who suffered because they tried to apply their (philosophically-based) ethical principles in politics. *Thrasea* Paetus, a Stoic, was forced to kill himself under the emperor Nero (AD 66). *Helvidius*: two men (relatives) with this name were executed under Vespasian (AD 74) and Domitian (AD 93). *Cato*: fighting on the Republican side, killed himself rather than surrender to Julius Caesar (46 BC). *Brutus*: Cato's son-in-law, one of the assassins of Caesar (44 BC), killed himself after his defeat at Philippi (42 BC). *Dio*: probably the Syracusan who, influenced by Plato's teachings, tried unsuccessfully to improve or replace the rule of the tyrant Dionysius II in the mid-4th century BC.

Figures such as Thrasea and Helvidius are sometimes characterised as the 'Stoic opposition' to imperial rule. This is misleading in that Stoicism was not opposed to imperial role as such but only to its abuse; Stoics believed that all types of regime, including monarchy, could be conducted in a virtuous way; the ideal described here (*government founded on equity* etc.) reflects Stoic as well as Roman political ideals. See further Brunt (1975); Griffin (1992), 363–6; also Introd. 10–12.

1.15

Maximus: Claudius Maximus, consul *c.*142; as governor of the province of Africa in 158 he presided over the trial of the writer and intellectual Apuleius; he is described in Apuleius' *Apology* as philosophically educated and wise; mentioned again in 1.16, 17.

1.16

adoptive father: Antoninus Pius, emperor 138–161, who adopted Marcus (and Verus) as heirs and sucessors in 138 at Hadrian's order. Marcus presents Antoninus as someone who, though supportive of *genuine philosophers*, acted virtuously on the basis of character and traditional Roman ethics rather than philosophical principles. However, the comparison with the philosopher Socrates (469–399 BC), famous for his principled life-style, suggests that Antoninus achieved in this way standards equal to those achieved by others through philosophy. (The specific reference is to Socrates' ability to refrain from, or to enjoy, food and drink: Plato, *Symposium* 176c, 220a.) Marcus' tribute to Antoninus (see also 1.17 and 6.30) illuminates Marcus' own ethical and political objectives; he apparently tried to live by the best Roman standards, while understanding these in the light of Stoic philosophy; see Introd. 10–12.

pederastic love affairs: Roman traditional ethics (by partial contrast with Greek) disapproved of homosexuality; there is an implied contrast with the pederasty of some previous emperors, especially Hadrian, whose love for the young Bithynian Antinous was notorious.

Council: not the Roman Senate, but an advisory group used by all emperors.

1.17

the gods: here and throughout *Med.*, Marcus treats the practices (e.g. prayer, prophecy) of traditional Greco-Roman polytheism as compatible with Stoic theology. For Stoicism, the divine (characterised as 'god, gods, Zeus, providence') represented the element of order and rationality both in the cosmos and in human beings ('the guardian-spirit within us', as Marcus often puts it). God is conceived in physical terms as 'designing fire'; see LS 46, esp. A, 54. By contrast with the Epicureans, the Stoics tried to reconcile conventional religious practices and ideas with their philosophical theories; see Cicero, *On the Nature of the Gods*, esp. Book 2. On Marcus and religion, see Rutherford (1989), ch. 5.

grandfather's concubine: Marcus was brought up in the house of his grandfather, Marcus Annius Verus, after his father's early death; his grandfather took a concubine (mistress) after his wife's death.

brother: Lucius Aelius Verus, adopted along with Marcus by Antoninus Pius in 138; he played an active role as (the more junior) co-emperor until his death in 169.

children: Marcus' wife Faustina (see note below) bore several children, including Commodus, Marcus' (unsuccessful) successor; Marcus' comment here restricts itself to the 'god-given' aspect of children (i.e. their being physically and mentally sound or not), and need not indicate lack of parental affection for the children thus given.

proficient at rhetoric: Marcus' letters to Fronto (see note on 1.11) show that Marcus was influenced by Fronto's advocacy of the importance of rhetoric (style and expression) as well as Fronto's character. But it is clear from 1.7 as well as 1.17 (also Fronto 1.216, Haines) that Marcus was at some point in his youth decisively drawn rather to philosophy (especially through Rusticus) and remained so; see Rutherford (1989), 103–7.

Apollonius, Rusticus and Maximus: see notes on 1.7–8, 1.15; Apollonius and Rusticus were important in drawing Marcus towards philosophy, Rusticus and Maximus were examples of men who led political lives influenced by philosophical education.

life according to nature: the Stoic ideal (see Introd. 6), here combined with observance of conventional religious practices.

Benedicta and Theodotus: unknown, presumably a female and male slave in the household of Marcus' adoptive father (Antoninus); sexual relations with these slaves would have been permissible; on Marcus' sexual self-restraint, see note on 1.16 (*pederastic love affairs*).

mother: see note on 1.3.

wife: Faustina, daughter of Antoninus, to whom Marcus was married from 145 until her death in 175. Although she was rumoured to have had an affair with Avidius Crassus and to have supported his unsuccessful revolt in 174, Marcus writes of her with affection and respect.

syllogisms . . . speculations about matters in the heavens: Marcus here makes plain that, in spite of his evident adoption of Stoic ethical principles, and his aspiration to the 'cosmic' perspective of the Stoic sage, he did not complete the full Stoic philosophical curriculum of logic–ethics–physics (study of nature). Since Stoics stressed the interdependence of these three areas of study (LS 26), his understanding of Stoicism is thus incomplete, though this does not, by itself, mean that *Med.* fails to reflect the Stoic world-view; see Introd. 9–14.

BOOK 2

Books 2 and 3 have headings indicating they were written during Marcus' campaigns in Germany; the *Quadi* were among the tribes Marcus was fighting in the 170's, the *Gran* is a tributary of the Danube.

2.2

Here, as elsewhere in Marcus, we find a distinctive three-part division between body, soul (*psyche*, identified with animating breath or air), and mind or 'governing faculty' (*hêgemonikon*). Soul (as breath) is sometimes identified (negatively) with the body (here and in 5.33, 8.56, 9.36, 12.3, 14), and sometimes identified (positively) with the mind (e.g. 6.32, 8.45, 10.1). The detachment from the body (*Despise the flesh*) recalls Plato, e.g. in *Phaedo* (see note on 3.6), though Plato tends to identify soul with mind.

Marcus' threefold division seems to diverge from standard Stoic psychology, in which psychological processes (including those of the 'governing faculty') are also physical, and are functions of animating 'breath' (*pneuma*); see LS 46, 53; Asmis (1989), 2240; Long (1996), ch. 10. However, this division may result from Marcus' emphatic stress on the role of our governing faculty as the seat of rationality and virtue, combined with his aspiration towards a sage-like, 'cosmic' perspective (bringing detachment from our body and animating life-force); see Introd. 9, 13–14. Marcus may be describing Stoic psychology from his own standpoint rather than putting forward a distinctively new psychological model.

2.3

On Stoic providence and god/gods, see note on 1.17 (*the gods*).

2.5

as suits a Roman and a man: on Marcus' attempt to combine allegiance to the best Roman standards and the universal (human, cosmic, rational) principles also presented as ideals in Stoicism, see Introd. 10–12.

2.10

Theophrastus succeeded Aristotle as head of the Lyceum (or Peripatos) in 322 BC. The relevant work of Theophrastus has been lost, but the contrast between appetite (*epithumia*) and anger (*thumos*) is important elsewhere in Aristotelian ethical psychology. Stoic ethics, by contrast, treats all wrongdoing as on the same level, as expressing 'folly', i.e. the failure to achieve full wisdom (LS 61).

2.11

If they do not exist: here, put forward only as a hypothesis to be rejected (for the linkage between gods and providence, see note on 1.17, *the gods*); for the 'providence or atoms' contrast, see Introd. 14 and note on 4.27.

2.13

the poet says: the quotation is a fragment of Pindar (fr. 292 Snell), the famous Greek lyric poet of the 5th century BC, cited by Plato, *Theaetetus* 173e.

the guardian-spirit within him: this signifies not just the human mind or governing-faculty (see note on 2.2), but also the rationality and virtue of which humans at their best are capable, which is the 'divine' element in their make-up (see note on 1.17, *the gods*). The term translated 'guardian-spirit' is *daimôn*, and suggests that which bridges human and god. This 'divine' element finds expression in proper (virtuous, rational) behaviour towards fellow-humans as well as gods. See also Introd. 9.

2.14

This chapter recalls the stock Greco-Roman genre of the 'consolation' (attempt to relieve grief at death); a key aim of philosophical practical ethics was to replace conventional with philosophical consolation; see Cicero, *Tusculans* 3, esp. 76, for a survey of approaches. The Stoics, like the Epicureans, maintained that length of life is not in itself a good thing. What matters is the quality of life, i.e. (for Stoics) living virtuously and rationally, and aspiring to the 'cosmic' perspective of the sage (see Cicero, *On Ends* 1.88, 3.45–7). Stoics also believed that world-historical events *recur in cycles* over time, LS 52. On Marcus' preoccupation with death and dissolution, see Rutherford (1989), 244–50. For similar expressions of this theme, see e.g. 3.3, 3.10, 4.32, 6.47, 7.49, 10.27, 12.27.

2.15

Everything is what you think it is: these words were both spoken *by* Monimus (a Cynic of the 4th century BC) and retorted *to* him, showing that his own claim is 'self-refuting' (*his* claim is just 'what he thinks'). Marcus seems to be referring to his recurrent theme (e.g. 3.9, 4.39) that what matters most is not what happens to us externally but forming correct judgements, i.e. judgements which are in line with what is rational or 'natural'; see also Epictetus, e.g. *Handbook* 5.

2.16

abscess . . . morbid outgrowth on the universe . . . reason and law of the most venerable of cities and constitutions: Marcus here combines two central Stoic ideas, that we are all part of the 'body' of the cosmos, and all fellow-citizens of the universal 'city and constitution' that is the cosmos; see Stanton (1968); Schofield (1991), esp. ch. 3.

2.17

Marcus here combines Heraclitean images (e.g. *flux, stream in flow, constantly changing*) with Cynic ones (e.g. *dream and delusion, fame* as *oblivion*), to reinforce the essentially Stoic point that death and dissolution are 'matters of indifference', and that what is important is maintaining 'the guardian-spirit within us', i.e. our capacity for virtuous rationality. See Introd. 9, 14.

BOOK 3

As in Book 2, the heading, *Written at Carnuntum* (just south of the boundary between Germany and the Roman province of Pannonia) suggests that this book was written on campaign.

3.1

the right moment . . . to depart from life: as well as arguing that length of life was not necessarily a good thing (note on 2.14), Stoics argued that suicide was 'well-reasoned' if performed for friends or country or to avoid mutilation or incurable illness (LS 66G–H and vol. 1, pp. 428–9); cf. 5.29, 8.47.

3.2

by-products of natural processes: the Stoics believed that there were certain necessary by-products of the rational, providential character of the cosmos, which we can learn to recognise (LS vol. 1, p. 332); cf. 6.36, 8.50.

3.3

Hippocrates: Greek founder of medicine, dated to the 5th century BC, but few facts are known about him; *Chaldaean* (i.e. Babylonian) astrologers; *Alexander* the Great, *Pompey* and *Gaius* Julius *Caesar*: famous Greek and Roman generals; *Heraclitus* (6th–5th century BC) and *Democritus* (born *c*.460 BC) were pre-Socratic philosophers; together with *Socrates* (469–399 BC), they are selected as famous instances of philosophers to whose names memorable stories of this type had become attached. Democritus has been confused with Pherecydes, another pre-Socratic, supposed to have been eaten *by lice*; the *lice of quite another kind* are the Athenian court which condemned Socrates to death in 399 BC.

3.4

[which may be of real benefit]: here and elsewhere words and phrases in square brackets have been added by the translation to fill apparent gaps in the Greek text to supply the needed sense.

3.5

one who is manly and mature, a statesman, a Roman, and a ruler: see 2.5 and Introd. 10–12.

3.6

as Socrates used to say: here as elsewhere (e.g. 3.16, 6.16, 28, 8.41), Marcus contrasts 'impulses' (*hormai*), as well as sensations, to the 'judgements' of reason (*the guardian-spirit within you*). As in 2.2, Marcus' language recalls the mind-body contrast of Plato's *Phaedo*. However, Marcus elsewhere (e.g. 8.1) expresses the orthodox Stoic view that human 'impulse' (i.e. motivation to action) depends on belief or judgement (LS 65 A–K, also Inwood (1985), ch. 3); and that is also implied here: reason *has subjected your impulses to its own authority*. Thus, as in 2.2, Marcus seems to be using Platonic language to underline an essentially Stoic idea. This is that virtue (and rationality) is the only good, and that to recognise this is to enable your governing-faculty (*guardian-spirit*) to determine your impulses. See Asmis (1989), 2241, and Introd. 9.

The final part of the chapter, esp. *examination*, recalls Epictetus' stress on the idea of examining our impressions to ensure our desire is directed only at virtue (which is 'up to us') and not 'indifferents' such as those mentioned by Marcus (wealth, pleasure), which are not; see e.g. Epictetus, *Discourses* 1.4.1–5, 3.2.1–5, *Handbook* 1, and Introd. 7–8. See also note on 3.11.

3.11

examine methodically . . . this object which now produces an impression in my mind: this account of Marcus' characteristic form of reflection also recalls Epictetus' theme of 'examining impressions (*phantasiai*)' (see note on 3.6). The focus here is on the analogue for the third stage of Epictetus' three-stage programme: the aim is to aspire to the sage-like, cosmic perspective, from which humans are seen as citizens of the cosmos and events as the outcome of the interwoven threads of fate. However, Marcus also stresses that aiming at this perspective helps us to recognise the fundamental importance of the virtues (*such as gentleness, courage* etc.) and to treat other people properly (*as the natural law of fellowship requires*), i.e. the equivalents of stages 1 and 2 of Epictetus' three-stage programme. For the idea of *stripping* naked, cf. 6.13, 9.34, 12.2.

3.13

Marcus here combines two standard ideas of ancient philosophical practical ethics (see Introd. 5): (1) the idea of philosophy as medicine or therapy, (2) the importance of basing practical precepts on doctrines (LS 66 I–J). These are linked with his characteristic appeal to the cosmic, 'divine', perspective.

3.14

The works mentioned (private notes, drafts and commonplace books) are not otherwise known; the 'notebooks' may be the *Meditations* themselves.

3.15

A satirical comment in the oracular style of Heraclitus; see also 4.29 and quotations from Heraclitus in 4.46.

3.16

Here the threefold division (*body, soul, mind*) is combined with a threefold division of functions (*impressions, impulses, judgements*); see notes on 2.2, 3.6. The idea of humans as 'puppets' on the strings of competing motives (see also 6.16, 28, 7.3, 29, 12.19) goes back to Plato, *Laws* 644d–645b.

effeminates: *androgunoi*, signifying passive homosexuals, men who give themselves up to any available sexual pleasure, however debased. *Phalaris*, tyrant of Acragas (sixth century BC), famous for cruelty, and *Nero*, Roman emperor in AD 54–68, famous both for cruelty and a colourful sex-life, are coupled as tyrants who are 'tyrannised' by their (bad) impulses.

BOOK 4

4.1

sets out to attain its primary objects, but not without reservation; wishing to obtain 'primary objects' or 'preferables' (*proêgoumena*) (e.g. good health) 'with reservation' is a standard part of the Stoic ethical ideal; see LS 58 on preferables, and Inwood (1985), 119–26, 165–75, on wishing 'with reservation'.

4.3

People seek retreats: the ideal that you can only retreat into 'yourself', not elsewhere, is a recurrent theme of ancient philosophy; see e.g. (another Stoic) Seneca, *Epistles* 28.

when people do wrong, they do so involuntarily: a Socratic paradox, developed by the Stoics in their ideas about folly and wisdom; see also 7.22, 63.

'either providence or atoms': see note on 4.27.

4.4

A closely argued statement of the idea of rational, universal law, which may derive from the great Stoic theorist Chrysippus (3rd century BC), except that the Stoic ideal is normally that of a city of *gods and* humans; cf. Cicero, *On Laws* 1.23, 33; also Schofield (1991), 68, n. 13.

4.21

Despite seeing human psychology as physical (note on 2.2), Stoics sometimes suggested that all, or some, souls might survive physical death at least until the end of the present time-cycle. Marcus here considers this possibility, without rejecting it; but seems more inclined to see souls, like bodies, as reabsorbed, more or less quickly, into the totality of the universe. See also 6.24, 7.32, 8.25, 58; Rutherford (1989), 248–50.

4.23

'*Dear city of Cecrops*': Aristophanes fr. 112; Cecrops was a mythical king of Athens; note also Marcus' related idea that we should *combine* allegiance to our local and universal city (7.44); see Introd. 10, 12.

4.27

One of many statements of the two alternatives, that the universe is a providentially ordered whole (as Stoics believed) or a fortuitous combination of atoms (as Epicureans believed). Marcus sometimes suggests that we can live rational lives and achieve peace of mind whichever option is true; but sometimes, as here, he signals his acceptance of the Stoic view, which is pervasive elsewhere in *Med.*; see Introd. 14, esp. n. 15.

4.29

For similar ideas about 'estranging' yourself from the city or body of the universe, see 8.34, 11.8.

4.30

Marcus seems to be contrasting himself, in style and in philosophical certainty, with the Cynics, who combined extreme simplicity (*no tunic*) with intense conviction.

4.32

A recurrent theme (e.g. 4.33, 48, 50, 8.25): *Vespasian*, emperor 69–79, *Trajan* 98–117.

4.33

Camillus . . . Dentatus: heroes of the early Roman republic; *Scipio*: probably Publius Cornelius Scipio Africanus, who defeated Hannibal; on *Cato*, see note on 1.14. *Augustus*: the first Roman emperor (lived 63 BC–AD 14).

4.41

Not in our surviving texts based on Epictetus' teachings; fr. 26 Schenkl, also cited in 9.24.

4.43

For other river imagery, see 2.17, 5.23, 6.15; it may derive from Heraclitus (e.g. fr. B 49a Diels–Kranz); see 4.46.

4.46

Quotations are from Heraclitus, frs. B 76, B 71–4 Diels–Kranz.

4.48

Helice: Greek city suddenly destroyed in 373 BC; *Pompeii, Herculaneum*: famously destroyed by the eruption of Vesuvius in AD 79.

4.49

headland . . . which yet stands firm: cf. the Roman–Stoic image in Virgil, *Aeneid* 7.586–90.

4.50

Caedicanus etc.: these names cannot be firmly identified.

BOOK 5

5.8

Asclepius: Greek god of healing, with a famous cult-centre at Epidaurus; his remedies (transmitted by dreams) were often bizarre, as in the case of Aelius Aristides, a 2nd-century AD sophist. Marcus compares accepting such remedies with accepting the mysterious workings of Fate.

5.10

A rather rapid and episodic chapter. Marcus moves from issues about knowledge generally (in Stoic terms, giving correct *assent* to *sense impressions*) to achieving ethical knowledge; and so to the ethical misunderstandings (the failure to form correct impressions) of most people, thus leading to the negative description of the majority of people and events (*murk and filth* etc.). This is qualified by the final, characteristic reassertion that it is within our power as humans to express our capacity for rationality and virtue, our *guardian-spirit*. On Stoic thinking about knowledge, see LS 41.

5.12

An uncharacteristically satirical chapter. It turns on the contrast between what Stoics regard as the only real good (virtue) and conventional so-called 'goods' (Stoic 'indifferents'), e.g. wealth. But, Marcus suggests, we need to bear in mind the popular misuse of this notion to make sense of the *old verses* quoted, which conclude with the rather coarse joke at the end of the chapter. Marcus also claims, less plausibly, that the initial offence felt at the joke by *even the average person* depends on the fact that he too takes 'goods' to signify 'virtue' in the first instance. That all humans have a natural capacity to form this conception of what 'good' means is a standard Stoic claim; see e.g. Epictetus, *Discourses* 1.22.

5.13

material . . . formal: one version of a recurrent contrast in *Med.* between the active, causal, formal principle (animating soul, mind, god) and the passive, material principle (body or matter). See e.g. 4.22, 7.29, 8.11, 9.25, 10.38, 12.10; also LS 44, in which the two principles form part of a materialist world-view. For the Stoic belief in eternal recurrence of cycles of *finite periods*, each terminated by conflagration of the cosmos, see 10.7, 11.1, and LS 52.

5.16

it is possible to live well at court: for the studied detachment from the idea that the royal life is inherently attractive, cf. 6.12, 8.9 (more positively, 11.7); on Marcus' Stoic political thinking, with which this chapter is consistent, see Introd. 10–12.

5.20

This chapter combines the Stoic ideas of (1) our natural kinship to other humans, (2) wishing 'with reservation' (see note on 4.1), (3) making the best use of circumstances, e.g. by responding virtuously to events which are not 'preferable', and accepting them as fated.

5.26

The first part of this chapter suggests the quasi-Platonic contrast (between *governing . . . part* and *movement . . . in flesh*) found elsewhere in Marcus (see note on 2.2). The second part suggests rather the Stoic view that the human being functions as *a unified* (psychophysical) *organism*, but that the mind still has the capacity to form correct judgements about what is *good or bad*.

5.33

from the broad-pathed earth: refers to Hesiod, *Works and Days* 197.

poor soul: as sometimes elsewhere (see note on 2.2) the soul/animating force is identified with the body (here, the blood, cf. 6.15).

be extinguished or to depart: for similar alternatives, see 4.21 (and note).

5.36

Text corrupt (see square brackets) and thought not wholly clear. The gist is that, even if you help those who have lost 'indifferents' (e.g. wealth, health) you should not share their false over-valuation of these, but act *like the old man*, presumably in a mime or comedy.

BOOK 6

6.4

The alternatives are either (Stoic) that the cosmos is a unified whole, although it suffers periodic conflagration (*turned to a vapour*, i.e. fiery air) or (Epicurean) that it is eventually dispersed into its component atoms. See notes to 4.27, 5.13; on Epicurean thinking about the universe, see LS 13.

6.10

See note to 4.27.

6.13

lay them naked: this brutal realism (cf. 2.2, 8.24, 37, 9.36) is the outcome of the method of stripping things to their essentials described in 3.11 and of adopting the 'cosmic' perspective. The bluntness evokes Cynic style; see also Rutherford (1989), 143–7. The comment of *Crates* (a Cynic of the 4th–3rd century BC) about *Xenocrates* (4th-century Platonist) is lost.

6.14

The central Stoic contrast between the value of virtue (the only real good) and of indifferents is stated in terms of a scale of types of things admired. In the first three stages are indifferents of increasing complexity and worth; in the final stage, we find virtue and rationality, which alone merit unqualified admiration. For a related scale of nature, see LS 57 A.

6.15

Another strongly Heraclitean chapter (e.g. *flux and transformation*); see Introd. 14.

6.24

See note to 6.4.

6.30

See note to 1.16.

6.32

A restatement, strongly reminiscent of Epictetus, of the central contrast between virtue, which is 'within our control', and 'indifferents' (*adiaphora*), e.g. wealth, which are not. On Epictetus, see Introd. 7–8. This is combined with a quasi-Platonic contrast between body and soul (*psyche*) or mind (*dianoia*) (see note on 2.2), and a focus (characteristic of Marcus) on living in the present (for the last point, see e.g. 3.10, 12.3, 36).

6.36

Mount Athos: a large promontory and mountain in Northern Greece; *secondary effect . . . by-products*: see note to 3.2.

6.42

Heraclitus: fr. B 75 Diels–Kranz.

Chrysippus: the main Stoic theorist (3rd century BC); the reference seems to be to a comment preserved in Plutarch *Moralia* 1065D (= *Stoicorum Veterum Fragmenta* 2.1181), suggesting that funny lines in comedies, like vice in the universe (when seen from a providential standpoint) can serve a beneficial function; on this issue in Stoic debate, see LS 54, esp. vol. 1, pp. 332–3.

6.43

On *Asclepius*, see note on 5.8.

the goddess who brings the harvest: Ceres (Greek Demeter).

6.44

On whether gods concern themselves with the good of individuals as well as of the cosmos as a whole, see Cicero, *On the Nature of the Gods* 2.164–7, 3.86; on the uselessness of *sacrifice* and *prayer* if the gods do not, see Cicero, *ibid.* 1.116, 122; also LS 54.

As Antoninus . . . : see Introd. 10.

6.45

Here Marcus moves from the standard Stoic claim that all that happens to individuals benefits the whole (providentially) to the more dubious claim that what benefits one person also benefits others, and that *benefit* here means conferring preferable 'indifferents' such as health and wealth (see note on 6.32). The idea, presumably, is that my health and prosperity benefits that of my friends and family. On the more normal Stoic idea that the wise (not all people) are benefited by the goods (virtues) of all other wise people, see Schofield (1991), 97–101; Annas (1993), 266–7.

6.46
See also note on 1.5.

6.47
For the theme, cf. 3.3, 4.48. *Philistion* etc. (unknown) must be recently dead people; *Pythagoras* (6th century BC), like Heraclitus, a Presocratic thinker; *Eudoxus*: 4th-century BC astronomer and mathematician; *Hipparchus*: 2nd-century astronomer; *Archimedes*: famous 3rd-century BC mathematician. *Menippus*: important Cynic writer (3rd century BC), who originated the genre of Menippean satire.

6.50
On wishing 'with reservation' (*the original impulse was not unconditional*), and on responding to the failure to obtain indifferents *with equanimity*, see note on 4.1.

6.57
On the influence on the foolish of false impresssions or opinions, cf. 5.10, 12.

BOOK 7

7.3
The colourful images are largely Cynic (esp. *pageantry, stage*), see Introd. 14 and note on 12.36; on *puppets*, see note on 3.16.

7.12
cf. 7.7, and contrast the final sentence of 3.5.

7.15
The underlying idea is that, since all human beings are fundamentally capable of virtue (LS 61 L), for each of us to act virtuously is to express our nature, though in our own specific way. The images, *gold* and *purple*, thus imply both distinctive character and high quality. See Epictetus 1.2, which uses 'purple (1.2.18) in the same way; also Cicero *On Duties* 1.107–17 (= LS 66 E), on the related theory of the four *personae* (roles or masks). See also C. Gill, 'Personhood and Personality: the Four-*Personae* Theory in Cicero, *De Officiis* I', *Oxford Studies in Ancient Philosophy* 6 (1988), 169–99.

7.17

In traditional Greek thought, *happiness* (*eudaimonia*) is identified with good external (god-given) circumstances; in most Greek philosophies, it is identified with internal qualities, such as virtue. This is described here as the work of a good governing-faculty or guardian-spirit (*daimôn*) within us; see Introd. 9. On the need to examine, and not be 'pulled' by, *impressions* (*phantasiai*), see 7.28 and notes on 3.11, 16.

7.22

do wrong through ignorance; see note on 4.3.

7.26

pity and not feel *anger*: cf. 6.27, 7.22, 9.3. The point is not that the Stoics valued pity positively (strictly, it is an irrational 'passion', LS 65 E4). The point is that Stoics should avoid the passionate reactions (e.g. anger) that result from overvaluing 'indifferents' (e.g. when someone wrongs you by taking your property); cf. Epictetus, *Discourses* 1.18, 1.28, esp. 9; on 'passions', see Introd. 7, n. 7.

7.29

puppet: see note on 3.16.

material and causal: see note on 5.13.

7.31

Democritus: 5th–4th century BC founder of atomic theory; reference is to frs. B 9 or B 125 Diels-Kranz.

7.32

See note on 4.21.

7.35

The first of a series of quotations from Greek philosophy and literature; citing poetic passages that support philosophical claims is characteristic of Stoicism, esp. of Chrysippus; see P. De Lacy, 'Stoic Views of Poetry', *American Journal of Philology* 69 (1948), 241–71; also note to 11.6. The quotation is from Plato, *Republic* 486a, describing the virtues of the 'philosophical nature' in a way that anticipates the 'cosmic' perspective ascribed to the Stoic sage.

7.36

Antisthenes fr. 20b Caizzi; also quoted by Epictetus, *Discourses* 4.6.20.

7.38

Euripides, *Bellerophon* fr. 287, 1 ff. Nauck, also quoted in 11.6.

7.39

source unknown.

7.40

Euripides, *Hypsipyle*, fr. 757, 6 ff., also quoted by Cicero, *Tusculan Disputations* 3.59, alluded to in Epictetus, *Discourses* 2.6.11–14.

7.41

Euripides, *Antiope* fr. 208, 1–2, also quoted in 11.6.

7.42

Euripides fr. 918, 3 ff.

7.43

source unknown.

7.44–6

Passages from Plato, *Apology* 28b, 28d, *Gorgias* 512d–e, respectively. Passages of this type, depicting the Platonic Socrates as morally tough and uncompromising, were much quoted by Stoics, such as Epictetus, and taken to anticipate Stoic thinking about virtue and 'indifferents', and about 'passions'.

7.50

Euripides, *Chrysippus* fr. 838, 9–11.

7.51

Euripides, *Suppliants* 1110–1, and an unknown passage.

7.52

The opening quotation recalls a Spartan anecdote: a defeated wrestler, told that his opponent was 'the better man', said, 'No, better at throwing his opponent.' Marcus adapts the idea of being 'better', making it refer to moral superiority.

7.60

On bodily movements as expressions of character, cf. 11.15; also Cicero, *On Duties* 1.98, 126–7, 130–1.

7.63

The quotation recalls Plato, *Republic* 382a–a, 412e–413a, 228c, and is related to the Socratic paradox that no one does wrong willingly (see note on 4.3); see also Epictetus, *Discourses* 1.28.4.

7.64

Epicurus, fr. 447, paraphrased in 7.33; see LS 21, esp. C, for Epicurus' theory of pleasure and pain.

7.66

Telauges: a little-known figure, who appeared in a lost Socratic dialogue by Aeschines. The point is that Socrates' superiority does not inhere just in external behaviour but in character and understanding; *frosty night*: Plato, *Symposium* 220b–d; *man from Salamis*: Plato, *Apology* 32c–d; Socrates ignored the order of the thirty tyrants who ruled Athens in 404–3 BC to arrest (without justification) Leo of Salamis; *strutted through the streets*: Aristophanes, *Clouds* 362, also quoted in Plato, *Symposium* 221b. See note to 7.44–46.

7.67

Nature etc: the translation assumes that the *compound* is the combination of body and soul; despite being such a compound, we can *circumscribe* (separate off) our soul (and mind) to exercise our capacity for rationality and virtue and so *ensure that what is yours is subject to yourself*, i.e. that we control what is 'up to us' (see notes on 2.2, 3.6). The *compound* is sometimes taken to be the cosmos of which we are a part, but the point of the chapter is less clear in this interpretation.

dialectic and natural philosophy: see note on 1.17, *syllogisms . . . speculations*.

7.75

Another version of the 'providence or atoms theme' (see note on 4.27), but here the second alternative is presented in a way that implies that it is inconceivable, or at least implausible (that a cosmic rational governing-faculty should directs its efforts to things that are non-rational). The overall effect, then, is to reaffirm universal causation and the *calmer mind* based on this. On fate and human agency, see also note on 10.33.

BOOK 8

8.1

For Marcus' limitations as a philosopher, see note on 1.17, *syllogisms . . . speculations* and on 7.67.

8.3

Diogenes: the 4th-century BC founder of Cynicism, often contrasted with his contemporary, *Alexander* the Great, in attitude and life-style. For the matter–cause distinction, see note on 5.13.

8.7

Marcus' statement of the standard Stoic view that, although all natural kinds have their own goodness and place in the whole cosmos, 'rational animals' (adult humans) have a special place in basing their responses ('assent to impressions') and actions, including social actions, on rational (verbal) impressions and assent. See LS vol. 1, p. 322; LS 57 A, F; Inwood (1985), chs. 2–3.

8.11

see notes on 3.11, 5.13.

8.13

knowledge of nature etc.: i.e. physics, ethics, and logic, the standard three parts of the Stoic philosophical curriculum (LS 26).

8.16

On the importance of being corrected, if mistaken, cf. 4.12, 5.28, 8.17.

8.19

Marcus rejects (from a teleological and providential standpoint) the Epicurean view that pleasure is the supreme good (LS 21).

8.21

earth . . . a mere point (*stigmê*): cf. 3.10, 4.3, 6.36.

8.24

A graphic statement of Marcus' quasi-Platonic rejection of (purely) physical reality, not here balanced by the corresponding emphasis on the 'formal' or providential aspect of reality; for fuller treatment, see 6.13, taken with 3.11.

8.25

Lucilla: presumably, Marcus' mother; *Verus*: either Marcus' natural father or brother (died 169); *Maximus*: see note on 1.15;

Secunda must be his wife; *Epitynchanus*: not known; *Diotimus*: mentioned as mourning (the emperor) Hadrian in 8.37 (a freedman or lover?); *Faustina*: not Marcus' wife, but his aunt, who died early in Antoninus' reign; *Celer*: taught Marcus rhetoric (not mentioned in 1); *Hadrian*: may be a sophist of that name, rather than the emperor; *Charax*: possibly a philosopher; *Demetrius*: probably, a Cynic philosopher, banished by Vespasian; *Eudaemon*: someone of this name was Marcus' Greek secretary for a time.

8.27
vessel . . . divine cause: a variant of the matter–form or body–soul/mind distinction, including social relations as a third category; see notes on 2.2, 5.13.

8.30
cf. 11.15. Truthful openness was valued in both traditional Roman and Stoic ethics, and seems to have been characteristic of Marcus from an early age, causing Hadrian to call him *Verissimus* ('Most truthful'), adapting the family name Verus.

8.31
Agrippa and *Maecenas*: the two chief associates of Augustus in power, Agrippa most effective as a general, Maecenas as a political leader who was also patron of poets such as Horace and Virgil; *Areios*: Stoic philosopher, resident in Augustus' court.

8.37
Pantheia: courtesan and mistress of Verus, Marcus' brother; *Pergamos*: unknown; *Chabrias*, *Diotimus* (cf. 8.25), otherwise unknown, may be freedmen or lovers of Hadrian.

8.41
'well-rounded sphere': Empedocles (pre-Socratic thinker (B 27.4 Diels-Kranz), referring to the cosmos as a unity and harmony; cf. 11.12, 12.3.

8.45
soul (*psyche*): here seems to be identified with 'mind/governing-faculty' (i.e. *guardian-spirit*), elsewhere sometimes contrasted with it; see note on 2.2.

8.48
mind as *citadel* (*akropolis*): a favourite Stoic image, see e.g. Cicero,

Tusculan Disputations 2.58, Epictetus, *Discourses* 4.1.86, 4.5.25 ff;
the image goes back to Plato, *Republic* 560b–c.

8.49

A variation on Epictetus' recurrent theme of 'examining
impressions' (see second part of note on 3.6); the proper response
to a sick child figures prominently in Epictetus, *Discourses* 1.11.
Marcus' advice is that we should not supplement our initial
impressions by judgements about 'indifferents' (e.g. 'that my
child's life is at risk and that this is a bad thing') which produce
'passions' (see Introd. 7).

8.51

sweet, clear-flowing spring: cf. Plutarch, *On Contentment, Moralia*
467A, 477B; the image fits the standard Stoic claim that all
humans have the capacity for virtue (e.g. LS 61 L).

8.54

This comparison takes on added point from the fact that, in
Stoicism, the mind functions through 'breath' (*pneuma*); god (the
divine mind) is associated with fire rather than air, but both air and
fire are conceived as active, animating elements, by contrast with
water and earth. See LS 46–7, esp. 47 D, H.

8.57

'rays' (aktines) . . . extended (ekteinesthai): a false etymology but
reflecting Stoic interest in etymologies with allegorical significance;
see e.g. Cicero, *On the Nature of the Gods* 2. 63–9. This is an
unusual instance of natural observation, momentarily recalling
Lucretius (see his treatment of sunlight and shadow in *On the
Nature of the Universe* 4.364–76); but Marcus' interest is really in
the moral conclusion, that our mind (cf. sun) should accept what
we find (our fate) and so make the most of it.

BOOK 9

9.1

This chapter gives extended treatment to some characteristic Stoic themes: that the universe is permeated by order/fate/god; that all humans have the natural capacity for virtue; that to mistake 'indifferents' for good or bad things is to go against our nature as rational beings and to fight against the rationality/fate/providence that permeates the universe and all events within it.

9.2

plague: although the point is general, it may have been sharpened by Marcus' experience of the plague brought back from the East by Verus' armies in 166–7.

9.9

This chapter gives a distinctive, 'aspirational', colour to certain central Stoic ideas. These are: (1) that the universe is composed of the four elements, of which the highest is fire, seen as permeating and 'designing' the whole, and identified with god; (2) that all animals, including human (rational) ones, are naturally disposed to form bonds of associations. See LS 46 esp. A–B, 47, 57 esp. A and F. Marcus presents the social instinct of animals as the 'fiery' element in their make-up striving to express itself; for rational animals (adult humans) not to take this process further is to fail to express their higher, more 'fiery', rational nature.

9.20

cf. 7.29, 9.38.

9.24

The overall thought is not clear. *Children's wrangles and pranks* (or 'toys') seems to be a sardonic picture of human life. *'little souls carrying their corpses around'*: cf. 4.41, a fragment of Epictetus (fr. 26 Schenkl) from a context now lost. The *journey* etc. may signify the accounts of such journeys we find in (e.g.) Homer, *Odyssey* 11.

9.25

For the causal–material distinction, see note on 5.13.

9.27

dreams and oracles: see note on 1.17, *the gods*.

9.29

This chapter sums up Marcus' general political position (Introd.

10–12): you should try to express *what universal nature wishes* by effective, practical action within your present role and community. He distances himself both from Utopian political theorising (*Plato's ideal state*, i.e. in the *Republic*) and from rulers (*Alexander* etc.), who failed to do what nature (rationality and virtue) wished, and who in that sense merely play-acted (*strutted around like stage heroes*) at being proper rulers; *snotty children*: may evoke Thrasymachus' taunt to Socrates in Plato, *Republic* 343a; *Philip* is the father of Alexander the Great; *Demetrius:* probably Poliorcetes ('Besieger of Cities'), famous general, king of Macedon, (like Philip and Alexander) in 294–87 BC.

9.34

in their naked state: cf. Plato, *Gorgias* 523, god judging souls naked after death; also 12.2.

9.36

cf. 6.13, 8.24.

9.39

'Providence or atoms' again (see Introd. 14) with no explicit preference for providence.

9.41

A fragment of Epicurus not found elsewhere (fr. 191), consistent with the attitude of Epicurus' deathbed letter, preserved in Diogenes Laertius 10.22. The appeal of this attitude to Marcus is clear; he follows here Seneca's practice (*Epistles*) of citing a philosophical opponent who recognises the truth of certain ideas which he sees as better explained by Stoicism.

9.42

An extended statement of the point that Stoic ethics requires us to refrain from the reactive attitudes (e.g. anger, condemnation) that are a normal part of social interchange and are linked with an overvaluation of 'indifferents' (see note on 7.26). Instead, we should concentrate on doing what is 'up to us', i.e exercising our own capacity for rational exercise of virtue, and trying to benefit others by teaching them to do the same.

BOOK 10

10.1
For the soul–body distinction, see note on 2.2.

10.6
'Providence or atoms' again. Although Marcus does not argue formally for providence, the whole chapter presupposes the truth of the Stoic providential world-view. For the linkage between universal and local citizenship (final sentence), see Introd. 10–12.

10.7
consumed periodically by fire: see note on 5.13.

10.8
The idea of following the ethical guidance of titles is also found in Epictetus, *Discourses* 2.10, though there the titles are social roles, not the virtues which, in Stoic theory, form part of playing the role of a human being or rational animal (see Cicero, *On Duties* 1. 98). It is by doing *the work of a human being* in this way (final sentence) that humans can *resemble* the gods, i.e. by expressing their shared rationality. See note to 7.15.

beast-fighters in the arena: for the negative attitude to the games, see also 1.5, 6.46.

Isles of the Blest: traditional image of location of the dead.

10.10
Sarmatians: here Marcus perhaps views from a 'cosmic' perspective his own conquest of (or plan to conquer) the Sarmatians, for which he took the title *Sarmaticus* in 175.

10.11
On this *method*, see note on 3.11.

10.12
within your power: cf. Epictetus' emphasis on the idea that virtue is 'up to us' or 'within our power' (e.g. *Discourses* 1.1, *Handbook* 1); *suspend your judgement*: for the idea that you should delay your desire until you are sure what you should desire, i.e. what is right or virtuous, cf. Epictetus, *Discourses*, 1.4.1, *Handbook* 2.

10.21
Euripides fr. 898 Nauck, interpreted in the light of the Stoic idea of the universe (or its immanent divinity) as a positive and creative

force (e.g. LS 46 A) to which we should respond by exercising our own rationality (divinity); *the expression*: the Greek *philei*, 'loves to' also means 'is accustomed to'; the regular, accustomed patterns in nature express her *love* or desire to create order in the cosmos.

10.23

'*penned* etc.': the quotation, from Plato, *Theaetetus* 174d, is obscurely linked with the main theme, that change of place makes no real difference. Plato's sentence is part of a sardonic description of a busy, exploitative ruler; it forms part of a contrast between the philosopher and the politician or worldly person.

10.27

Croesus: king of Lydia famous for wealth, overcome by the Persian king, Cyrus, in 547–6 BC.

10.28

pig: about to be sacrificed; *alone* etc.: probably someone ill. The final sentence combines two ideas: (1) that all must yield to fate, whether they want to or not (cf. Cleanthes, *Stoicorum Veterum Fragmenta* 1.527, Seneca, *Epistles* 107.11; Epictetus, *Handbook* 53); that rational animals (adult humans) can yield to fate freely, i.e. rationally, by accepting fate as providential. See also note on 10.33.

10.30

See note on 7.28. The idea that 'fools' are 'compelled' by their false beliefs, and the 'passions' these produce, is common in Stoicism.

10.31

When you see a living person, think of a comparable dead person and so remind yourself of human mortality. So the first three names (unknown) must be members of the contemporary Academy (followers of Socrates/Plato); *Eutychion*, *Silvanus* must be contemporary Stoics, like Euphrates, teacher of the younger Pliny (1st century AD); *Tropaeophorus* and (the relevant) *Alciphron* cannot be identified; *Severus* (see note on 1.14) is perhaps a friend of philosophers, like the friends of Socrates, *Crito* and *Xenophon*; Marcus compares himself with one of the Caesars (i.e. Roman rulers from Julius Caesar to Nero).

10.33

The main point of this relatively complex chapter arises out of

Stoic thinking on fate, which is 'compatibilist' in seeing human agency and rationality as compatible with universal causation and fate. Physical objects (e.g. a cylinder on a slope) can only exercise their nature if there are no external obstacles to doing so. But human nature can express its distinctive (rational) character, whatever the circumstances, by putting apparent obstacles to a good use (e.g. by accepting them as fated). In this way humans use their 'material' (their nature); and, in doing so, they exercise their 'citizenship' of the cosmic city, whose laws (rational principles) cannot be affected by events. For Stoic thinking on fate, see LS 55, 62, esp. 62 C–D on the cylinder example.

10.34

On the moral function of poetry, see note to 11.6; 'Leaves etc.': Homer, *Iliad* 6.146–9, shortened, a famous passage.

10.36

serious minded and wise: Marcus has in mind not himself (though he turns to *our own case* a little later) but how people would react to a Stoic sage (if one ever existed, except as an ideal).

10.38

Marcus here reuses the puppet image (see note on 3.16), presenting the strings as pulled not by impressions or passions, but by the governing-faculty, the *person* or *human being* (*anthrôpos*) himself, identified with the active *cause*, not the bodily *instruments* it uses. Interestingly, Plato, in his use of the image (*Laws* 644e–645c), also envisages human beings yielding, ideally, to the 'golden string' of reason or law.

BOOK 11

11.2

pass to the component parts: for the method of analysis, see note on 3.11.

11.3

contrariness as with the Christians: the words 'as with the Christians' are thought by some scholars to be a later addition to the manuscript tradition. If the words go back to Marcus, they reflect the same view that is shown in an exchange of letters between Pliny, as provincial governor, and the emperor Trajan (*Epistles*

10.96, 97), that the Christians' refusal to renounce their faith and sacrifice to the emperor showed a perverse 'stubbornness' (*pertinacia*), which, in itself, merited punishment. This is the only reference to the Christians in *Med.*; the religion may not at this date have been important in the Western part of the Empire; see Brunt (1979).

11.5
The Stoic conception of the goal (*telos*) was sometimes defined in terms of realising human (rational) nature, and sometimes in terms of universal (cosmic) nature. See LS 63, esp. C–E; also Annas (1993), 159–79.

11.6
Marcus here treats a theme more commonly treated in works of literary theory, such as Aristotle, *Poetics* ch. 4 and Horace, *Art of Poetry*, 202–32. The strongly moralistic treatment of poetry (recalling that of Plato, *Republic* 2–3) is characteristic of Stoicism. See e.g. Epictetus, *Discourses*, 1.28; also C. Gill, 'Did Chrysippus Understand Medea?', *Phronesis* 28 (1983), 136–49, and De Lacy (note to 7.35). *Ah Cithaeron!*: Sophocles, *Oedipus the King*, 1391; for the other quotations, see 7.38–41 and notes. The preference for Old Comedy over New (Aristophanes rather than Menander) reflects Marcus' fondness for 'Cynic' *outspokenness* (note the mention of *Diogenes*, 4th-century BC founder of Cynicism, and see Introd. 9).

11.7
See note on 5.16.

11.8
See note on 2.16, also 8.34.

11.10
'*In no case* etc.': source of quotation unknown; cf. Cicero, *On the Nature of the Gods* 2.81.

11.12
sphere: see note on 8.41.

11.13
Phocion: 4th-century BC Athenian politician and general, executed ᵇy his city after a successful but controversial career; before his execution, he was said to have sent his son the message not to bear a grudge against the Athenians for his death: Plutarch, *Phocion* 36 (and other sources).

11.15

On bodily appearance as an expression of character, see note on 7.60. On truthfulness, see note on 8.30.

11.18

Marcus' longest chapter, on a central theme of ancient practical ethics (see Introd. 5); the essays most relevant to Marcus are Seneca's Stoic *On Anger* and Plutarch's more eclectic *On the Control of Anger*. As Brunt shows (1974), 11–12, when compared with these other essays, Marcus' chapter has two main emphases. (1) It focuses on anger that is objectively justified rather than on responses to personal slights (which an emperor would rarely receive). (2) It focuses on the implications of our nature as sociable creatures, on the importance of taking into account the mistaken beliefs that lead people to act in a way that arouses anger, and on the need to teach them (tactfully) how to act better; there is less focus than in other essays on controlling your own personal reactions and so avoiding passionate agitation. See also note to 7.26.

11.19

more divine part: the governing-faculty; for the quasi-Platonic contrast with the body, see note on 2.2; cf. 3.3, end.

11.20

Although the airy or breathy and fiery elements in our composition (the higher, more 'god-like' elements, LS 46–7) are naturally inclined to rejoin their kind (cf. 9.9), they should also remain part of the bodily compound until the fated time for death; *the signal sounds from there* (*ekeithen*): i.e. from divine providence (cf. 2.3, 6.36, 12.26). The argument against suicide is a more theoretically developed version of Socrates' in *Phaedo* 61b–c; on Stoic thinking on suicide, see LS vol. 1, 428–9.

11.21

'*He whose aim . . .* ': for an example of this kind of statement, see Cicero, *On Duties* 1.111, which, however, also recognises the need to aim at the objectively good and the socially beneficial (98–9, see also note to 7.15) as well as self-consistency as an individual.

11.22

For the fable of the town and mountain (usually, 'country') mouse, see Horace, *Satires* 2.6; presumably, this incomplete comment (like, e.g. 7.3, *the scurryings of startled mice*), reflects the Cynic side of Marcus' world-view.

11.23

cf. Epictetus, *Discourses* 2.1.15, referring to Plato, *Phaedo* 77e, both passages dealing with popular stories about the after-life (though the earlier passages do not use the term *lamiae*, monstrous female vampires).

11.25

Perdiccas is a slip for Archelaus, 5th-century ruler of Macedon and Perdiccas' father. The point is not very clear.

11.26

cf. Epicurus fr. 210 Usener, cited in Seneca, *Epistles*, 11.8, 25.5–6.

11.27

On the stars as a model of cosmic order, see e.g. Cicero, *On the Nature of the Gods* 2. 43, 56; also Plato, *Timaeus* 90c–d. The Pythagoreans (6th–5th century BC Greek thinkers), are presented here as anticipating this idea; *nakedness*: a recurrent idea in *Med.*; see end of note on 3.11.

11.28

Socrates is presented in our sources as wearing only a cloak (*himation*), with a loin-cloth underneath, and not the usual tunic (*chitôn*); this anecdote (otherwise unknown) depends on this point and on Socrates' characteristic indifference to social convention.

11.30

The point of this quotation is obscure.

11.31

Homer, *Odyssey* 9.413 (Odysseus pleased at his triumph over the Cyclops); the point is obscure.

11.32

Hesiod, *Works and Days* 186, made more moralistic by inserting the word *virtue* (*aretê*).

11.33–9.

These passages are based on Epictetus, *Discourses*, 3.24.86–7 (33); 3.24.88, 91 (34); 3.24.91–2 (35); 3.22.105, and often elsewhere (36); fr. 27 Schenkl (37); fr. 28 Schenkl (38). On Epictetus and Marcus, see Introd. 7–8.

11.39
Socratic in character, but not otherwise known.

BOOK 12

12.2
For god seeing humans naked, see note on 9.34; on the mind-body dualism, see note on 2.2.

12.3
body, breath, and mind: on this threefold division, see note on 2.2. As sometimes elsewhere, *breath* (or soul, *psyche*) is linked with the body (*body . . . and the breath conjoined with it*); *sphere*: see note on 8.41.

12.5
Here Marcus meets the objection that it is wrong that the best and most 'divine' people should, none the less, be *extinguished* by death. He argues that, if this extinction does occur, it must be consistent with the providential goodness that is characteristic of the gods. Although some Stoics envisaged more or less temporary survival of all human souls, or of the wise, no Stoic envisaged the permanent immortality of human souls; see Rutherford (1989), 248–50; also note on 4.21.

12.10
On *matter* and *cause*, see note on 5.3. The relevant type of *relation* or reference (*anaphora*) must be that which derives from our nature, e.g. our relation to fellow humans (see 9.23, 12 20) or to the cosmos.

12.14
A variant on the 'providence or atoms' theme: the second option considered is a providence that can be appeased by making *yourself worthy of the divine* (i.e. by self-improvement?). If the second option is genuinely Stoic, it can only be a version of the first (providence allows room for us to improve our 'destiny' by making ethical progress). The third option is not entirely coherent, since the Epicurean world-view (*confusion without a governor*) is combined with a Stoic governing faculty and a quasi-Platonic mind–body distinction. So only the first option (Marcus' normal preference) emerges as wholly coherent.

12.18

For the method, see note on 3.11. On *relation*, see note on 12.10.

12.20

reference, refer: see note on 12.10.

12.24

The main point is the contrast between the divine (rational) elements in nature, which humans partly share, and the transient and material. Humans can share in the divine by just action and by accepting the power of providence. Also, we are capable of aspiring to the 'cosmic' perspective (*raised aloft* etc.) from which the transient affairs in which we normally take *pride* (final words) seem relatively unimportant; *host of beings*: probably, the stars etc., seen as exemplifying cosmic order (see note on 11.27); possibly, a non-Stoic adoption of the traditional idea, sometimes adopted by philosophers (e.g. Plutarch) that a variety of types of spirits (*daimones*) are found in the heavens.

12.26

from there (ekeithen): see note on 11.20.

12.27

Fabius Catullinus: perhaps the Fabius of 4.50, otherwise unknown, as is *Lusius Lupus*; *Stertinius at Baiae*: perhaps the rich doctor of Naples noted in Pliny, *Natural History* 29.5; *Tiberius*: emperor 14–37, spent most of his last ten years of power in Capri, in semi-retirement and, allegedly, depravity; *Velius Rufus*, a correspondent of Fronto (2.86–8 Haines).

12.28

visible to our eyes: as stars, see 8.19 and note on 11.27.

12.30

On the unity of the cosmos, cf. 4.40.

12.34

The Epicureans, who regarded pleasure as the supreme good, also claimed that 'death is nothing to us'; see LS 21, 24; also note on 9.41.

12.36

On the unimportance in Stoicism of length of life, see note on 2.14. The image of life as a play is common in *Med.*; see e.g. 3.8, 7.3, 10.27, which combine Stoic ideas with Cynic colour.

APPENDICES

ACKNOWLEDGEMENTS

The extracts from Robin Hard and Christopher Gill's *Epictetus* are by kind permission of Orion Books.

The extracts from R. W. Sharples, *Stoics, Epicureans and Sceptics: An Introduction to Hellenistic Philosophy,* are by kind permission of Routledge Ltd.

The extract from Elizabeth Asmis, *The Stoicism of Marcus Aurelius,* is by kind permission of Walter De Gruyter & Co.

AN ESSAY ON MARCUS AURELIUS BY MATTHEW ARNOLD*

Mr Mill says, in his book on Liberty, that 'Christian morality is in great part merely a protest against paganism; its ideal is negative rather than positive, passive rather than active.' He says that, in certain most important respects, 'it falls far below the best morality of the ancients.' Now, the object of systems of morality is to take possession of human life, to save it from being abandoned to passion or allowed to drift at hazard, to give it happiness by establishing it in the practice of virtue; and this object they seek to attain by prescribing to human life fixed principles of action, fixed rules of conduct. In its uninspired as well as in its inspired moments, in its days of languor and gloom as well as in its days of sunshine and energy, human life has thus always a clue to follow, and may always be making way towards its goal. Christian morality has not failed to supply to human life aids of this sort. It has supplied them far more abundantly than many of its critics imagine. The most exquisite document after those of the New Testament, of all the documents the Christian spirit has ever inspired — the *Imitation* — by no means contains the whole of Christian morality; nay, the disparagers of this morality would think themselves sure of triumphing if one agreed to look for it in the *Imitation* only. But even the *Imitation* is full of passages like these: '*Vita sine proposito languida et vaga est*' — '*Omni die renovare debemus propositum nostrum, dicentes: nunc hodie perfecte incipiamus, quia nihil est quod hactenus fecimus*' — '*Secundum propositum nostrum est cursus profectus nostri*' — '*Raro etiam unum vitium perfecte vincimus, et ad*

* This essay appeared under the title 'Marcus Aurelius' in *Essays in Criticism: First Series* (London, 1865) pp. 217–41.

quotidianum profectum non accendimur' — *'Semper aliquid certi proponendum est'* — *'Tibi ipsi violentiam frequenter fac'* (A life without a purpose is a languid, drifting thing — Every day we ought to renew our purpose, saying to ourselves: This day let us make a sound beginning, for what we have hitherto done is naught — Our improvement is in proportion to our purpose — We hardly ever manage to get completely rid even of one fault, and do not set our hearts on daily improvement — Always place a definite purpose before thee — Get the habit of mastering thine inclination.). These are moral precepts, and moral precepts of the best kind. As rules to hold possession of our conduct, and to keep us in the right course through outward troubles and inward perplexity, they are equal to the best ever furnished by the great masters of morals — Epictetus or Marcus Aurelius.

But moral rules, apprehended as ideas first, and then rigorously followed as laws, are, and must be, for the sage only. The mass of mankind have neither force of intellect enough to apprehend them clearly as ideas, nor force of character enough to follow them strictly as laws. The mass of mankind can be carried along a course full of hardship for the natural man, can be borne over the thousand impediments of the narrow way, only by the tide of a joyful and bounding emotion. It is impossible to rise from reading Epictetus or Marcus Aurelius without a sense of constraint and melancholy, without feeling that the burden laid upon man is well-nigh greater than he can bear. Honour to the sages who have felt this, and yet have borne it! Yet, even for the sage, this sense of labour and sorrow in his march towards the goal constitutes a relative inferiority; the noblest souls of whatever creed, the pagan Empedocles as well as the Christian Paul, have insisted on the necessity of an inspiration, a joyful emotion, to make moral action perfect; an obscure indication of this necessity is the one drop of truth in the ocean of verbiage with which the controversy on justification by faith has flooded the world. But, for the ordinary man, this sense of labour and sorrow constitutes an absolute disqualification; it paralyses him; under the weight of it, he cannot make way towards the goal at all. The paramount virtue of religion is, that it has *lighted up* morality; that it has supplied the emotion and inspiration needful for carrying the sage along the narrow way perfectly, for carrying the ordinary man along it at all.

Even the religions with most dross in them have had something of this virtue; but the Christian religion manifests it with unexampled splendour. 'Lead me, Zeus and Destiny!' says the prayer of Epictetus, 'whithersoever I am appointed to go; I will follow without wavering; even though I turn coward and shrink, I shall have to follow all the same.' The fortitude of that is for the strong, for the few; even for them the spiritual atmosphere with which it surrounds them is bleak and grey. But, 'Let thy loving spirit lead me forth into the land of righteousness' – 'The Lord shall be unto thee an everlasting light, and thy God thy glory' – 'Unto you that fear my name shall the sun of righteousness arise with healing in his wings,' says the Old Testament; 'Born, not of blood, nor of the will of the flesh, nor of the will of man, but of God' – 'Except a man be born again, he cannot see the kingdom of God' – 'Whatsoever is born of God, overcometh the world,' says the New. The ray of sunshine is there, the glow of a divine warmth – the austerity of the sage melts away under it, the paralysis of the weak is healed; he who is vivified by it renews his strength; 'all things are possible to him'; 'he is a new creature'.

Epictetus says: 'Every matter has two handles, one of which will bear taking hold of, the other not. If thy brother sin against thee, lay not hold of the matter by this, that he sins against thee; for by this handle the matter will not bear taking hold of. But rather lay hold of it by this, that he is thy brother, thy born mate; and thou wilt take hold of it by what will bear handling.' Jesus, being asked whether a man is bound to forgive his brother as often as seven times, answers: 'I say not unto thee, until seven times, but until seventy times seven.' Epictetus here suggests to the reason grounds for forgiveness of injuries which Jesus does not; but it is vain to say that Epictetus is on that account a better moralist than Jesus, if the warmth, the emotion, of Jesus's answer fires his hearer to the practice of forgiveness of injuries, while the thought in Epictetus's leaves him cold. So with Christian morality in general: its distinction is not that it propounds the maxim, 'Thou shalt love God and thy neighbour,' with more development, closer reasoning, truer sincerity, than other moral systems; it is that it propounds this maxim with an inspiration which wonderfully catches the hearer and makes him act upon it. It is because Mr Mill has attained to the perception of truths of this nature, that he is –

instead of being, like the school from which he proceeds, doomed to sterility – a writer of distinguished mark and influence, a writer deserving all attention and respect; it is (I must be pardoned for saying) because he is not sufficiently leavened with them, that he falls just short of being a great writer.

That which gives to the moral writings of the Emperor Marcus Aurelius their peculiar character and charm, is their being suffused and softened by something of this very sentiment whence Christian morality draws its best power. Mr Long has recently published in a convenient form a translation of these writings, and has thus enabled English readers to judge Marcus Aurelius for themselves; he has rendered his countrymen a real service by so doing. Mr Long's reputation as a scholar is a sufficient guarantee of the general fidelity and accuracy of his translation; on these matters, besides, I am hardly entitled to speak, and my praise is of no value. But that for which I and the rest of the unlearned may venture to praise Mr Long is this; that he treats Marcus Aurelius's writings, as he treats all the other remains of Greek and Roman antiquity which he touches, not as a dead and dry matter of learning, but as documents with a side of modern applicability and living interest, and valuable mainly so far as this side in them can be made clear; that as in his notes on Plutarch's *Roman Lives* he deals with the modern epoch of Caesar and Cicero, not as food for schoolboys, but as food for men, and men engaged in the current of contemporary life and action, so in his remarks and essays on Marcus Aurelius he treats this truly modern striver and thinker not as a Classical Dictionary hero, but as a present source from which to draw 'example of life, and instruction of manners'. Why may not a son of Dr Arnold say, what might naturally here be said by any other critic, that in this lively and fruitful way of considering the men and affairs of ancient Greece and Rome, Mr Long resembles Dr Arnold?

One or two little complaints, however, I have against Mr Long, and I will get them off my mind at once. In the first place, why could he not have found gentler and juster terms to describe the translation of his predecessor, Jeremy Collier – the redoubtable enemy of stage plays – than these: 'a most coarse and vulgar copy of the original?' As a matter of taste, a translator should deal leniently with his predecessor; but putting that out of the question, Mr Long's language is a great deal too hard. Most English people who knew Marcus Aurelius before Mr Long appeared as his introducer, knew him through Jeremy Collier. And the acquaintance of a man like Marcus Aurelius is such an imperishable benefit, that one can never lose a peculiar sense of obligation towards the man who confers it. Apart from this claim upon one's tenderness, however, Jeremy Collier's version deserves respect for its genuine spirit and vigour, the spirit and vigour of the age of Dryden. Jeremy Collier too, like Mr Long, regarded in Marcus Aurelius the living moralist, and not the dead classic; and his warmth of feeling gave to his style an impetuosity and rhythm which from Mr Long's style (I do not blame it on that account) are absent. Let us place the two side by side. The impressive opening of Marcus Aurelius's fifth book, Mr Long translates thus:

> In the morning when thou risest unwillingly, let this thought be present: I am rising to the work of a human being. Why then am I dissatisfied if I am going to do the things for which I exist and for which I was brought into the world? Or have I been made for this, to lie in the bedclothes and keep myself warm? – But this is more pleasant. – Dost thou exist then to take thy pleasure, and not at all for action or exertion?

Jeremy Collier has:

> When you find an unwillingness to rise early in the morning, make this short speech to yourself: 'I am getting up now to do the business of a man; and am I out of humour for going about that which I was made for, and for the sake of which I was sent into the world? Was I then designed for nothing but to doze and batten beneath the counterpane? I thought action had been the end of your being.'

In another striking passage, again, Mr Long has:

> No longer wonder at hazard; for neither wilt thou read thy own memoirs, nor the acts of the ancient Romans and Hellenes, and the selections from books which thou wast reserving for thy old age. Hasten then to the end which thou hast before thee, and, throwing away idle hopes, come to thine own aid, if thou carest at all for thyself, while it is in thy power.

Here his despised predecessor has:

> Don't go too far in your books and overgrasp yourself. Alas,
> you have no time left to peruse your diary, to read over the
> Greek and Roman history: come, don't flatter and deceive
> yourself; look to the main chance, to the end and design of
> reading, and mind life more than notion: I say, if you have a
> kindness for your person, drive at the practice and help
> yourself, for that is in your own power.

It seems to me that here for style and force Jeremy Collier can
(to say the least) perfectly stand comparison with Mr Long. Jeremy
Collier's real defect as a translator is not his coarseness and
vulgarity, but his imperfect acquaintance with Greek; this is a
serious defect, a fatal one; it rendered a translation like Mr Long's
necessary. Jeremy Collier's work will now be forgotten, and Mr
Long stands master of the field; but he may be content, at any rate,
to leave his predecessor's grave unharmed, even if he will not
throw upon it, in passing, a handful of kindly earth.

Another complaint I have against Mr Long is, that he is not
quite idiomatic and simple enough. It is a little formal, at least, if
not pedantic, to say *Ethic* and *Dialectic*, instead of *Ethics* and
Dialectics, and to say '*Hellenes* and Romans' instead of '*Greeks* and
Romans'. And why too – the name of Antoninus being
preoccupied by Antoninus Pius – will Mr Long call his author
Marcus *Antoninus* instead of Marcus *Aurelius*? Small as these
matters appear, they are important when one has to deal with the
general public, and not with a small circle of scholars; and it is the
general public that the translator of a short masterpiece on morals,
such as is the book of Marcus Aurelius, should have in view; his
aim should be to make Marcus Aurelius's work as popular as the
Imitation, and Marcus Aurelius's name as familiar as Socrates's. In
rendering or naming him, therefore, punctilious accuracy of
phrase is not so much to be sought as accessibility and currency;
everything which may best enable the Emperor and his precepts
volitare per ora virum. It is essential to render him in language
perfectly plain and unprofessional, and to call him by the name by
which he is best and most distinctly known. The translators of the
Bible talk of *pence* and not *denarii*, and the admirers of Voltaire do
not celebrate him under the name of Arouet.

But, after these trifling complaints are made, one must end, as one began, in unfeigned gratitude to Mr Long for his excellent and substantial reproduction in English of an invaluable work. In general the substantiality, soundness, and precision of Mr Long's rendering are (I will venture, after all, to give my opinion about them) as conspicuous as the living spirit with which he treats antiquity; and these qualities are particularly desirable in the translator of a work like that of Marcus Aurelius, of which the language is often corrupt, almost always hard and obscure. Any one who wants to appreciate Mr Long's merits as a translator may read, in the original and in Mr Long's translation, the seventh chapter of the tenth book; he will see how, through all the dubiousness and involved manner of the Greek, Mr Long has firmly seized upon the clear thought which is certainly at the bottom of that troubled wording, and, in distinctly rendering this thought, has at the same time thrown round its expression a characteristic shade of painfulness and difficulty which just suits it. And Marcus Aurelius's book is one which, when it is rendered so accurately as Mr Long renders it, even those who know Greek tolerably well may choose to read rather in the translation than in the original. For not only are the contents here incomparably more valuable than the external form, but this form, the Greek of a Roman, is not exactly one of those styles which have a physiognomy, which are an essential part of their author, which stamp an indelible impression of him on the reader's mind. An old Lyons commentator finds, indeed, in Marcus Aurelius's Greek, something characteristic, something specially firm and imperial; but I think an ordinary mortal will hardly find this: he will find crabbed Greek, without any great charm of distinct physiognomy. The Greek of Thucydides and Plato has this charm, and he who reads them in a translation, however accurate, loses it, and loses much in losing it; but the Greek of Marcus Aurelius, like the Greek of the New Testament, and even more than the Greek of the New Testament, is wanting in it. If one could be assured that the English Testament were made perfectly accurate, one might be almost content never to open a Greek Testament again; and, Mr Long's version of Marcus Aurelius being what it is, an Englishman who reads to live, and does not live to read, may henceforth let the Greek original repose upon its shelf.

The man whose thoughts Mr Long has thus faithfully reproduced, is perhaps the most beautiful figure in history. He is one of those consoling and hope-inspiring marks, which stand for ever to remind our weak and easily discouraged race how high human goodness and perseverance have once been carried and may be carried again. The interest of mankind is peculiarly attracted by examples of signal goodness in high places; for that testimony to the worth of goodness is the most striking which is borne by those to whom all the means of pleasure and self-indulgence lay open, by those who had at their command the kingdoms of the world and the glory of them. Marcus Aurelius was the ruler of the grandest of empires; and he was one of the best of men. Besides him, history presents one or two sovereigns eminent for their goodness, such as St Louis or Alfred. But Marcus Aurelius has, for us moderns, this great superiority in interest over St Louis or Alfred, that he lived and acted in a state of society modern by its essential characteristics, in an epoch akin to our own, in a brilliant centre of civilisation. Trajan talks of 'our enlightened age' just as glibly as *The Times* talks of it. Marcus Aurelius thus becomes for us a man like ourselves, a man in all things tempted as we are. Saint Louis inhabits an atmosphere of mediaeval Catholicism, which the man of the nineteenth century may admire, indeed, may even passionately wish to inhabit, but which, strive as he will, he cannot really inhabit. Alfred belongs to a state of society (I say it with all deference to the *Saturday Review* critic who keeps such jealous watch over the honour of our Saxon ancestors) half barbarous. Neither Alfred nor Saint Louis can be morally and intellectually as near to us as Marcus Aurelius.

The record of the outward life of this admirable man has in it little of striking incident. He was born at Rome on the 26th of April, in the year 121 of the Christian era. He was nephew and son-in-law to his predecessor on the throne, Antoninus Pius. When Antoninus died, he was forty years old, but from the time of his earliest manhood he had assisted in administering public affairs. Then, after his uncle's death in 161, for nineteen years he reigned as emperor. The barbarians were pressing on the Roman frontier, and a great part of Marcus Aurelius's nineteen years of reign was passed in campaigning. His absences from Rome were numerous and long. We hear of him in Asia Minor, Syria, Egypt,

Greece; but, above all, in the countries on the Danube, where the war with the barbarians was going on – in Austria, Moravia, Hungary. In these countries much of his *Journal* seems to have been written; parts of it are dated from them; and there, a few weeks before his fifty-ninth birthday, he fell sick and died. The record of him on which his fame chiefly rests is the record of his inward life – his *Journal*, or *Commentaries*, or *Meditations*, or *Thoughts*, for by all these names has the work been called. Perhaps the most interesting of the records of his outward life is that which the first book of his work supplies, where he gives an account of his education, recites the names of those to whom he is indebted for it, and enumerates his obligations to each of them. It is a refreshing and consoling picture, a priceless treasure for those, who, sick of the 'wild and dreamlike trade of blood and guile', which seems to be nearly the whole of what history has to offer to our view, seek eagerly for that substratum of right thinking and well-doing which in all ages must surely have somewhere existed, for without it the continued life of humanity would have been impossible. 'From my mother I learnt piety and beneficence, and abstinence not only from evil deeds but even from evil thoughts; and further, simplicity in my way of living, far removed from the habits of the rich.' Let us remember that, the next time we are reading the sixth satire of Juvenal. 'From my tutor I learnt' (hear it, ye tutors of princes!) 'endurance of labour, and to want little, and to work with my own hands, and not to meddle with other people's affairs, and not to be ready to listen to slander.' The vices and foibles of the Greek sophist or rhetorician – the *Graeculus esuriens* – are in everybody's mind; but he who reads Marcus Aurelius's account of his Greek teachers and masters, will understand how it is that, in spite of the vices and foibles of individual *Graeculi*, the education of the human race owes to Greece a debt which can never be overrated. The vague and colourless praise of history leaves on the mind hardly any impression of Antoninus Pius: it is only from the private memoranda of his nephew that we learn what a disciplined, hard-working, gentle, wise, virtuous man he was; a man who, perhaps, interests mankind less than his immortal nephew only because he has left in writing no record of his inner life – *caret quia vate sacro*.

Of the outward life and circumstances of Marcus Aurelius, beyond these notices which he has himself supplied, there are few of much interest and importance. There is the fine anecdote of his speech when he heard of the assassination of the revolted Avidius Cassius, against whom he was marching; *He was sorry*, he said, *to be deprived of the pleasure of pardoning him.* And there are one or two more anecdotes of him which show the same spirit. But the great record for the outward life of a man who has left such a record of his lofty inward aspirations as that which Marcus Aurelius has left, is the clear consenting voice of all his contemporaries – high and low, friend and enemy, pagan and Christian – in praise of his sincerity, justice, and goodness. The world's charity does not err on the side of excess, and here was a man occupying the most conspicuous station in the world, and professing the highest possible standard of conduct – yet the world was obliged to declare that he walked worthily of his profession. Long after his death, his bust was to be seen in the houses of private men through the wide Roman empire. It may be the vulgar part of human nature which busies itself with the semblance and doings of living sovereigns, it is its nobler part which busies itself with those of the dead; these busts of Marcus Aurelius, in the homes of Gaul, Britain, and Italy, bear witness, not to the inmates' frivolous curiosity about princes and palaces, but to their reverential memory of the passage of a great man upon the earth.

Two things, however, before one turns from the outward to the inward life of Marcus Aurelius, force themselves upon one's notice, and demand a word of comment; he persecuted the Christians, and he had for his son the vicious and brutal Commodus. The persecution at Lyons, in which Attalus and Pothinus suffered, the persecution at Smyrna, in which Polycarp suffered, took place in his reign. Of his humanity, of his tolerance, of his horror of cruelty and violence, of his wish to refrain from severe measures against the Christians, of his anxiety to temper the severity of these measures when they appeared to him indispensable, there is no doubt: but, on the one hand, it is certain that the letter, attributed to him, directing that no Christian should be punished for being a Christian, is spurious; it is almost certain that his alleged answer to the authorities of Lyons, in which he directs that Christians persisting in their profession shall be dealt with according to law, is genuine. Mr Long seems inclined to try and throw doubt over the persecution at Lyons, by pointing out that the letter of the Lyons Christians relating it, alleges it to have been attended by miraculous and incredible incidents. 'A man,' he says, 'can only act consistently by accepting all this letter or rejecting it all and we cannot blame him for either.' But it is contrary to all experience to say that because a fact is related with incorrect additions and embellishments, therefore it probably never happened at all; or that it is not, in general, easy for an impartial mind to distinguish between the fact and the embellishments. I cannot doubt that the Lyons persecution took place, and that the punishment of Christians for being Christians was sanctioned by Marcus Aurelius. But then I must add that nine modern readers out of ten, when they read this, will, I believe, have a perfectly false notion of what the moral action of Marcus Aurelius, in sanctioning that punishment, really was. They imagine Trajan, or Antoninus Pius, or Marcus Aurelius, fresh from the perusal of the Gospel, fully aware of the spirit and holiness of the Christian saints, ordering their extermination because he loved darkness rather than light. Far from this, the Christianity which these emperors aimed at repressing was, in their conception of it, something philosophically contemptible, politically subversive, and morally abominable. As men, they sincerely regarded it much as well-conditioned people, with us, regard Mormonism; as rulers, they regarded it much as Liberal statesmen, with us, regard the Jesuits. A kind of Mormonism, constituted as a vast secret society, with obscure aims of political and social subversion, was what Antoninus Pius and Marcus Aurelius believed themselves to be repressing when they punished Christians. The early Christian apologists again and again declare to us under what odious imputations the Christians lay, how general was the belief that these imputations were well-grounded, how sincere was the horror which the belief inspired. The multitude, convinced that the Christians were atheists who ate human flesh and thought incest no crime, displayed against them a fury so passionate as to embarrass and alarm their rulers. The severe expressions of Tacitus, *exitiabilis superstitio — odio humani generis convicti*, show how deeply the prejudices of the multitude imbued the educated class also. One asks oneself with astonishment how a doctrine so benign

as that of Jesus Christ can have incurred misrepresentation so
monstrous. The inner and moving cause of the misrepresentation
lay, no doubt, in this – that Christianity was a new spirit in the
Roman world, destined to act in that world as its dissolvent; and it
was inevitable that Christianity in the Roman world, like
democracy in the modern world, like every new spirit with a
similar mission assigned to it, should at its first appearance occasion
an instinctive shrinking and repugnance in the world which it was
to dissolve. The outer and palpable causes of the misrepresentation
were, for the Roman public at large, the confounding of the
Christians with the Jews, that isolated, fierce, and stubborn race,
whose stubbornness, fierceness, and isolation, real as they were,
the fancy of a civilised Roman yet further exaggerated; the
atmosphere of mystery and novelty which surrounded the
Christian rites; the very simplicity of Christian theism. For the
Roman statesman, the cause of mistake lay in that character of
secret assemblages which the meetings of the Christian community
wore, under a State-system as jealous of unauthorised associations
as is the State-system of modern France.

A Roman of Marcus Aurelius's time and position could not well
see the Christians except through the mist of these prejudices.
Seen through such a mist, the Christians appeared with a thousand
faults not their own; but it has not been sufficiently remarked that
faults really their own many of them assuredly appeared with
besides, faults especially likely to strike such an observer as Marcus
Aurelius, and to confirm him in the prejudices of his race, station,
and rearing. We look back upon Christianity after it has proved
what a future it bore within it, and for us the sole representatives
of its early struggles are the pure and devoted spirits through
whom it proved this; Marcus Aurelius saw it with its future yet
unshown, and with the tares among its professed progeny not less
conspicuous than the wheat. Who can doubt that among the
professing Christians of the second century, as among the
professing Christians of the nineteenth, there was plenty of folly,
plenty of rabid nonsense, plenty of gross fanaticism? Who will
even venture to affirm that, separated in great measure from the
intellect and civilisation of the world for one or two centuries,
Christianity, wonderful as have been its fruits, had the development
perfectly worthy of its inestimable germ? Who will venture to

affirm that, by the alliance of Christianity with the virtue and intelligence of men like the Antonines – of the best product of Greek and Roman civilisation, while Greek and Roman civilisation had yet life and power – Christianity and the world, as well as the Antonines themselves, would not have been gainers? That alliance was not to be. The Antonines lived and died with an utter misconception of Christianity; Christianity grew up in the Catacombs, not on the Palatine. And Marcus Aurelius incurs no moral reproach by having authorised the punishment of the Christians; he does not thereby become in the least what we mean by a *persecutor*. One may concede that it was impossible for him to see Christianity as it really was – as impossible as for even the moderate and sensible Fleury to see the Antonines as they really were; one may concede that the point of view from which Christianity appeared something anti-civil and anti-social, which the State had the faculty to judge and the duty to suppress, was inevitably his. Still, however, it remains true that this sage, who made perfection his aim and reason his law, did Christianity an immense injustice and rested in an idea of State-attributes which was illusive. And this is, in truth, characteristic of Marcus Aurelius, that he is blameless, yet, in a certain sense, unfortunate; in his character, beautiful as it is, there is something melancholy, circumscribed, and ineffectual.

For of his having such a son as Commodus, too, one must say that he is not to be blamed on that account, but that he is unfortunate. Disposition and temperament are inexplicable things; there are natures on which the best education and example are thrown away; excellent fathers may have, without any fault of theirs, incurably vicious sons. It is to be remembered, also, that Commodus was left, at the perilous age of nineteen, master of the world; while his father, at that age, was but beginning a twenty years' apprenticeship to wisdom, labour, and self-command, under the sheltering teachership of his uncle Antoninus. Commodus was a prince apt to be led by favourites; and if the story is true which says that he left, all through his reign, the Christians untroubled, and ascribes this lenity to the influence of his mistress Marcia, it shows that he could be led to good as well as to evil. But for such a nature to be left at a critical age with absolute power, and wholly without good counsel and direction, was the

more fatal. Still one cannot help wishing that the example of
Marcus Aurelius could have availed more with his own only son.
One cannot but think that with such virtue as his there should go,
too, the ardour which removes mountains, and that the ardour
which removes mountains might have even won Commodus.
The word *ineffectual* again rises to one's mind; Marcus Aurelius
saved his own soul by his righteousness, and he could do no more.
Happy they who can do this! But still happier, who can do more!
Yet, when one passes from his outward to his inward life, when
one turns over the pages of his *Meditations* – entries jotted down
from day to day, amid the business of the city or the fatigues of the
camp for his own guidance and support, meant for no eye but his
own, without the slightest attempt at style, with no care, even, for
correct writing, not to be surpassed for naturalness and sincerity –
all disposition to carp and cavil dies away, and one is overpowered
by the charm of a character of such purity, delicacy, and virtue.
He fails neither in small things nor in great; he keeps watch over
himself both that the great springs of action may be right in him,
and that the minute details of action may be right also. How
admirable in a hard-tasked ruler, and a ruler, too, with a passion
for thinking and reading, is such a memorandum as the following:

> Not frequently nor without necessity to say to any one, or to
> write in a letter, that I have no leisure; nor continually to
> excuse the neglect of duties required by our relation to those
> with whom we live, by alleging urgent occupation.

And, when that ruler is a Roman emperor, what an 'idea' is this to
be written down and meditated by him:

> The idea of a polity in which there is the same law for all, a
> polity administered with regard to equal rights and equal
> freedom of speech, and the idea of a kingly government which
> respects most of all the freedom of the governed.

And, for all men who 'drive at practice', what practical rules may
not one accumulate out of these *Meditations*:

> The greatest part of what we say or do being unnecessary, if a
> man takes this away, he will have more leisure and less
> uneasiness. Accordingly, on every occasion a man should ask
> himself: 'Is this one of the unnecessary things?' Now a man

should take away not only unnecessary acts, but also unnecessary thoughts, for thus superfluous acts will not follow after.

And again:

We ought to check in the series of our thoughts everything that is without a purpose and useless, but most of all the over-curious feeling and the malignant; and a man should use himself to think of those things only about which if one should suddenly ask, 'What hast thou now in thy thoughts?' with perfect openness thou mightest immediately answer, 'This or That'; so that from thy words it should be plain that everything in thee is simple and benevolent, and such as befits a social animal, and one that cares not for thoughts about sensual enjoyments, or any rivalry or envy and suspicion, or anything else for which thou wouldst blush if thou shouldst say thou hadst it in thy mind.

So, with a stringent practicalness worthy of Franklin, he discourses on his favourite text, *Let nothing be done without a purpose*. But it is when he enters the region where Franklin cannot follow him, when he utters his thoughts on the ground-motives of human action, that he is most interesting, that he becomes the unique, the incomparable Marcus Aurelius. Christianity uses language very liable to be misunderstood when it seems to tell men to do good, not, certainly, from the vulgar motives of worldly interest, or vanity, or love of human praise, but 'that their Father which seeth in secret may reward them openly'. The motives of reward and punishment have come, from the misconception of language of this kind, to be strangely overpressed by many Christian moralists, to the deterioration and disfigure-ment of Christianity. Marcus Aurelius says, truly and nobly:

One man, when he has done a service to another, is ready to set it down to his account as a favour conferred. Another is not ready to do this, but still in his own mind he thinks of the man as his debtor, and he knows what he has done. A third in a manner does not even know what he has done, *but he is like a vine which has produced grapes, and seeks for nothing more after it has once produced its proper fruit*. As a horse when he has run, a dog when he has caught the game, a bee when it has made its honey, so a man when he has done a good act, does not call out for others to come and see, but he goes on to another act, as a vine goes on to produce again the grapes in season. Must a man, then, be one of these, who in a manner acts thus without observing it? Yes.

And again:

What more dost thou want when thou hast done a man a service? Art thou not content that thou hast done something conformable to thy nature, and dost thou seek to be paid for it, *just as if the eye demanded a recompense for seeing, or the feet for walking*?

Christianity, in order to match morality of this strain, has to correct its apparent offers of external reward, and to say: *The kingdom of God is within you.*

I have said that it is by its accent of emotion that the morality of Marcus Aurelius acquires a special character, and reminds one of Christian morality. The sentences of Seneca are stimulating to the intellect; the sentences of Epictetus are fortifying to the character; the sentences of Marcus Aurelius find their way to the soul. I have said that religious emotion has the power to *light up* morality: the emotion of Marcus Aurelius does not quite light up his morality, but it suffuses it; it has not power to melt the clouds of effort and austerity quite away, but it shines through them and glorifies them; it is a spirit, not so much of gladness and elation, as of gentleness and sweetness; a delicate and tender sentiment, which is less than joy and more than resignation. He says that in his youth he learned from Maximus, one of his teachers, 'cheerfulness in all circumstances as well as in illness; *and a just admixture in the moral character of sweetness and dignity*': and it is this very admixture of sweetness with his dignity which makes him so beautiful a moralist. It enables him to carry even into his observation of nature a delicate penetration, a sympathetic tenderness, worthy of Wordsworth; the spirit of such a remark as the following has hardly a parallel, so far as my knowledge goes, in the whole range of Greek and Roman literature:

Figs, when they are quite ripe, gape open; and in the ripe olives the very circumstance of their being near to rottenness adds a peculiar beauty to the fruit. And the ears of corn bending down, and the lion's eyebrows, and the foam which flows from the mouth of wild boars, and many other things – though they are far from being beautiful, in a certain sense – still, because they come in the course of nature, have a beauty in them, and they please the mind; so that if a man should have a feeling and a deeper insight with respect to the things which are produced in the universe, there is hardly anything which comes in the course of nature which will not seem to him to be in a manner disposed so as to give pleasure.

But it is when his strain passes to directly moral subjects that his delicacy and sweetness lend to it the greatest charm. Let those who can feel the beauty of spiritual refinement read this, the reflection of an emperor who prized mental superiority highly:

Thou sayest, 'Men cannot admire the sharpness of thy wits.' Be it so, but there are many other things of which thou canst not say, 'I am not formed for them by nature.' Show those qualities, then, which are altogether in thy power – sincerity, gravity, endurance of labour, aversion to pleasure, contentment with thy portion and with few things, benevolence, frankness, no love of superfluity, freedom from trifling, magnanimity. Dost thou not see how many qualities thou art at once able to exhibit, as to which there is no excuse of natural incapacity and unfitness, and yet thou still remainest voluntarily below the mark? Or art thou compelled, through being defectively furnished by nature, to murmur, and to be mean, and to flatter, and to find fault with thy poor body, and to try to please men, and to make great display, and to be so restless in thy mind? No, indeed; but thou mightest have been delivered from these things long ago. Only, if in truth thou canst be charged with being rather slow and dull of comprehension, thou must exert thyself about this also, not neglecting nor yet taking pleasure in thy dullness.

The same sweetness enables him to fix his mind, when he sees the isolation and moral death caused by sin, not on the cheerless thought of the misery of this condition, but on the inspiriting thought that man is blest with the power to escape from it:

Suppose that thou hast detached thyself from the natural unity – for thou wast made by nature a part, but now thou hast cut thyself off – yet here is this beautiful provision, that it is thy power again to unite thyself. God has allowed this to no other part, after it has been separated and cut asunder, to come together again. But consider the goodness with which he has privileged man; for he has put it in his power, when he has been separated, to return and be united and to resume his place.

It enables him to control even the passion for retreat and solitude, so strong in a soul like his, to which the world could offer no abiding city:

Men seek retreat for themselves, houses in the country, seashores, and mountains; and thou, too, art wont to desire such things very much. But this is altogether a mark of the most common sort of men, for it is in thy power whenever thou shalt choose to retire into thyself. For nowhere either with more quiet or more freedom from trouble does a man retire than into his own soul, particularly when he has within him such thoughts that by looking into them he is immediately in perfect tranquillity. Constantly, then, give to thyself this retreat, and renew thyself; and let thy principles be brief and fundamental, which, as soon as thou shalt recur to them, will be sufficient to cleanse the soul completely, and to send thee back free from all discontent with the things to which thou returnest.

Against this feeling of discontent and weariness, so natural to the great for whom there seems nothing left to desire or to strive after, but so enfeebling to them, so deteriorating, Marcus Aurelius never ceased to struggle. With resolute thankfulness he kept in remembrance the blessings of his lot; the true blessings of it, not the false:

I have to thank Heaven that I was subjected to a ruler and a father (Antoninus Pius) who was able to take away all pride from me, and to bring me to the knowledge that it is possible for a man to live in a palace without either guards, or embroidered dresses, or any show of this kind; but that it is in such a man's power to bring himself very near to the fashion of a private person, without being for this reason either meaner in thought or more remiss in action with respect to the things which must be done for public interest . . . I have to be thankful that my children have not been stupid nor deformed in body; that I did not make more proficiency in rhetoric, poetry, and the other studies, by which I should perhaps have been completely engrossed, if I had seen that I was making great progress in them; . . . that I knew Apollonius, Rusticus, Maximus; . . . that I received clear and frequent impressions about living according to nature, and what kind of a life that is, so that, so far as depended on Heaven, and its gifts, help, and inspiration, nothing hindered me from forthwith living according to nature, though I still fall short of it through my own fault, and through not observing the admonitions of Heaven, and, I may almost say, its direct instructions; that my body has held out so long in such a kind of life as mine; that though it was my mother's lot to die young, she spent the last years of her life with me; that whenever I wished to help any man in his need, I was never told that I had not the means of doing it; that, when I had an inclination to philosophy, I did not fall into the hands of a sophist.

And, as he dwelt with gratitude on these helps and blessings vouchsafed to him, his mind (so, at least, it seems to me) would sometimes revert with awe to the perils and temptations of the lonely height where he stood, to the lives of Tiberius, Caligula, Nero, Domitian, in their hideous blackness and ruin; and then he wrote down for himself such a warning entry as this, significant and terrible in its abruptness:

A black character, a womanish character, a stubborn character, bestial, childish, animal, stupid, counterfeit, scurrilous, fraudulent, tyrannical.

Or this:

About what am I now employing my soul? On every occasion I must ask myself this question, and enquire, What have I now in this part of me which they call the ruling principle, and whose soul have I now? – that of a child, or of a young man, or of a weak woman, or of a tyrant, or of one of the lower animals in the service of man, or of a wild beast?

The character he wished to attain he knew well, and beautifully he has marked it, and marked, too, his sense of shortcoming:

When thou hast assumed these names — good, modest, true, rational, equal-minded, magnanimous — take care that thou dost not change these names; and, if thou shouldst lose them, quickly return to them. If thou maintainest thyself in possession of these names without desiring that others should call thee by them, thou wilt be another being, and wilt enter on another life. For to continue to be such as thou hast hitherto been, and to be torn in pieces and defiled in such a life, is the character of a very stupid man, and one overfond of his life, and like those half-devoured fighters with wild beasts, who though covered with wounds and gore still entreat to be kept to the following day, though they will be exposed in the same state to the same claws and bites. Therefore fix thyself in the possession of these few names: and if thou art able to abide in them, abide as if thou wast removed to the Happy Islands.

For all his sweetness and serenity, however, man's point of life 'between two infinities' (of that expression Marcus Aurelius is the real owner) was to him anything but a Happy Island, and the performances on it he saw through no veils of illusion. Nothing is in general more gloomy and monotonous than declamations on the hollowness and transitoriness of human life and grandeur: but here, too, the great charm of Marcus Aurelius, his emotion, comes in to relieve the monotony and to break through the gloom; and even on this eternally used topic he is imaginative, fresh, and striking:

Consider, for example, the times of Vespasian. Thou wilt see all these things, people marrying, bringing up children, sick, dying, warring, feasting, trafficking, cultivating the ground, flattering, obstinately arrogant, suspecting, plotting, wishing for somebody to die, grumbling about the present, loving, heaping up treasure, desiring to be consuls or kings. Well then that life of these people no longer exists at all. Again, go to the times of Trajan. All is again the same. Their life too is gone. But chiefly thou shouldst think of those whom thou hast thyself known distracting themselves about idle things, neglecting to do what was in accordance with their proper constitution, and to hold firmly to this and to be content with it.

Again:

> The things which are much valued in life are empty, and rotten, and trifling; and people are like little dogs, biting one another, and little children quarrelling, crying, and then straightway laughing. But fidelity, and modesty, and justice, and truth, are fled
>
> > Up to Olympus from the wide-spread earth.
>
> What then is there which still detains thee here?

And once more:

> Look down from above on the countless herds of men, and their countless solemnities, and the infinitely varied voyagings in storms and calms, and the differences among those who are born, who live together and die. And consider too the life lived by others in olden time, and the life now lived among barbarous nations, and how many know not even thy name, and how many will soon forget it, and how they who perhaps now are praising thee will very soon blame thee, and that neither a posthumous name is of any value, nor reputation, nor anything else.

He recognised, indeed, that (to use his own words) 'the prime principle in man's constitution is the social'; and he laboured sincerely to make not only his acts towards his fellow-men, but his thoughts also, suitable to this conviction:

> When thou wishest to delight thyself, think of the virtues of those who live with thee; for instance, the activity of one, and the modesty of another, and the liberality of a third, and some other good quality of a fourth.

Still, it is hard for a pure and thoughtful man to live in a state of rapture at the spectacle afforded to him by his fellow-creatures; above all it is hard, when such a man is placed as Marcus Aurelius was placed, and has had the meanness and perversity of his fellow-creatures thrust, in no common measure, upon his notice – has had, time after time, to experience how 'within ten days thou wilt seem a god to those to whom thou art now a beast and an ape.' His true strain of thought as to his relations with his fellow-men is rather the following. He has been enumerating the higher consolations which may support a man at the approach of death, and he goes on:

> But if thou requirest also a vulgar kind of comfort which shall reach thy heart, thou wilt be made best reconciled to death by observing the objects from which thou art going to be removed and the morals of those with whom thy soul will no longer be mingled. For it is no way right to be offended with men, but it is thy duty to care for them and to bear with them gently; and yet to remember that thy departure will not be from men who have the same principles as thyself. For this is the only thing, if there be any, which could draw us the contrary way and attach us to life, to be permitted to live with those who have the same principles as ourselves. But now thou seest how great is the distress caused by the difference of those who live together, so that thou mayest say: 'Come quick, o death, lest perchance I too should forget myself.'

O faithless and perverse generation! how long shall I be with you? how long shall I suffer you? Sometimes this strain rises even to passion:

> Short is the little which remains to thee of life. Live as on a mountain. Let men see, let them know, a real man, who lives as he was meant to live. If they cannot endure him, let them kill him. For that is better than to live as men do.

It is remarkable how little of a merely local and temporary character, how little of those *scoriae* which a reader has to clear away before he gets to the precious ore, how little that even admits of doubt or question, the morality of Marcus Aurelius exhibits. Perhaps as to one point we must make an exception. Marcus Aurelius is fond of urging as a motive for man's cheerful acquiescence in whatever befalls him, that 'whatever happens to every man *is for the interest of the universal*'; that the whole contains nothing *which is not for its advantage*; that everything which happens to a man is to be accepted, 'even if it seems disagreeable, *because it leads to the health of the universe*.' And the whole course of the universe, he adds, has a providential reference to man's welfare: '*all other things have been made for the sake of rational beings*.' Religion has in all ages freely used this language, and it is not religion which will object to Marcus Aurelius's use of it; but science can hardly accept as severely accurate this employment of terms *interest* and *advantage*. To a sound nature and a clear reason the proposition that things happen 'for the interest of the universal', as men conceive of interest, may seem to have no meaning at all, and the proposition that 'all things have been made for the sake of rational beings' may seem to be false. Yet even to this language, not irresistibly cogent when it is thus absolutely used, Marcus Aurelius gives a turn which makes it true and useful, when he says: 'The ruling part of man can make a material for itself out of that which opposes it, as fire lays hold of what falls into it, and rises higher by means of this very material;' – when he says: 'What else are all things except exercises for the reason? Persevere then until thou shalt have made all things thine own, as the stomach which is strengthened makes all things its own, as the blazing fire makes flame and brightness out of everything that is thrown into it;' – when he says: 'Thou wilt not cease to be miserable till thy mind is in such a condition, that, what luxury is to those who enjoy pleasure, such shall be to thee, in every matter which presents itself, the doing of the things which are conformable to man's constitution; for a man ought to consider as an enjoyment everything which it is in his power to do according to his own nature – and it is in his power everywhere.' In this sense it is, indeed, most true that 'all things have been made for the sake of rational beings'; that 'all things work together for good'.

In general, however, the action Marcus Aurelius prescribes is action which every sound nature must recognise as right, and the motives he assigns are motives which every clear reason must recognise as valid. And so he remains the especial friend and comforter of all clear-headed and scrupulous, yet pure-hearted and upward-striving men, in those ages most especially that walk by sight, not by faith, but yet have no open vision. He cannot give such souls, perhaps, all they yearn for, but he gives them much; and what he gives them, they can receive.

Yet no, it is not for what he thus gives them that such souls love him most! It is rather because of the emotion which lends to his voice so touching an accent, it is because he too yearns as they do for something unattained by him. What an affinity for Christianity had this persecutor of the Christians! The effusion of Christianity, its relieving tears, its happy self-sacrifice, were the very element, one feels, for which his soul longed; they were near him, they brushed him, he touched them, he passed them by. One feels, too, that the Marcus Aurelius one reads must still have remained, even had Christianity been fully known to him, in a great measure himself; he would have been no Justin – but how would Christianity have affected him? In what measure would it have changed him? Granted that he might have found, like the *Alogi* of modern times, in the most beautiful of the Gospels, the Gospel which has leavened Christendom most powerfully, the Gospel of St John, too much Greek metaphysics, too much *gnosis*; granted that this Gospel might have looked too like what he knew already to be a total surprise to him: what, then, would he have said to the Sermon on the Mount, to the twenty-sixth chapter of St Matthew? What would have become of his notions of the *exitiabilis superstitio*, of the 'obstinacy of the Christians'? Vain question! Yet the greatest charm of Marcus Aurelius is that he makes us ask it. We see him wise, just, self-governed, tender, thankful, blameless; yet, with all this, agitated, stretching out his arms for something beyond – *tendentemque manus ripae ulterioris amore.*

MARCUS AURELIUS AND STOICISM

How much of a Stoic was Marcus Aurelius? This is a question that everyone must face who tries to find an intellectual context in which to place *The Meditations*. It is one which experts on ancient philosophy have debated in recent years, but which still remains very much open. This section provides two kinds of material with which readers can make their own start with this question. First, there are passages from Epictetus which illustrate important themes in Stoicism which Marcus developed in his own way. Second, there are extracts from recent discussions of Stoic ethics, and of Marcus' place within Stoicism, by two experts in Hellenistic and Roman thought. See the Bibliography for details of books referred to by author and date, and for further reading on this question.

As stressed in the Introduction (7–8) and Notes (especially those to 3.6, 3.11, 6.32, 7.26), Epictetus was a very important influence on Marcus. Since Epictetus was a recognised teacher of Stoicism, the writings based on his teachings provide a useful bench-mark against which to place Marcus' thinking. A key theme in Epictetus is the contrast between trying to be morally good people, something which is in principle 'up to us' or 'within our power' as humans beings, and trying to obtain 'preferable indifferents' (e.g. wealth, health), which are not. A related emphasis is on 'examining impressions', to ensure that what seems 'good' and worth pursuing is virtue and not the indifferents. Both points come out clearly in this passage (*Handbook* 1; all translations of Epictetus are taken from Gill and Hard (1995)):

> Some things are up to us and others are not. Up to us are opinion, impulse, desire, aversion, and, in a word, whatever is

our own action. Not up to us are body; property, reputation, office, and, in a word, whatever is not our own action. The things that are up to us are by nature free, unhindered and unimpeded; but those that are not up to us are weak, servile, subject to hindrance, and not our own. Remember, then, that if you suppose what is naturally enslaved to be free, and what is not your own to be your own, you will be hampered, you will lament, you will be disturbed, and you will find fault with both gods and men. But if you suppose only what is your own to be your own, and what is not your own not to be your own (as is indeed the case), no one will ever coerce you, no one will hinder you, you will find fault with no one, you will accuse no one, you will not do a single thing against your will, you will have no enemy, and no one will harm you because no harm can affect you.

Since you aim, then, at such great things, remember that it is not sufficient for you to be just moderately motivated to gain them, but that you must give up some things entirely and postpone others for the time being. But if you want to have both these and public office and riches too, you will perhaps not gain even the latter, because you are aiming also at the former, but you will certainly fail to get the former, by which alone happiness and freedom are obtained.

Practise, then, from the start to say to every harsh impression, 'You are an impression, and not at all the thing you appear to be.' Then examine it and test it by these rules which you have, and firstly, and chiefly, by this: whether the impression has to do with the things which are up to us, or those which are not; and, if it has to do with the things that are not up to us, be ready to reply, 'It is nothing to me.'

In the next passage (*Discourses* 1.4.1–4), Epictetus outlines the idea of moral 'progress' implied by his method, namely, gradually recognising that virtue is the only real good, and moving closer to the peace of mind that comes from this recognition.

The man who is making progress, having learned from the philosophers that desire has good things for its object, and aversion bad things, and having also learned that peace of mind and serenity can only be attained by a man if he achieves what he desires and does not fall into what he wants to avoid – such a man has either rid himself of desire altogether or put it off to another time, and applies aversion only to things that are within the sphere of choice. For if he should try to avoid anything that lies outside the sphere of choice, he knows that he will sometimes fall into it despite his aversion, and be unhappy. Now if virtue promises happiness, an untroubled mind and serenity, then progress towards virtue is certainly progress towards each of these. For whatever is the definitive end to which the perfection of a thing leads, progress is always an approach towards it.

Next, Epictetus outlines the three-stage programme of practical ethics that can help to bring people closer to this goal. These stages are (1) directing our desires at virtue (which is 'up to us'), rather than the indifferents, which are not; (2) shaping our social relationships in the light of this aim; and (3) examining our ethical beliefs to make sure they are consistent and correct (*Discourses* 3.2.1–5, see further Introd. 7).

There are three areas of study, in which a person who is going to be good and noble must be trained. That concerning desires and aversions, so that he may neither fail to get what he desires nor fall into what he would avoid. That concerning the impulse to act and not to act, and, in general, appropriate behaviour; so that he may act in an orderly manner and after due consideration, and not carelessly. The third is concerned with freedom from deception and hasty judgement, and, in general, whatever is connected with assent.

Of these, the principal, and most urgent, is that which has to do with the passions; for these are produced in no other way than by the disappointment of our desires, and the incurring of our aversions. It is this that introduces disturbances, tumults, misfortunes, and calamities; and causes sorrow, lamentation and envy; and renders us envious and jealous, and thus incapable of listening to reason.

The next has to do with appropriate action. For I should not be unfeeling like a statue, but should preserve my natural and acquired relations as a man who honours the gods, as a son, as a brother, as a father, as a citizen.

The third falls to those who are already making progress and is concerned with the achievement of certainty in the matters already covered, so that even in dreams or drunkenness or melancholy no untested impression may catch us off guard.

In the following discourse (1.14, complete), Epictetus treats cosmic and human rationality in a way that anticipates two of Marcus' most common themes: the unification of the cosmos by divine providence and our possession of a governing faculty that is our inner guardian-spirit.

When a person asked him how a man might be convinced that each of his actions is observed by god, Epictetus said: Do you not think that all things are bound together in a unity?

I do.

Well; and do you not think that things on earth feel the influence of what is in the heavens?

Yes.

Else how could it come about so regularly, as if by god's express command, that when he tells plants to flower, they flower, and to bud, they bud, and to bear fruit, they bear it, and to bring their fruit to ripeness, it ripens; and when again, he tells them to shed their fruit and drop their leaves and, gathered in upon themselves, remain at peace and take their rest, they remain at peace and take their rest? And how else could it come about that as the moon waxes and wanes and as the sun approaches and recedes we behold amongst the things on earth so great a transformation and change? But if the plants and our bodies are so intimately bound to the universe and affected by its influences, must our souls not be much more so? But if our souls are thus bound and fastened to god, as being particles and portions of his being, must he not be aware of their every motion, as a motion that is akin to and connatural to himself? For you have the power to reflect on the divine governance and each of its accomplishments, and likewise on human affairs also, and you have the capacity to be moved by thousands of things at once both in your senses and in your intelligence, assenting to some, dissenting from others and sometimes suspending your judgement; and preserve in your mind so many impressions from so many and various objects, and whenever you are moved by these impressions, you hit on ideas corresponding to the objects which first impressed you, and from these thousands of objects, you derive and maintain both arts, one after another, and memories. If you are capable of all this, is not god capable of surveying all things, and being present with all, and having a certain communication with all? Now the sun is capable of illuminating so great a part of the universe, and of leaving only that small part of it unilluminated which is covered by the shadow of the earth; so cannot he who made the sun (which is but a small part of himself when compared with the whole) and causes it to revolve, can such a being not perceive all things?

'But I cannot', say you, 'attend to all these things at once.' Why, does any one tell you that you possess a power equal to Zeus? No! but nevertheless he has assigned to each man a director, his own personal daemon, and committed him to his guardianship; a director whose vigilance no slumbers interrupt, and whom no false reasonings can deceive. For to what better and more careful guardian could he have committed us? So when you have shut your doors, and darkened your room, remember never to say that you are alone; for you are not, but god is within, and your daemon is within, and what need have they of light to see what you are doing? To this god you also should swear such allegiance as soldiers do to Caesar. For they, in order to receive their pay, swear to put the safety of Caesar before all things; so will you not swear your oath to god, who have received so many and such great favours, or if you have sworn, will you not abide by your oath? And what must you swear? Never to disobey, never to accuse, never to find fault with anything that god has bestowed, never to do or suffer unwillingly and with a bad grace anything that is inevitable. Is this oath like the former? In the first case, men swear not to honour any other beyond Caesar; but we swear to honour our true selves above all things.

In a recent introduction to Hellenistic philosophy, R. W. Sharples (1996) first outlines the main principles of Stoic ethics, and subsequently identifies certain key features in Marcus' version of this. He begins by contrasting Stoic thought with other ancient ethical approaches (pp. 100–2, with minor omissions).

Plato had made Socrates argue that a wicked person cannot be happy, however prosperous that person is in worldly terms. But he does not make him explicitly argue the converse, that a virtuous person will be happy just by being virtuous, regardless of the material circumstances. Plato's Socrates is challenged *(Republic* 2.361) to show only that the righteous person who is being tortured is happier than the wicked person who is prosperous, not that he or she is happy *tout court*. And Aristotle for his part describes the claim that a person who is suffering the greatest misfortune is happy as one that no one would defend who was not arguing for the sake of argument *(EN* 1.5 1096a1; cf. 7.13 1153b19) – though he nevertheless suggests that a virtuous person cannot ever be truly wretched, either. *(EN* 1.10 1101a34; we will have occasion to return to this passage later.) In his *Rhetoric* (1.5 1360b14ff.; adopting a more popular view to suit the context, but cf. also *EN* 1.8 1099b3) Aristotle regards happiness as including wealth, good children, health, honour and much else besides; later writers picked out his follower Theophrastus as 'weakening' virtue by claiming that it was not sufficient for happiness (Cicero, *Tusculan Disputations* 5.24; *Academica* 1.33ff.).

They did so because they required a view to contrast with that of the Stoics. For the Stoics did hold that virtue or wisdom (the two being equated) is sufficient in itself for happiness (DL 7.127 = LS 61I; Cicero, *Tusculan Disputations* 5.82 = LS 63M), and that virtue alone is good, wickedness alone evil (DL 7.102 = LS 58A). Where others might say that virtue was so important that no other considerations could outweigh it or come anywhere near doing so – so that between virtue plus poverty and wickedness plus riches there is no real contest – the Stoics went further and denied that riches and virtue could enter into the same calculation at all; in judging what is good our only concern should be to behave virtuously:

Indeed, if wisdom [i.e. virtue] and wealth were both *desirable*, the combination of both would be more desirable than wisdom alone; but it is not the case that, if both are *deserving of approbation*, the combination is worth more than wisdom alone on its own. For we judge health deserving of a certain degree of approbation but do not place it among goods, and we consider that there is no degree of approbation so great that it can be preferred to virtue. This the Peripatetics do not hold, for they must say that an action which is both virtuous and without pain is more desirable than the same action accompanied by pain. We [Stoics] think otherwise.

(Cicero, *On Ends* 3. 44; my emphasis)

Virtuous behaviour, however, needs to be defined. For the Cynics virtue consisted in 'living according to nature', and Zeno, the founder of the Stoic school, who had been a pupil of the Cynic Crates before founding his own school, took over this definition; his successors modified the formulation but preserved its essence (Stobaeus, *Selections* 2.7.6a, p. 75.11ff. Wachsmuth–Hense, DL 7.87-9 = LS 63BC). For the Cynics it seems that 'life according to nature' was largely a negative slogan, involving the rejection of conventional ways of behaving; but for Zeno and for orthodox Stoics after him it had positive content, indicating that we should live in accordance with our own human nature, and also with the nature of the universe of which we are parts. No human being, not even the Stoic sage, can foresee everything that the future – which is to say, fate and providence – has in store; since our knowledge is limited we should follow the guidance of our own nature, but if things turn out otherwise we should accept this as for the best.

What, then, is the guidance of our own nature? Where Epicurus claimed that the first instinct of any new-born living creature was for pleasure, the Stoics claimed that it was for self-preservation (DL 7 85–6 = LS 57A). The instinct for self-preservation is described in terms of the creature's 'appropriation' to itself – its recognition of its body, first of all, as its own. 'Appropriation', *oikeiôsis*, is a term with no very natural English equivalent; its force can perhaps be more easily grasped by contrasting it with its more familiar opposite, 'alienation'. Significantly, for the Stoics it is usually a matter of us being appropriated to things by nature, rather than appropriating them to ourselves. Bulls are instinctively aware of their horns (Hierocles, *Elements of Ethics* 2.5 = LS 57C); a tortoise placed on its back struggles to right itself, and endures pain in order to do so (Seneca, *Letters on Morals* 121.8 = LS 57B) – the point presumably being that if the animal could calculate it might be trading off present pain for future pleasure, but if it cannot it must be instinct that drives it to strive for its natural condition. As Long and Sedley stress (p. 352) the appeal to nature is not intended to imply that we should behave in a certain way because animals do so; rather, observation of animals can help to reinforce our understanding of what is natural for us and for them, and to refute the Epicureans.

As the infant human being grows and develops, its 'appropriation' develops in two ways; it comes to recognise more fully what its own nature involves, and it builds links with other human beings, in its family, its city and so on (DL 7.86 = LS 57A). A human being thus comes to recognise that it is natural to pursue certain things and avoid others; health and wealth, for example, will fall in the first group, sickness and poverty in the latter. Ordinary people think that these are respectively goods and evils; but the person who eventually comes to be a Stoic sage will realise that they are not (Cicero, *On Ends* 3.21 = LS 59D). For one's own true nature, what really matters is one's reason; virtue, the only good, consists in making the right selections (not choices, for virtue alone is worthy of *choice*) among external and bodily goods and in attempting to put one's selections into effect as far as one can. This is in our own individual control; whether we succeed is not, and is irrelevant to our happiness.

Virtue alone is good; health and wealth are indifferent, but they fall into a class of 'preferred indifferents'. Wealth is preferred as a means to an end – it can be used to perform virtuous actions; bodily fitness, however, is preferred both for this reason and for its own sake, because it is natural (DL 7.107; cf. LS vol. 2, p. 355). Sickness and poverty are 'unpreferred indifferents'; that is to say, we should try to avoid them if we can do so without compromising our virtue (we should not steal to pay the doctor's bill, for example), but what is important is that we behave rationally, i.e. virtuously, by *trying* to avoid them, not that we should succeed in doing so. Other things of no importance at all, such as having an odd or even number of hairs, are indifferents that are neither preferred nor unpreferred (DL 7.104 = LS 58B)

Sharples also discusses the Stoic ideal 'wise person' or sage, whose validity is assumed by Marcus and other Stoic writers (pp. 105–8, with omissions).

The Stoic sage, and the ordinary person who is doing what he or she should, will make the same selections – e.g., in most circumstances, health rather than sickness, wealth rather than poverty – and will try to put them into effect. The difference is in their attitude and motivation. For the ordinary person thinks that it is achieving health that matters, while the Stoic sage will realise that the important thing is trying to do so.

The sage's virtue consists in possession not just of individual true judgements but of *truth* – a systematic body of moral knowledge. Virtue cannot therefore be easily lost – or so one might expect, though in fact there was a debate within the school over whether virtue could be lost, by senility or, more oddly, through the sage's getting drunk (DL 7.127 = LS 61I). There is no middle ground between virtue and wickedness, wisdom and folly; though some people who are not virtuous are 'making progress (*prokoptontes*) towards virtue, everyone who is not wise and virtuous is mad and bad (Plutarch, *SR* 31 1048E; Alexander of Aphrodisias, *On Fate* 28 199.14 = LS 61N):

> Whoever is driven blindly along by evil stupidity and ignorance of the truth, him the porch and herd of Chrysippus declares to be insane. This rule applies to all nations and to great kings, to everyone except the wise.
>
> (Horace, *Satires* 2.3.43ff.)

Any falling short of the ideal is a falling short; one can drown just as well half a yard below the surface as at the bottom of the sea (Plutarch, *CN* 1063A = LS 61T). The Stoics thus insisted that all wrong actions were equal (Stobaeus, *Selections* 2.7.11o, p. 113.18 Wachsmuth–Hense = LS 59O); this is a deliberate paradox – true from one point of view, false from another – which incurred the derision of their critics:

> Nor will this principle prevail, that the fault is equal and the
> same of the person who breaks off young cabbages in
> someone else's garden and of the one who at night carries
> off the sacred emblems of the gods. Let there be a rule to
> demand punishments that fit the crimes, so that you do not
> use the terrible scourge on what only deserves the whip.
>
> (Horace, *Satires* 1.3.115ff.)

And indeed the very passage of Stobaeus just cited allows that,
even if all wrong actions are equally wrong, there is a
difference between those that result from inveterate wickedness and those that do not. The latter will presumably include
the inevitable mistakes made by the *prokoptontes*.

Not surprisingly, the Stoic sage is as rare as the phoenix
(Alexander of Aphrodisias, *loc. cit.*); and Chrysippus did not
claim that either he himself or any of his teachers or
acquaintances was a sage (Plutarch, *SR* 31 1048E). The final
change to virtue when you become a sage is so slight you do
not notice it (*ibid.*). Since death is not in itself an evil, suicide
may sometimes be the rational, and therefore virtuous, course
to follow (Cicero, *On Ends* 3.60–1 LS 66G; DL 7.130 = LS
66H). Seneca in particular – perhaps because of his personal
situation under Nero – lays great emphasis on suicide as the
guarantee of personal freedom, but is perhaps unorthodox in
the extent to which he does so.

Modern criticism of Stoic ethics has centred on the seeming
inhumanity of the Stoic sage. The objection is well illustrated
by the example, not found in this form in ancient sources but
reconstructed according to Stoic principles, of the Stoic sage
who comes home to find the house on fire and his child inside.
(I take the example from Long, *Hellenistic Philosophy*, pp. 197–
8.) If there is any possibility of saving the child, the Stoic sage
will try to do so. (It would be foolhardy, and so not virtuous,
to try if there was no hope; it would be failing to act in
accordance with nature not to try to save the child if there was
any hope of doing so.) But the sage will try to save the child
not, ultimately, from concern about saving the child, but from
concern to do the right thing. And if the sage is beaten back by
the flames and the child dies, there will be no regrets – and

that, it would seem, for three reasons. First, because the sage did the right thing; that is what being a Stoic sage, and hence virtuous, *means*, and hence it is a logically demonstrable truth that a sage will have no regrets. Saving the child was not in the sage's power; trying to save it was, and that the sage did. Second, death is not an evil but an 'unpreferred indifferent', so nothing really bad has happened either to the child or to the sage himself (Anaxagoras, in the fifth century BC, when he heard of his son's death, said that he knew he had begotten a mortal (Cicero, *Tusculan Disputations* 3.30) and Epictetus said that, if you kiss your wife, you should be aware she is a mortal (*Discourses* 1.1.22)). And third, everything that happens is ordered for the best by Providence, even if we cannot understand how. It would not be alien to Stoic thought to argue that the apparent disaster has given the sage an opportunity to put virtue into practice, both in trying to save the child and in not grieving afterwards, and also that it may have forestalled some real evil for the child if not for the sage (i.e. it may have been destined that the child would grow up to be wicked).

The Stoic attitude may seem harsh, even repulsive. But we should note two things: first, that as far as actions are concerned the Stoic sage acts in just the same way as anyone else, and tries just as hard to save the child; if that is the proper thing to do, it would not be virtuous to do otherwise. Second, the Stoic distinction between what is in our power and what is not has a point. The Stoics certainly push the importance of intentions, as opposed to results, to paradoxical extremes, like so much else in their doctrine; we should beware of watering down the paradoxes in order to make the Stoic position seem more acceptable, but equally we should not disregard what there is to be said in its favour. The claim that virtue alone is good can be seen as an attempt to stress the distinction between moral and non-moral values; the implication that it is not only more in our own self-interest to be unjustly tortured than to do wrong, but that we will be just as happy in those circumstances as if we were virtuous and prosperous, may seem bizarre, but is it any more so than the belief that we should do our duty regardless of the consequences, or the belief that we should act for the greatest happiness of the greatest number even if that does not include ourselves?

Sharples next (pp. 111–12, with minor omissions) takes up topics which are especially relevant to Marcus' thought, the relationship between physics (study of nature) and ethics in Stoicism, and the related significance of the 'cosmic' perspective that is so prominent in the *Meditations* (see Introd. 13).

There is, however, a more general question: *can* Stoic ethical theory be detached from its context in Stoic physics and remain coherent? Annas has argued (*The Morality of Happiness*, pp. 159ff., 176ff.) that the cosmic context was not important for early Stoic ethics, and that it is the later, Roman Stoics in particular who stress the idea of each human being as a part of a greater whole. The latter point is certainly true, and we will see some striking examples later. But the image of the dog tied to the wagon is attributed to Zeno and Chrysippus, and Chrysippus also said:

As long as what will follow is not clear to me, I always cling to the things better suited by nature for obtaining the things in accordance with nature; for God himself gave me the power of selecting these. But if I knew that it was fated for me to be ill now, I would eagerly seek that; for the foot too, if it had sense, would eagerly seek to be covered with mud.

(Chrysippus cited by Epictetus,
Discourses 2.6.9f. = LS 58J)

This suggests that the cosmic context was important for the early Stoa too. Annas asks (p. 162) what happiness there can be in conforming to an external standard; but it is important to recognise, first that the standard is not for the Stoics a purely external one, for each human being is part of the larger system, and second that the Stoics are not claiming that submissiveness is a virtue in itself, regardless of what one is submitting to.

There is, however, a distinction to be drawn. The Stoics, both early and late, may indeed introduce a cosmic aspect into ethics by holding that one should accept the failure of one's own attempts, as being in the interests of a greater whole. But Annas is right to stress that early Stoic ethical theory – and later Stoic theory too, for that matter – does not base on non-human nature its claims about what course of action is natural for a human being, about what we ought to *try* to achieve. There is no theoretical difficulty in claiming that human nature should guide our actions, without any reference to the ordering of the universe as a whole. The link (not confined to the Stoics) between human reason and the divine no doubt makes it *easier* to argue that reason is the most important human characteristic, but it is not essential to that argument; Aristotle too believes in the divinity of reason, but he does not appeal to it in the first book of the *EN*. What is more problematic is whether specifically Stoic ethics, and the claim that outcomes do not matter and the sage should therefore have no regrets, can be maintained in the absence of a belief that everything in the world happens for the best even if we cannot understand how. Could one adopt the Stoic view of virtue, and of human nature, and above all of *happiness*, in an essentially hostile and unfriendly world – an Epicurean one, for example? And could one do so in the absence *both* of any belief in personal immortality (which the Stoics did not accept, in the sense of an everlasting existence) *and* of belief that our selves, even if not everlasting, are ultimately parts of a greater whole?

Pursuing this question (pp. 128–31, with omissions), Sharples places in the larger context of Stoic thought Marcus' idea of the mind as a guardian-spirit, an idea linked to the 'cosmic' perspective.

The question how important physics was to Stoic ethics in the Hellenistic period was discussed earlier. In the Stoicism of the Roman Empire we find less concern with physics in general, though Seneca wrote eight books of *Questions* on natural science, with some moralising content. More typical of the period, however, is an emphasis not on the physical structure of the cosmos but on the divine spirit in each individual. The idea of such a spirit is already present in Chrysippus (DL 7.88), and the idea that the reason within us is part of the universal reason is standard in Stoicism from the beginning. Posidonius, too, contrasted the divine spirit within us with the lowest part of the Platonically divided soul, and described the former as akin to the spirit that rules the world:

The cause of the passions, that is, of discord and of an unhappy life, is failing to follow in everything the spirit (*daimôn*) within oneself, which is akin to and has the same nature as the spirit that manages the whole world, but [rather] falling away and being carried along with the inferior and animal-like spirit . . . it is of primary importance in no way to be led by the irrational and unhappy and godless aspect of the soul.

(Posidonius cited by Galen, *PHP* 5.6.4–5 = Posidonius F187 EK)

But Epictetus uses the image far more directly:

You are of primary importance, you are a portion of God; you have some part of him in yourself. Why then do you not recognise your kinship? Why do you not know whence you have come? Are you not willing to bear in mind, when you eat, who you are that is eating and whom you are nourishing? When you associate with people, who you are that is associating? When you are someone's companion, when you exercise, when you converse, do you not know that it is God you are nourishing, God you are exercising? You carry God round with you, wretch, and you do not know it.

(Epictetus, *Discourses* 2.8.11)

So, when you shut your doors and make darkness within, remember never to say that you are alone; you are not, but God is within and so is your guardian spirit (*daimôn*). And what need do these have of light to see what you are doing?

(*ibid.*, 1.14.13–14)

Seneca too has the idea of a divine spirit within us, and couples it with that of the virtuous person rising above fortune:

A holy spirit dwells within us, the observer and guardian of our good and bad deeds. He treats us in the way he is treated by us. No human being is good without God; can anyone rise above fortune unless aided by him? He gives splendid and upright counsels. In every good person 'what god it is is uncertain, but a god dwells there'.

(Seneca, *Letters on Morals* 41.2)

It is, however, in Marcus Aurelius, more than any earlier Stoic, that we find a contrast between the world of our experience and a superior region. Traditional Stoic themes of universal nature and the kinship of the human race are combined with a playing down of the importance of the here and now:

> When you are annoyed at something, you have forgotten that everything comes about in accordance with the nature of the whole; and that the error was not yours; and in addition to this that everything that happens always happened in this way and will happen and now happens everywhere; and how great is the kinship of a human being with the whole human race, for it is sharing not in a little blood or a little seed but in intellect. You have also forgotten that each person's mind is a god, and has flowed from There; and that nothing is private to anyone, but the little child, and the little body, and the little soul itself have come from There; and that everything is supposition; and that each person lives only in the present and at once loses that.
>
> (Marcus Aurelius, *Meditations* 12.26)

('There', *ekei*, was a traditional, originally euphemistic, expression for the underworld; in Neoplatonism it would come to indicate the incorporeal Platonic Forms by contrast with what is bodily, apprehensible by the senses and subject to change.) Marcus sometimes sounds not unlike Plato in certain of his moods, and with hindsight his view of human experience can be seen as pointing to the replacement of Stoicism by Platonism as the dominant philosophy of late antiquity:

> Empty seriousness of a show, plays upon the stage, flocks, herds, battles with spears, a bone thrown to dogs, a morsel to the fish that receive it; strugglings of ants to bear their burdens, the travels of fluttering blowflies, puppets pulled by strings. Among these one must take one's stand graciously and without snorting insolently; but one should take note that each person is worth just as much as the things he or she takes seriously.
>
> (*ibid.*, 7.3)

with which one may compare from Plato himself:

Human affairs, then, are not deserving of much serious concern; but it is necessary to be concerned, and this is not fortunate . . . I say that it is necessary to be seriously concerned about what is serious, but not about what is not; and that by nature God is deserving of all blessed concern, but human beings, as I said before, are contrived as a sort of plaything of God, and in reality this is the best thing about them.

(Plato, *Laws* 7 803bc)

Not that such ideas started with Plato; the idea that human activities provide amusement for the gods is as old as Homer's *Iliad*. The difference is that for Plato, and later for the Neoplatonists, immmortality and rationality can give human beings a stake in the other, superior world. Marcus, however, is still a Stoic; he shares, indeed, the Stoic belief in a limited survival of the soul after the death of the body, but there is little emphasis on this, and an absence of the Platonic sense that human beings truly belong in another world or that there are rewards for virtue there. Cicero, named Father of his Country and by his own estimation greater than its founder Romulus (*Against Catiline* 3.2), presents rewards in heaven for great statesmen after death in his *Republic* as Scipio's dream. But in Marcus, ruler of the Roman Empire, even the dreams seem absent. For him we are very definitely part of the physical world and its processes:

Consider continually how many doctors have died, after often knitting their brows over their patients; how many astrologers, having foretold the deaths of others as if this were something important; how many philosophers, who contended endlessly about death or immortality . . . Go over how many people you have known, one after the other; one buried another and was then laid out for burial himself, and another another; all in a short time. In general, consider always how ephemeral and cheap human affairs are; yesterday slime, tomorrow pickle or ashes. Go through this momentary time in accordance with nature, and come to an end cheerfully, like an olive that falls when

it is ripe, speaking well of earth who bore you and giving
thanks to the tree that begat you.

(*ibid.*, 4.48)

In the final discussion, Elizabeth Asmis (1989, 2249–52, with
omissions) explores Marcus' repeated use of the alternative,
'providence or atoms', and asks how far Marcus is working within,
or going outside, a Stoic framework of thought.

The only philosophers with whom Marcus expresses outright
disagreement are the atomists, traditionally the chief opponents
of Stoicism. But even here Marcus adjusts his beliefs to those of
others. Prior to Marcus, some Stoics, especially Seneca, had
admitted some Epicurean teachings into Stoicism. Marcus
continues this tendency when he lauds Epicurus' attitude to
pain (7.64, 9.41). But Marcus goes further than his Stoic
predecessors in making concessions to the atomists. On the
one hand, he wants to correct their mistakes; on the other
hand, he is willing, at times, to concede to them their most
basic physical doctrine, that the world is made of atoms.

Marcus quotes Democritus twice in order to improve upon
him. At 4.24, he takes Democritus' saying 'do few things if you
are going to be content' and proposes that one should choose
necessary things instead, as demanded by one's nature as a
political being. These necessary things are indeed few; but they
just happen to be so. At 7.31, he quotes Democritus' claim that
'all things are by law, but in truth there are only elements'.
Affirming Stoic doctrine, Marcus writes that it is sufficient to
keep in mind that 'all things are by law'.

Marcus' belief in cosmic law, however, is subject to doubt.
Overwhelmingly in his writings, Marcus takes the Stoic
position that he is part of a rational, provident universal nature,
which binds all things together in mutual cooperation. But
occasionally Marcus wavers. While he often affirms his belief
in providence, he also repeatedly puts to himself the
disjunction: 'Providence or atoms'. The Stoics regularly used
disjunctions to argue their case; but Marcus' use of the
disjunction has sceptical overtones. Marcus weighs both sides
of the question; and, although he inclines toward the Stoic

alternative he sometimes suspends judgement and is willing to accept either possibility. In either case, he argues, there is no reason to be disturbed or to assign blame. If everything happens at random, he, at any rate, should not act at random. Marcus also puts the threefold possibility: there is fated necessity, or a gracious providence, or a random mixture (12.14). Here he modifies Stoicism by making a disjunction between necessity and providence. In case everything is unguided mixture, Marcus has a refuge: let flesh and breath be swept away, he writes; the mind will not be swept away.

In weighing providence against atomic randomness, Marcus is particularly concerned about death. If the world is an organised whole, he writes, he will be extinguished or change to another place; if there are atoms moving at random, he will be scattered. In neither case, he concludes, is there any reason to be disturbed. Marcus describes extinction as an absorption into the whole, that is, into the 'seminal logoi' of the cosmos. The Stoics believed that the soul is ultimately absorbed in the cosmic organism; but the early Stoics held that the individual soul remains for a while after death, whereas Panaetius and other later Stoics believed that the soul is absorbed immediately upon death. Marcus thus opposes two alternatives within the Stoic tradition to the atomist position, and is willing to accept any of these alternatives.

At the same time, Marcus' view of the alternatives is influenced by Socrates. With an allusion to Socrates, Marcus explains change of place as 'being posted in another place' (8.25). He also puts the alternatives as non-perception or different perception (8.58), and as non-perception or a different life not devoid of gods (3.5.2). These formulations are versions of Socrates' proposition in the *Apology* (40c) that death is either a state of non-perception or an 'alteration and change of abode' to a better place. In proposing a different perception or different life, as well as a change of abode simply, Marcus appears to open the range of possibilities not only to a limited Stoic survival of the soul, but also to an enduring, Platonic survival. The many passages in which Marcus regards death as dissolution show that he did not adopt the Platonic position. But he is not entirely dogmatic in his rejection. At

12.5, he asks how the gods, who arranged everything so beautifully and with a love for humankind, overlooked that worthwhile and pious people do not come into being again once they have died. He answers that 'if this is so', the gods arranged it just as it ought to be. Marcus is strongly committed to the view that the individual is ephemeral, but he does not presume to conclude for certain what will happen after death.

Influenced by the Epicureans, Marcus pursues his doubts about providence by putting to himself the disjunction whether the gods exist, or either don't exist or don't concern themselves with human affairs (2.11). He affirms the first alternative by noting that in the latter case he has no reason to live. He also asks whether the gods have power or not (9.40). Here he dismisses the latter alternative with the question: 'Then why do you pray?' At 6.44, he makes an important concession. He discusses whether the gods take counsel about him personally, or take counsel about the common good (from which his particular circumstances follow), or do not take counsel about anything at all. The last possibility, he says, is impious to believe. But if it is true and the gods do not take counsel about any human affairs, he continues, he can still take counsel about himself. Having granted this much to the Epicureans, Marcus immediately distances himself from them by asserting that his nature is both rational and political: as Antoninus, he is a citizen of Rome, and as a human being, he is a citizen of the world; and his good is identical with the good of these two cities. Even if the belief in providence must be abandoned, his obligations as a member of human society remain.

At certain moments of doubt, Marcus is willing to concede to the Epicureans that there may be no rational plan in human life except what a person has thought out for oneself. At these times, Marcus reduces all his beliefs to a single conviction: there is one thing of value, his inner deity, the intellect. This epistemological retreat is an extreme form of his fundamental ethical belief that he must serve his intellect. Marcus is usually convinced that his intellect is part of a rationally organised, divinely guided whole. But he is willing to concede that his belief in a rationally ordered world may be without foundation.

In that case, he still has his inner self: sceptical doubt cannot take away from him his awareness of himself as a rational being.

In sum, Marcus has an unshakeable belief in his intellectual self. For the rest, he has a range of beliefs, carrying different degrees of conviction and admitting much variation. Reflecting upon Stoic ethical doctrines in a broad philosophical context, he mixes doubt with conviction and makes additions and alterations. His philosophical statements are ever changing responses to his own circumstances; they are fluid, yet remarkably coherent as an expression of his faith in human reason.

WORDSWORTH CLASSICS
OF WORLD LITERATURE

SIR THOMAS MORE
Utopia

FRIEDRICH NIETZSCHE
Thus Spake Zarathustra

OVID
Metamorphoses

THOMAS PAINE
Rights of Man

SAMUEL PEPYS
The Concise Pepys

PLATO
Republic
*Symposium and
the Death of Socrates*

PLUTARCH
Lives
(SELECTED)

MARCO POLO
The Travels

LA ROCHEFOUCAULD
Maxims

JEAN-JACQUES ROUSSEAU
The Confessions
The Social Contract

WILLIAM SHAKESPEARE
Five Great Comedies
Five Great Tragedies
Five Great History Plays
*Five Great Plays of
Greece and Rome*

SUETONIUS
Lives of the Twelve Caesars

LAO TZU
Tao te ching

THUCYDIDES
*The History of the
Peloponnesian War*

ALEXIS DE TOCQUEVILLE
Democracy in America
(ABRIDGED)

SUN TZU
The Art of War
(with The Book of Lord Shang)

VIRGIL
The Aeneid

ANONYMOUS
The Koran
The Newgate Calendar
Njal's Saga
*Sir Gawain and the Green
Knight*
The Upanishads